MW01537392

Know and Follow the
STRAIGHT PATH

Know and Follow the
STRAIGHT PATH

FINDING COMMON GROUND
BETWEEN SUNNIS AND SHI'AS

Tallal Alie Turfe

Visiting Professor
Department of Religious Studies
University of Detroit Mercy

TRUE DIRECTIONS
AN AFFILIATE OF TARCHER BOOKS

iUniverse®

KNOW AND FOLLOW THE STRAIGHT PATH
FINDING COMMON GROUND BETWEEN SUNNIS AND SHI'AS

Copyright © 2015 Tallal Alie Turfe.

All rights reserved. No part of this book may be used or reproduced by any means, graphic, electronic, or mechanical, including photocopying, recording, taping or by any information storage retrieval system without the written permission of the publisher except in the case of brief quotations embodied in critical articles and reviews.

iUniverse books may be ordered through booksellers or by contacting:

iUniverse
1663 Liberty Drive
Bloomington, IN 47403
www.iuniverse.com
1-800-Authors (1-800-288-4677)

Because of the dynamic nature of the Internet, any web addresses or links contained in this book may have changed since publication and may no longer be valid. The views expressed in this work are solely those of the author and do not necessarily reflect the views of the publisher, and the publisher hereby disclaims any responsibility for them.

Certain stock imagery © Thinkstock.
Any people depicted in stock imagery provided by Thinkstock are models, and such images are being used for illustrative purposes only.

ISBN: 978-1-4917-5756-7 (e)
ISBN: 978-1-4917-5755-0 (sc)
ISBN: 978-1-4917-5757-4 (hc)

Library of Congress Control Number: 2015900144

Print information available on the last page.

iUniverse rev. date: 04/27/2015

A gift to my lovely and dedicated wife, Hajjah Neemat, for her support and inspiration in being my partner in life and a great mother, guide, and leader to our children and grandchildren. As a volunteer in social services, she has won acclaim and distinction from the Islamic centers in the community, as her efforts have touched the hearts of many who are in dire need of assistance. A truly remarkable person, she has enriched my life with love and devotion.

Contents

Preface

I am American born, and I had no formal training in Islamic studies. I taught myself the Arabic alphabet so I could read the Qur'an in its original language. English translations of the Qur'an aided my understanding of the Arabic verses. For more than a half century, I taught young people about the Islamic faith, which further strengthened my knowledge and understanding of the religion. I also spoke to adult groups and at interfaith institutions.

As the growing Muslim community needed more Islamic centers and teachers, I became more involved in studying, writing, and lecturing about Islamic topics. Religious scholars recognized my knowledge of Islam, and they frequently invited me to give presentations on the topic. Some of these topics centered on the common ground between Sunnis and Shi'as, such as the Qur'an, hadiths (traditions), and the core fundamentals of Islam as well as the respect for unity in diversity. In addition, I made presentations to the broader interfaith community.

I have authored four other books on religion, some of which are in several languages: (1) *Patience in Islam: Sabr*; (2) *Unity in Islam: Reflections and Insights*; (3) *Energy in Islam: A Scientific Approach to Preserving Our Health and the Environment*; and (4) *Children of Abraham: United We Prevail, Divided We Fail.*

I have served on a number of boards and was chairman of the Greater Detroit Interfaith Round Table of the National Conference for Community and Justice, currently the Michigan Roundtable for Diversity and Inclusion. I was a member of former president Bill Clinton's Call to

Action: One America race relations group. Dubai Television identified me as a prominent and influential Arab American.

In October 1995, I was the first Muslim to be presented with the Knight of Charity award by the Vatican-based Pontifical Institute for Foreign Missions. I was inducted into the International Heritage Foundation Hall of Fame for my global humanitarian efforts.

In August 2000, I was one of two hundred political and religious leaders from around the world who participated in the Millennium World Peace Summit at the United Nations in New York. I have given other presentations on Islam at the United Nations—for example, education and parenting for peace, global ethics, and public diplomacy.

My wife, Neemat, and I have been married for fifty years, and we have five children and twelve grandchildren.

Tallal Alie Turfe

Acknowledgments

This book is dedicated to the Twelfth Infallible Imam, Mohammad al-Mahdi, and may he pardon me for any errors I may have made.

This book is also dedicated to my parents, Hajj Alie Turfe and Hajjah Hassaney Turfe, who were constant and steadfast in their Islamic faith and good deeds. They inspired me to learn about Islam and its message to mankind.

It is hoped that this book will inspire those who wish to obtain a greater understanding of Islam as well as introspective reflection of what is important in becoming a more unified and knowledgeable Muslim.

The eminent and renowned scholar Ayatollah Imam Abdul Latif Berry, founder of the Islamic Institute of Knowledge, spurred me to enhance my knowledge of Islam and write books on the subject. I am very grateful to him for opening my mind to the many facets of the religion and for nurturing me to explore the depths of its philosophy. He always urged me to undertake a study of the contemporary facets of Islam, thereby enlightening Muslims and non-Muslims in America and abroad.

Imamat: A Poem
by Tallal Alie Turfe

Like stars in the sky shining so bright,
Transmitting down an array of light.
As a guide showing us the straight way,
Cleansing our souls each and every day.
O' glowing spark of heaven above,
Stimulating thy heart with its love.
Awaken thy spirit as I pray,
Shining bright from its eternal ray.

Bismillahi al-Rahmani al-Rahim
(In the name of Allah, the Beneficent, the Merciful)
Praise be to Allah, the Lord of the Worlds, and blessings and
peace be upon Prophet Mohammad and his Ahl al-Bayt. May
Allah grant peace and honor on him and his family.

Introduction

Disputes between Sunnis and Shi'as are rooted in disagreements over the succession to Prophet Mohammad and the nature of leadership of the Islamic *ummah* (community). The topic of succession and leadership has been an historic debate since the death of Prophet Mohammad. Over the centuries, these disputes have led to violence, terrorism, and even wars, further fragmenting the global Islamic community. It is the intent of the author to come to an understanding of how these differences can be resolved for the sake of unity within the Islamic arena. In researching the topic of succession and leadership, the author focused on three aspects: (1) issue, (2) argument, and (3) hypothesis.

> *Issue:* In order to lead the Islamic ummah, is it necessary to transfer succession exclusively to the *Imamat* (doctrine of leadership of the Twelve Infallible Imams) of *Ahl al-Bayt* (house of the family of Prophet Mohammad), or can others assume the leadership?

> *Argument:* Shi'as' claim that the Twelve Infallible Imams of Ahl al-Bayt are the heirs as well as religious and political leaders of the Islamic ummah, while Sunnis claim leadership does not necessitate infallibility or Ahl al-Bayt.

Hypothesis: The right of succession to lead the Islamic ummah was declared and demanded by Prophet Mohammad to be Imam Ali ibn Abi Talib and the Imamat of Ahl al-Bayt.

This book is written to address these three aspects as well as to explore the concept of Imamat and its significance and importance to Muslims. Moreover, the book is guided by the following Qur'anic verse: "Mix ye not the truth with falsehood and hide ye not the truth when ye know (it)" (Qur'an 2:42).

In searching for the truth, one should be cautious about making statements that are untrue. The search for truth requires one to accurately understand the Qur'an, hadiths (traditions), and various viewpoints of the Islamic schools of thought. Often, we witness the unnecessary derogatory remarks against fellow Muslims by both sides of the equation: Sunnis and Shi'as. This has led to further fragmentation within the Islamic arena, causing violence, fighting, and even wars. The end result is chaos and confusion for the Muslim society and generations of Muslims to follow. One such misunderstanding is that of the concept of Imamat and Ahl al-Bayt.

Understanding the term "Imam" has been somewhat confusing with respect to who should be addressed with this title and the duties and responsibilities that are associated with it. As we shall discover, the term Imam has a number of meanings that refer to destinations and books as well as people. It is the intent of the author to shed light on the term Imam and how it relates to the concept of Imamat. It is hoped that scholars will use this book as a benchmark to further research and explore the concept and importance of Imamat.

Overview

As defined by al-Alama al-Hilli, the Imamat is "the general leadership in all-religious and secular affairs performed by a person deputizing for or in place of the Prophet" (al-Hilli 1986). This definition underscores the significance of the Imamat in the Islamic ummah and its position in continuing and perpetuating Prophet Mohammad's mission of safeguarding the divine message of Allah and leading the ummah. The Imamat are the Twelve Infallible Imams of Ahl al-Bayt. These Imams are the successors of Prophet Mohammad. As such, they are entrusted by Allah to perform all of the prophet's functions and responsibilities, except that of revelation, which is the domain of prophets and messengers.

The Qur'an and Prophet Mohammad's hadiths stress the importance of the Imamat and its role in leading the religious and other affairs of the Muslim ummah. The Imams of the prophet's household were recognized as the supreme intellectual leaders, the authorities on religion from which theologians and religious scholars learned and whose teachings they followed. Additionally, the Imams undertook two major tasks: the responsibility of political and intellectual leadership and acting as role models to be followed and imitated. Therefore, the caliphate and political and intellectual leadership are all combined in the persons of prophets and Imams for the purpose of achieving mankind's material and spiritual objectives in this life and the hereafter (Al-Musawi 1996).

Prophets, messengers, and the Imamat personified the character, personality, and disposition of flawlessness, submission, and devotion. They were gifted with knowledge and armored with courage to convey to humanity the importance of faith, righteous deeds, truth, and patience. The miracle for the Imamat was that their knowledge, qualifications, and conduct, by the grace of Allah, were molded in perfection and inherited from the lineage of Prophet Mohammad.

Prophet Mohammad and the Imamat have illuminated our spirits, as their energy flows through every facet of our soul, body, and mind. As heirs of this energy, we must own up to our responsibility to be the guardians and trustees of the faith of Islam. We must instill this radiant energy within our children so they can carry on the legacy of Islam.

Muslims believe that the concept of divine unity is based on the Qur'an and recognition of the unity of Allah in all his attributes, in particular that Allah alone must be worshipped. Based on their belief in the divine unity, Muslims maintain that while Allah is just in the obligations he imposes on his worshippers, he does not impose obligations on mankind beyond their capabilities. Man is essentially free to choose between right and wrong. Mankind's choice to be good or bad is of their own free will, as they will bear the reward or consequence of their choice. The Twelve Infallible Imams expounded upon the concept of free will and volition. The Twelve Infallible Imams are manifested in the divine light of guidance, as this light is passed from one Imam to the next. The Twelve Infallible Imams are unified strands within the rope of Allah.

Picture the rope of Allah as having two ends. At one end is the Qur'an, and at the other end is Ahl al-Bayt. Just as the prophets were a continuation of the previous prophet, the infallible Imams are a continuation of Prophet Mohammad who was also an Imam. They are called the Twelve Infallible Imams. They were infallible and immune to sin, but they were not prophets. Prophet Mohammad was the seal of the prophets. Nonetheless, these Imams possessed similar qualities to those of prophets. The first of the Twelve Imams is Imam Ali Ibn Abi Talib, first cousin and son-in-law to Prophet Mohammad. The last Imam is Imam Mohammad al-Mahdi, who is still alive in his major occultation. Since man is not self-sufficient to guide himself in terms of faith and religious doctrines, Allah has necessitated Imams.

While patients may be able to read a book on medicine, they still need a physician to help diagnose and administer a cure for their ailment. Similarly, Imams are needed to continue the work of the prophet in explaining what the many verses in the Qur'an mean. Centuries have followed since the passing of Prophet Mohammad, and the world has dramatically changed, owing in large part to technology and space travel as well as easy access around the globe. The major role of Imams was to guide the people from ignorance, tyranny, and disputes. After the death of Prophet Mohammad, the Imam was entrusted with the guardianship and continuation of the prophet's accomplishments and leadership. In short, as leaders, the Imam's role was to guide mankind in all aspects of existence.

Concept of Khalifa

The concept of *khalifa* in the Qur'an has evolved in meaning:

> (Recollect O' Our Apostle Mohammad) When said thy
> Lord unto the angels: "Verily I (intend to) appoint a
> vicegerent in the Earth" they said, "Will Thou (O' our
> Lord) appoint therein one who will cause mischief and
> shed blood, while we celebrate by Thy praise and hallow
> Thee alone?" Said (the Lord to the angels) "Verily I know
> what ye know not." (Qur'an 2:30)

The majority of Qur'anic translations define the term khalifa as
Allah's vicegerent or steward, while other translations have described it
to mean successor, substitute, replacement, or deputy. In the Qur'anic
verse above, the word khalifa refers to Adam as the inhabitant, settler of
the earth. According to the Qur'an (verse 38:26), Allah bestowed upon
Prophet David the title of Khalifa fi l-Ard (Caliph on Earth). Hence, for
Prophet David, the khalifa indicates one who exercises authority and can
judge between people justly. After the death of Prophet Mohammad, the
word khalifa was defined to mean the head of the Islamic community,
which began with Abu Bakr as the first caliph. Subsequently, with the
rise of the Umayyad caliphate, the term khalifa began to acquire new
meanings, such as representative of Allah. The Umayyad caliphs took the
position that to disobey them or their agents was a refusal to acknowledge
Allah and, therefore, was tantamount to disbelief (Watt 1968).

The Shi'as recognize blood kinship with Prophet Mohammad
as the most important criterion for picking his successor. Moreover,
according to the Shi'as, the designation of Imam Ali by the prophet as his
successor was one of divine appointment. Hence, Allah appointed Imam
Ali through the mediation of the prophet. Shi'as use the term Imam as
the religious and political leader, while Sunnis use the term khalifa as
their leader. Furthermore, Sunnis contend that the term Imam usually
refers to a prayer leader. Prophet Mohammad was both the prophet

(warner) and Imam (guide) of Islam and not referred to as the caliph of Islam. Therefore, when the prophet passed the baton of leadership to his successor, it was the leadership of Imam and not prophet, since he was the seal of the prophets. Hence, it stands to reason that since the prophet did not pass on the title of caliph to his successor, that term becomes null and void in determining the leadership of the Islamic ummah.

For purposes of this book, the author refers to the term caliph as the leader of the Islamic ummah. The term caliph appears in both the Sunni and Shi'a literature to address the issue of Prophet Mohammad's successor. However, it should be kept in mind that the Imam, not the caliph, is the successor of Prophet Mohammad and the true leader of the Islamic ummah.

This book will touch upon the importance, significance, and leadership of the Imamat (i.e., Prophet Mohammad and the Twelve Infallible Imams).

Leadership and Character

As Muslims, we must learn from the leadership and character of Prophet Mohammad and the Imamat. Here, leadership demands results and provides the courage to overcome ignorance, fear, and denial. Islam teaches us a code of ethics. Muslim leaders as well as Muslims in general must espouse admirable traits in life by being friendly, sociable, and kind. Another important trait is that of justice and the capacity to defend their own rights. As they must exhibit qualities of respect, equality, self-restraint, self-sacrifice, and self-denial, they must not misbehave or infringe upon other people's rights. This is the sound and actionable leadership that has been taught by Prophet Mohammad and the Imamat.

Character has a great deal to do with leadership. Character and leadership are complementary. Prophet Mohammad and his progeny taught us about character. The best of character is when we fully submit our will to the will of Allah and obey his commandments and the teachings of his prophets, messengers, and the Imamat. We strive to become like the best of role models (e.g., Prophet Mohammad and the Imamat). We try to imitate these role models and pattern our attitudes, behaviors, and lifestyles after them. Character, like personality, is comprised of different qualities. Strengths are elements of a person's basic personality, and they show themselves across circumstances and occasions. They are cultivated within the person through various occurrences and over time. The environment plays a major part in defining character. For the Imamat, at the core of character are a number of qualities: wisdom, courage, compassion, justice, self-control, and spirituality, to mention a few. Across this gamut of qualities and virtues, the Imamat begins with wisdom that deals with creativity and social intelligence, and it ends with spirituality that deals with forgiveness and gratitude.

Case Example of Leadership and Character

In AD 680, leadership was put to the test during the period of Caliph Yazid's illegal rule. Imam Hussein, the grandson of Prophet Mohammad and son of Imam Ali ibn Abi Talib and Fatima, fought and died for the protection and preservation of Islam. To him, Islam was not only threatened but on the verge of collapse and destruction. But threatened by whom? Many scholars believe it was a fight against the tyrannical and corrupt Yazid and his followers. A more in-depth analysis reveals that Imam Hussein's underlying mission was to put an end to those who compromised their Islamic values and ideals. The very essence of Islam was compromised, for Muslims had fallen back into the depths of ignorance.

What led up to Imam Hussein's martyrdom is a tragedy, a story that has been recounted over the centuries. Imam Hussein lived under the most difficult circumstances of oppression and persecution. After the death of Prophet Mohammad, Mu'awiyah (father of Yazid) and his followers made use of every possible scheme to destroy and dispose of Ahl al-Bayt and thus obliterate the name of Imam Ali ibn Abi Talib and his progeny.

Imam Hussein took over the leadership of Islam following the martyrdom of his brother, Imam Hassan. This was the time for Imam

Hussein to make public his authority and to fulfill his *jihad* (struggle) for the cause of justice, which resulted in his own martyrdom.

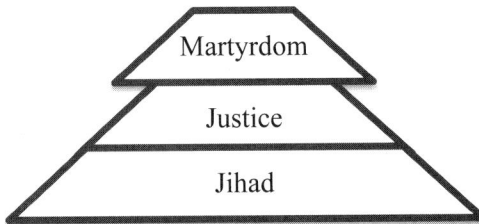

Mu'awiyah broke the truce he had with Imam Hassan by taking severe measures to implement his own plan, that of strengthening the basis of the caliphate for his son, Yazid. During that time, Imam Hussein had to endure every kind of mental and spiritual anguish and suffering from Mu'awiyah, Yazid, and their followers.

With deception and fraudulent means, Mu'awiyah gained the support of Muslims who pledged their allegiance to Yazid. Mu'awiyah, who did not impose this requirement upon Imam Hussein, had advised his son, Yazid, not to force the issue. But Yazid did not listen and continued to pursue Imam Hussein with impudence and treachery. Yazid's character was tantamount to that of the devil himself. Unrelenting, Yazid caused all kinds of disruption and interference in the precepts of Islam, as he practiced every malevolence and evil with the highest degree of insolence.

With determination and zeal for justice, Imam Hussein would not give his allegiance to Yazid's injustice and tyranny. Imam Hussein had to confront oppression and despotism by spreading the message of truth and justice to the Muslim ummah. In order to safeguard the sanctuary of the holy place of Mecca from war, Imam Hussein decided to leave Mecca and proceed to Iraq. In Kufa, Iraq, the people pledged their allegiance to Imam Hussein, guaranteeing him their trust and contract. However, the people of Kufa later broke their pledge and deserted him.

Karbala is a town located in a desert about fifty miles from Kufa. Here is where the battle for truth and justice took place. The army of

Yazid numbered in the thousands, and they surrounded Imam Hussein and his followers. The event at Karbala lasted ten days. Imam Hussein and his followers remained steadfast while the enemy's army continued to increase. However, on the seventh day, the water supply was cut off from Imam Hussein's camp. Now began the torture of thirst and hunger. The Imam strengthened his resolve as he informed his companions that martyrdom was inevitable. Many of his companions dispersed, and what was left was a small contingent of less than a hundred devout Muslims that remained loyal. On the ninth day, the last challenge was made by the enemy to Imam Hussein to choose either allegiance or war. Imam Hussein refused allegiance and became determined to enter battle on the next day, the tenth day of the month of Muharram, known as Ashura.

At Karbala, Imam Hussein fought and died for the sanctity of Islam. The Imam and his companions fought until they were all martyred. Among those killed were two children of Imam Hassan, who were only eleven and thirteen years old, and a five-year-old child and baby of Imam Hussein. The bodies of the martyrs were decapitated and denied burial.

Imam Hussein was the essence of *sabr* (patience), because he was firm in his purpose, maintained his consciousness of Allah, and was guided by *Sirat-al-Mustaqim* (Straight Path), leading to his ultimate sacrifice to save Islam. What Imam Hussein left at Karbala was an example, and the very essence of that example was prayer. His perseverance in prayer at Karbala was the light that drew even some of the enemies to his side. While Imam Hussein and his tiny contingent were in prayer, some of the opposition, such as the well-known soldier Hurr, were so drawn to the true believers that they crossed over and joined them.

It is important to understand that it was the prayer that Imam Hussein was safeguarding. He saw that Muslims were compromising their prayer. Make no mistake about this—the enemies at Karbala also prayed. But the prayers by the enemies were null and void. Can one pray and then proceed to murder the grandson of the Prophet Mohammad? No! So, you see, even prayer was distorted, and the reason was that the enemies lacked sabr in their prayer, and they had fallen from the Straight Path.

Imam Hussein's message is for people not to compromise Islam and to realize that one's salvation is through the practice of sabr and prayer. The symbol of prayer was so dynamic and powerful that it was the means by which the continuation of the root of Imam Hussein followed. And that continuation was Imam Hussein's son, Imam Ali al-Sajjad. Seeking knowledge, understanding, and wisdom, or striving toward prosperity and tranquility, cannot be meaningful without the security of the foundation of faith. That foundation is prayer.

While it is important to seek knowledge and understanding, these needs are nurtured in self-awareness once prayer is solidified. Imam Ali al-Sajjad was the leader of prayer, prostration, and supplication, and he restored Islam by these means. It was Imam Ali al-Sajjad who continued the cause of Islam that his father courageously died for. The Muslim world had to be reawakened to Islam, and it was Imam Ali al-Sajjad who successfully restored the Muslims back to the Straight Path. He did this by example, and his example was prayer, the root essence of Islam. His numerous prayers and supplications are recorded in volumes of books, and they are the standard for all Muslims to follow.

Message of the Imamat

The centuries following Imam Hussein's martyrdom saw Muslims time and again compromising their Islamic values and ideals. Whether with the Umayyads, the Abbasids, or in contemporary times, Islam has been and continues to be threatened throughout the world. For example, many Muslim countries grant fewer religious freedoms to their subjects than do leaders of Western nations. The problem here is deep-rooted; it is a problem of the Muslims themselves. In order to assimilate into the mainstream of a non-Islamic society, Muslims often feel it necessary to forego their Islamic traditions, lifestyles, and behaviors in order to be accepted by that society. These Muslims have fallen to the lowest form of degradation, for they have substituted Islam with convenience and social compatibility.

Let us reflect on the martyrdom of Imam Hussein and the martyrdom of the other infallible Imams so we can learn from their example. What we learn is that Imam Hussein carried out the legacy of his grandfather, Prophet Mohammad. It is a legacy that truth must prevail over evil, injustice, tyranny, and deviation. It is a legacy that faith must overcome disbelief. It is a legacy that Muslims must fulfill all obligations.

Remember that Islam cannot be compromised. To know whether we have compromised Islam requires that we have knowledge of at least the basic fundamentals of Islam. This requires an understanding of what Islam is and what it is not. We must submit our will to Allah, become certain of our faith, believe in Imam Hussein's message, and accept the challenge that we will strive in the way of Allah to better ourselves as Muslims. We must be steadfast and actionable in our obligations to Islam. We must display the right attitude so that our faith can endure. We must let our behavior be one for others to follow, and above all, we must be patient!

We should fulfill all obligations in order to strengthen our Islamic personality. Whether they are divine obligations to please Allah as we pray and fast, or moral obligations, such as avoiding backbiting and suspicion, or mutual obligations, such as keeping the promise relative to a marriage contract, or tacit obligations, such as empathy, gestures, intuitions, attitude, and behavior, we should fulfill them by our *thikr* (remembrance) of Allah and by our actions.

Developing a strong Islamic personality that is nurtured in the ideals of outer and inner cleanliness helps fulfill these obligations. It is not enough to just pray and fast. We have to make our prayers and fasting actionable by fulfilling all obligations. Each of us is responsible for fulfilling our own individual obligations by purifying ourselves and creating a healthy body and mind so that the soul may return to Allah.

Trials of wealth, trials of power and authority, and trials of courage test our resolve. Whether they are trials of ease or of hardship, only those who have understanding and whose hearts are filled with faith can remain steadfast. The foundation for fulfilling our obligations is unity, and that is the message of Prophet Mohammad and his Imamat: "And hold ye fast by the Rope of Allah all together, and be not divided (among yourselves) …" (Qur'an 3:103)

And it is the rope of Allah that we cling to in order to walk the Straight Path, for it is the path of the soul. As Muslims, we should invoke our blessings upon Prophet Mohammad and the Imamat to show our appreciation for their guidance, knowledge, and wisdom.

AHL AL-BAYT

Chapter 1

Blessings

Allah has showered his blessings on Ahl al-Bayt and empowered them as guides to the Straight Path. Every Muslim is obligated to recite blessings (*salawat*), especially during prayer. If it is not recited during the prayer, then one's prayer becomes invalid. The Qur'an reminds us that blessings were given to Prophet Mohammad:

> Verily Allah and His Angels bless the Prophet! O' ye who believe! Send ye blessings on him and ye greet him with a salutation worthy of the respect (due to him). ("ya ayyuha alladhena amanu sallu 'alayhi wa sallamu tasliman") (Qur'an 33:56)

> O' Allah! Please bless Mohammad and the Household of Mohammad. ("allahumma salli 'ala mohammadin wa ali mohammadin") (al-Haythami 1965; al-Suyuti 2000)

The first blessing is a directive from the Qur'an, and Prophet Mohammad declared the second blessing. The second blessing resulted from the companions of Prophet Mohammad asking him about the necessity of the second blessing, to which the Prophet responded:

> Narrated 'Abdur-Rahman bin Abi Laila: "... O Allah! Send Your Salat (Graces, Honours and Mercy) on Mohammad and on the family of Mohammad as You sent Your Salat (Graces, Honours and Mercy) on Ibrahim and on the family of Ibrahim, for You are the Most Praiseworthy, the Most Glorious. O Allah! Send Your Blessings on Mohammad and the family of Mohammad, as You sent Your Blessings on Ibrahim and the family of Ibrahim, for You are the Most Praiseworthy, the Most Glorious)." (*Sahih Bukhari*, Vol. 4, Book 60, Hadith 3370) (See appendix 4 for other Sunni sources.)

The question arises as to why the necessity for the two blessings:

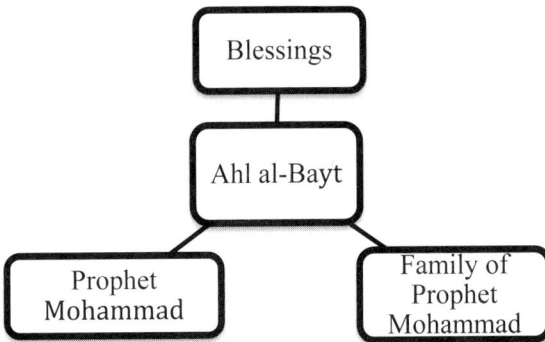

We are reminded by two verses in the Qur'an. The first verse is mentioned above (Qur'an 33:56), while the following verse is the basis for the first verse:

> And stay ye in your abodes and display not your finery like the display of the ignorance of yore, and establish

2

ye prayer and give away the poor-rate, and obey Allah and His Apostle (Mohammad); verily, Allah intendeth but to keep off from you (every kind of) uncleanness O' ye the People of the House, and purify you (with) a thorough purification. (Qur'an 33:33)

Sunni scholars concur that this verse is attributed to those whom Allah has purified: Prophet Mohammad, Imam Ali, Fatima, Imam Hassan, and Imam Hussein of Ahl al-Bayt (*Sahih Muslim*, V6, Book 44, Hadith 6220 [Sahih/Authentic]; *Ibn Majah*, Sunan, V1, p. 52; *Al-Tirmidhi*, V6, Book 46, Hadith 3724 [Sahih/Authentic]; *Ahmad ibn Hanbal*, V1, p. 185).

Therefore, it stands to reason that Allah had a purpose for those whom he purified. Allah does not make mistakes, so the purification of Ahl al-Bayt is sound and therefore a declaration for all Muslims to obey and follow. Furthermore, the word *intends* (*yoreedo*) in the verse means the continuous will and intention of Allah. Moreover, Prophet Mohammad mentioning his progeny in the blessing is testimony to the importance of the inclusion of his Ahl al-Bayt.

Islam is a way of life, and it establishes rules and responsibilities in an orderly fashion, not in a chaotic fashion. Therefore, it is logical to assume that as Prophet Mohammad received the orderly pronouncement of blessing and peace in the Qur'anic verse, then the house of the family of Prophet Mohammad (Ahl al-Bayt) should likewise receive the same blessing and peace that corresponds with the prophet's declaration. We find the following Sunni hadiths that confirm the above:

+ *Sahih Bukhari*, V4, Book 60, Hadith 3370 (Sahih/Authentic)
+ *Sahih Muslim*, V1, Book 4, Hadith 907 (Sahih/Authentic)
+ *Ibn Majah*, V2, Book 5, Hadith 904 (Sahih/Authentic)
+ *Abu Dawud*, V1, Book 2, Hadith 976 (Sahih/Authentic)
+ *Al-Tirmidhi*, V1, Book 3, Hadith 483 (Sahih/Authentic)
+ *Al-Nasa'i*, V2, Book 13, Hadith 1286 (Sahih/Authentic)
+ *Ahmad ibn Hanbal*, V4, pp. 241, 243–244

Another Sunni hadith also confirms the blessings upon Ahl al-Bayt:

> O' members of the Household (Ahl al-Bayt) of the
> Messenger of Allah! (Our) love for you is an obligation,
> which Allah has revealed in the Qur'an. Your lofty
> station such that if one does not invoke blessings on you
> (while offering prayers) one's prayers will be of no avail.
> (*Poem by Al-Shafi'i*; al-Haythami 1965)

Likewise, one of the many Shi'a hadiths that records the blessings
upon Ahl al-Bayt is the following:

> Ali bin Ibrahim reported from his fathers who reported
> from ibn Abu Umayr who reported from Abdulla bin
> Sinan who reported from Imam Sadiq that the Prophet
> said: "Invoking salawat upon me and my Ahl al-Bayt
> carries away hypocrisy." (Sarwar 2013, *Al Kafi*, Vol. 4,
> p. 251)

As noted, the above sources further confirm that blessings and
peace should be given to both Prophet Mohammad and his progeny
of Ahl al-Bayt. With the blessings that Allah bestowed upon Prophet
Mohammad, the prophet became the mercy for the universe (*rahmatun-lelalamin*). Let us give our blessings to Prophet Mohammad and the
Imamat as we pursue the Straight Path.

Chapter 2

Straight Path

The opening chapter of the Qur'an, *al-Fatiha*, is the most important and frequent recital in our lives, whether in daily prayers, upon the birth of a newborn baby, at funerals, at weddings, as an invocation or benediction at an event, or for other occasions. It is a prayer for guidance:

> In the name of Allah, the Beneficent, the Merciful (all) praise is (only) Allah's, the Lord of the Worlds, The Beneficent, the Merciful. Master of the Day of Judgment. Thee (alone) worship we and Thee (only) we seek help. Guide us (O' Lord) on the Straight Path. The Path of those upon whom Thou has bestowed Thy bounties, not (the path) of those inflicted with Thy wrath, nor (of those) gone astray. (Qur'an 1:1–7)

The five daily prayers constitute a total of seventeen parts (*rakats*). Al-Fatiha is the only chapter (*sura*) in the Qur'an that is compulsorily recited in the obligatory prayer. It is recited, at least, in each of the first two parts of the prayers, or ten times daily. However, al-Fatiha may be recited more often in each of the daily prayers. In addition to the five daily prayers and the recital of al-Fatiha for other occasions, Muslims recite al-Fatiha over five thousand times yearly. In our prayers, we ask Allah to guide us (*ihdina*) to the Straight Path (Sirat al Mustaqim), which is the Path of faith, righteous deeds, truth, and patience. It is the clear path that guides us to the *nur* (light). Whoever wants to find the Straight Path will find it, if they are sincere and righteous. The Straight Path is a *ni'mah* (blessing) from Allah, and the ultimate ni'mah is the ni'mah of Islam! In seeking the ni'mah, we must obey Allah and Prophet Mohammad to receive guidance:

> And whoever obeyeth Allah and the Apostle (Mohammad) these shall be with those Allah hath bestowed favors upon them; of the Prophets, and the Truthful, and the Witnesses, and the Righteous ones; and excellent are these as companions! (Qur'an 4:69)

Gift of Guidance

The words *hadiyya* (gift) and *hidaya* (guidance) are connected in that the Straight Path is a gift of guidance:

Straight Path
(Sirat al Mustaqim)

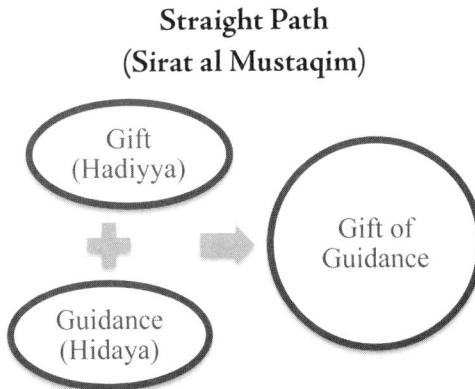

Any deviation from the Straight Path is regarded as misguidance. Daily, we seek Allah's grace to guide us (ihdina) to the Straight Path:

Verily, this my My Path, is the straight (right) one, so ye follow it, and follow ye not (other) ways for they will scatter you away from His Path; this doth He enjoin you with, so that ye may guard (yourselves against evil). (Qur'an 6:153)

As Allah has done us a favor by guiding us to the Straight Path, we must express our gratitude and be thankful for his guidance and blessing. There is no limit to the amount of hidaya (guidance) one can receive from Allah. Of course, Prophet Mohammad and Ahl al-Bayt received the most hidaya. As a guide, Allah revealed to us the Qur'an, which is a hidaya. As al-Fatiha reminds us of the basics of our faith, we must constantly remember to praise and worship Allah for his benevolence and mercy. We ask Allah to guide us to seek righteousness and to refrain from keeping the company of evil people. Even prophets, messengers, and infallible Imams were chosen and guided by Allah to perfect them as they walked the Straight Path. Not only did they walk the Straight Path, but they also became the Straight Path. For example, Prophet Mohammad was the Straight Path during his life, and his successor (wasi), Imam Ali ibn Abi Talib, and every succeeding infallible Imam thereafter was also the Straight Path. We must follow their example by walking the Straight Path in order to perfect ourselves in every circumstance and aspect of our lives.

To be mustaqim (straight) is vital to our proper behavior and attitude in life. Once it is followed, the Straight Path transforms the whole of life by bringing about a positive change in character and action that purifies the self. We seek Allah's guidance to remove any obstacle or bad intention so that we can remain steadfast along the Straight Path: "Whoever holdeth fast unto Allah, is already guided to the Straight Path." (Qur'an 3:101)

Psychology, as it is practiced in Western societies, neglects or pays little attention to the concept of the soul. As such, people forget their gratitude to Allah for his hidaya and ni'mah, thereby forgetting to follow the Straight Path. For Muslims, spiritual happiness and psychological health are connected and often reflect each other. Islamic beliefs are important for our psychological health because they instill proper direction in life, guiding us to the Straight Path, which leads to self-actualization of the Islamic personality. Even our *du'as* (supplications) are gifts of guidance, as we not only make du'as for ourselves but for others as well.

Concept of Shi'a

The Straight Path is the connection that links the Qur'an and Ahl al-Bayt (household of Prophet Mohammad):

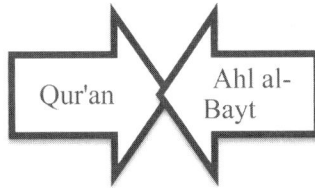

Those who follow Ahl al-Bayt are called Shi'a. Interestingly, according to the Qur'an, the Shi'a were also followers of Prophet Noah:

> Peace be on Noah in all the worlds! Verily thus do We recompense the doers of good. Verily he was (one) of Our faithful servants. Then We drowned the others. And verily of his persuasion was Abraham. (Qur'an 37:79–83)

Therefore, Prophet Abraham was a follower (Shi'a) of Prophet Noah. The followers of Prophet Moses were also Shi'a because Prophet Moses himself was a Shi'a:

> And he entered the city at a time when unvigilant were its people, and found he therein two men fighting: the one, of his own party (Shi'a); and the other of his

enemies; And the one of his own party (Shi'a) sought his help against the one who was of his enemies, and Moses smote him with his fist and passed (death) on him; Said (Moses): "This is of the Satan's doing; verily, he is an enemy, an open misleader." (Qur'an 28:15)

Even Prophet Jesus was a Shi'a in that he came to fulfill and follow the law of Prophet Moses in the Old Testament:

> Do not think that I (Jesus) have come to abolish the Law (of Moses) or the Prophets; I have not come to abolish them but to fulfill them ... (Matthew 5:17–18)

Moreover, we can conclude that Prophet Mohammad was a follower (Shi'a), as were Prophet Abraham, Prophet Moses, and Prophet Jesus. A well-known Sunni source states that the Shafi'i scholar Maghazli recorded a tradition from Anas bin Malik that he heard the Prophet say:

> Seventy thousand people will go to Heaven without questions; the Prophet then turned to Ali and said, "They will be from among your Shi'a and you will be their Imam." (ShiaPen Newsletter, *Revealing the Truth*, www.shiapen.com [*Manaqib Ali al Murtaza*, by al Maghazli al Shafi'i, p. 184])

Other well-known Sunni scholars revealed that Prophet Mohammad stated the following:

> I swear by the one who controls my life that this man (Ali) and his Shi'a shall secure deliverance on the Day of Resurrection. (LagosShia [*Fadha'il al-Sahaba*, by Ahmad ibn Hanbal, Vol. 2, p. 655]); (Revert Muslims Association [*Tafsir ibne Jarir*, Vol. 33, p. 146 by Hadhrath

Muhammad bin Ali; *Tafsir Durre Manthur* by Jalaladin
Suyuti, Vol. 6, p. 379])

As Shi'as, the prophets and infallible Imams followed the Straight
Path. Likewise, our self-realization becomes manifest when we obtain
a deeper understanding of the Straight Path and the inseparability of
the Qur'an and Ahl al-Bayt. They remain connected, complementing
each other in leading and guiding the people. In understanding the
significance and meaning of the Straight Path, we are guided by the
Qur'an and the hadiths.

AHL AL-BAYT

Chapter 3

Hadiths

Hadiths, or traditions, are a main part of Islam, occupying a place second only to the Qur'an. As both the hadiths and the Qur'an are crucial, Muslims practice Islam by consulting both of them. The role of hadiths is to focus on what is mentioned in the Qur'an and to interpret and explain it. Primarily, hadiths deal with the life of Prophet Mohammad, concentrating on his narrations, teachings, actions, accountings, statements, sayings, utterances, communications, deeds, and decisions. Shi'as make use of the hadiths of Prophet Mohammad that have been related by trustworthy and reliable sources, whether these sources are Shi'as or Sunnis.

Classification of Hadiths

During the time of Prophet Mohammad, these hadiths were declared orally. They were later compiled in written form, centuries after the death of Prophet Mohammad. The compilation of hadiths was based on narrations from the companions and followers of Islam who lived during the time of the prophet. Generations that followed conveyed these hadiths to those after them, which became known as the chain of narrators. As these hadiths multiplied to tens of thousands over the centuries, some hadiths contradicted other hadiths. Therefore, it became necessary for scholars to study the meaning and significance of each hadith and to classify it as authentic, good, weak, or fabricated.

Hadiths are classified as authentic (*sahih*), good (*hasan*), weak (*dha'eef*), or fabricated (*mawdoo'*). Another classification of hadiths is called *moothaq* (almost like sahih, but the narration is not as strong). Of course, fabricated hadiths are null and void. Usually, only the authentic (sahih, including moothaq) and good hadiths are used in deriving the rules in Islam. As for the weak hadiths, scholars have differed as to whether or not these hadiths have value. The value of any of the hadiths is often predicated on the basis of its text (*matn*) but also on the basis of its chain (*isnad*). Therefore, the weak hadiths could be the result of a lack of continuity or integrity in the chain of narrations (Ibrahim Syed).

The two main branches of Islam, Sunni and Shi'a, have their own collections of hadiths, some of which are agreed upon by both Sunni and Shi'a scholars. For example, *Hadith Qudsi* (Sacred Hadith) is a collection of forty narrations that are accepted by both Sunni and Shi'a schools of thought. The various schools of Islamic thought rely on hadiths as tools for understanding the Qur'an and various aspects of jurisprudence. In determining which hadiths to use, one must be very cautious to ensure that they are not in conflict with the Qur'an.

Sunni Hadiths

The most reliable hadiths accepted by Sunnis were collected and recorded by the following, which became known as *Kutub al-Sittah* (*The Six Books*):

+ *Sahih Bukari* (died AD 870)
+ *Sahih Muslim* (died AD 875)
+ *Sunan ibn Majah* (died AD 886)
+ *Sunan Abu Dawud* (died AD 888)

+ *Jami al-Tirmidhi* (died AD 892)
+ *Sunan al-Nasa'i* (died AD 915)

The foregoing hadiths are known as *musannaf*, which is a collection of hadiths in which the traditions relating to different topics are assembled and then classified into various books or chapters, each dealing with a particular topic (e.g., prayer). However, there are also collections known as *musnad* in which hadiths are arranged alphabetically under the names of the companions on whose authority these hadiths were reported (e.g., Abu Bakr). Musnad are also hadiths compiled and reported by the Imams of the four Sunni schools of thought (e.g., *Musnad Ahmad ibn Hanbal*, died AD 855) (Dindang 2004). Moreover, *Musnad Ahmad ibn Hanbal* contains numerous hadiths that pertain to the merits of Prophet Mohammad's Ahl al-Bayt. Following is a comparison table of the collection of Sunni hadiths:

Collection of Sunni Hadiths

Recorders of Hadiths	Number of Hadiths (Est.)	
Sahih Bukari	7,000 to 9,000	(2,200 to 4,000 without repetition)
Sahih Muslim	7,000 to 12,000	(2,200 to 4,000 without repetition)
Sunan Ibn Majah	4,300	
Sunan Abu Dawud	5,300	
Jami al-Tirmidhi	4,000	(None fabricated)
Sunan al-Nasa'i	5,800	

Sources: Data derived from various sources are estimates of the number of hadiths, including those without repetition.

A number of sources conflict as to the number of *collected* and *recorded* hadiths by the six Sunni references. Therefore, estimates were used based on the consensus of these sources. It is reported that *Sahih Bukhari* recorded 7,000 to 9,000 hadiths of the 600,000 collected (another source said 300,000 were collected), which means he decided that there were errors in the majority of the hadiths collected (Al-Khazraji 2005).

Likewise, *Sahih Muslim* recorded 7,000 to 12,000 hadiths of the 300,000 collected, while *Sunan Abu Dawud* recorded about 5,300 hadiths of the 500,000 collected. Additionally, the number of hadiths recorded without repetition is estimated. Since both *Sahih Bukhari* and Muslim each rejected over 97 percent of the hadiths they collected, and since neither was divinely inspired or infallible, how is it possible for them to know which hadiths were authentic and which were not?

Moreover, *Sahih Bukhari's* portrayal of Muawiyah as pure and righteous, despite his known corruption and defiance of Islam, is a reflection of his bias in listing the hadiths and the political corruption that influenced him. Furthermore, a number of the hadiths recorded by *Sahih Bukhari* and Muslim are insulting to Prophet Mohammad:

Aishah said, "I scented Allah's Messenger and he went round (had sexual intercourse with) all his wives and in the morning he was a Muhrim (after taking a bath)." (*Sahih Bukhari*, Vol. 1, Book 5, Hadith 270)

The Prophet used to visit all his wives in one night and he had nine wives at that time. (*Sahih Bukhari*, Vol. 1, Book 5, Hadith 284)

Allah's Messenger said, "Do not offer Salat (prayer) at the time of sunrise and at the time of sunset." (*Sahih Bukhari*, Vol. 1, Book 9, Hadith 582)

A group of eight men from the tribe of 'Ukl came to the Prophet ... and said, "O Allah's Messenger! Provide us with some milk." Allah's Messenger said, "I recommend that you should join the heard of camels." So, they went and drank the urine and the milk of the camels (as a medicine) till they became healthy and fat. Then they killed the shepherd and drove away the camels, and they became disbelievers after embracing Islam ... the Prophet ... sent some men in their pursuit ... they were caught ... and he had their hands and feet cut off. Then he ordered for nails that were heated and were branded with those nails, their eyes, and they were left in the Harra (i.e., rocky land in Al-Madina). And when they asked for water, no water was given to them till they died. (*Sahih Bukhari*, Vol. 4, Book 56, Hadith 3018)

Prophet Mohammad is compassionate and of high moral character. It is inconceivable that he would act as a barbarian gouging people's eyes out and cutting off their hands and legs. To further underscore the authenticity of *Sahih Bukhari*'s hadiths, let's examine the following hadith:

The Messenger of Allah said: "Allah, Glorified and Exalted is He, created Adam in His image ..." (*Sahih Muslim*, Vol. 7, Book 51, Hadith 7163)

Allah does not have an image; therefore, the above hadith is erroneous and incorrect, as the Qur'an states that Allah cannot be seen (Qur'an 6:103; 7:143).

Interestingly, there are no recorded fabrications in the estimated 4,000 hadiths of Jami al-Tirmidhi. We are reminded that al-Tirmidhi recorded a hadith in which Prophet Mohammad said, "I am the City of Knowledge (House of Wisdom) and Ali is its gate." (Al-Tirmidhi, Vol. 6, Book 46, Hadith 3723)

Al-Nasa'i found that people held erroneous views against Imam Ali ibn Abi Talib, due to the past influence of the Umayyads. In order to guide the people, he wrote a book on the merits of Imam Ali and wanted to read it from the pulpit in the mosque. But the congregation, instead of giving him a hearing, maltreated him, kicked him, and drove him from the mosque. He died a year later, perhaps as a result of this incident (Siddiqui 2006).

To underscore how numerous hadiths were omitted from *Kutub al-Sittah (The Six Books)*, let us examine the number of hadiths attributed to the following narrators:

Narrator	Number of Hadiths
Abu Hurayra	5,374
Abd Allah ibn Umar	2,630
Anas ibn Malik	2,286
Aisha	2,210
Abd Allah ibn Abbas	1,660
Jabr ibn Abd Allah	1,540
Abu Said al-Khudri	1,170
Umar ibn Khattab	537
Ali ibn Abi Talib	536
Uthman ibn Affan	146
Abu Bakr	142

Source: *Hadith Literature: Its Origin, Development & Special Features* by Muhammed Zubayr Siddiqui, Islamic Book Trust, 2006

It is inconceivable that the combined number of narrations by the four caliphs (Umar, Ali, Uthman, and Abu Bakr) is 1,361 hadiths, which is far less than the 2,210 hadiths narrated by Aisha. Moreover, only *Sahih Bukhari* of *Kutub al-Sittah* cites one hadith narrated by Fatima, the daughter of Prophet Mohammad. Undoubtedly, the Umayyads and other dynasties that followed did their utmost to discard and remove numerous hadiths attributed to Imam Ali and Fatima, as well as to Abu Bakr, Umar, and Uthman. Furthermore, with 5,374 hadiths narrated by Abu Hurayra (AD 603–681), which is more than any of the other narrators, the authenticity of these hadiths is questioned, especially since he spent only about three years with the prophet. Abu Hurayra lived in the royal palace of Muawiyah serving him and his political views. As a result, Abu Hurayra produced a number of hadiths that demean and insult Imam Ali ibn Abi Talib, only for the pleasure of Muawiyah (Kandemir 1994).

Other notable Sunni collectors of hadiths are:

+ *Muwatta Imam Malik* (died AD 795)
+ *Musnad al Tayalisi* (died AD 819)
+ *Musannaf al Sanani* (died AD 826)
+ *Musnad Ahmad ibn Hanbal* (died AD 855)
+ *Sunan al-Darimi* (died AD 868)
+ *Musnad al Najjar* (died AD 875)
+ *Musnad al Bazzar* (died AD 904)
+ *Musnad al Mawsili* (died AD 919)
+ *Sahih ibn Khuzaymah* (died AD 923)
+ *Sahih Abu Awana* (died AD 928)
+ *Sahih Ibn Hibban (al Busti)* (died AD 965)
+ *Al Mu'jam al Kabir (al Tabarani)* (died AD 970)
+ *Sunan al Daraqutni* (died AD 995)
+ *Mustadrak al Hakim al-Nishaburi* (died AD 1014)
+ *Sunan al Baihaqi* (died AD 1065)
+ *Masabih al Sunnah (al Baghawi)* (died AD 1122)

Fabricated Hadiths

The Umayyad and Abbasid rulers actively promoted hadith writing (Haq 2009). Forgery of hadiths was prevalent under the Umayyads, who considered the hadith a means of sustaining their rule and who actively circulated traditions against Imam Ali in favor of Muawiyah. The Abbasids followed the same pattern, circulating prophetic hadiths that predicted the reign of each successive ruler. Moreover, religious and ethnic conflicts further contributed to the forgery of hadiths (Brown 1999).

The Umayyads, who cared little for religion, encouraged and spread freely forged hadiths and fortified others to forge such traditions as were favorable to their plans and to their rule in general (MacDonald 1903). Additionally, the Sunni collectors of *Kutub al-Sittah* lived under Abbasid rule during the turbulent ninth century. The Abbasid hadith transmitters (narrators) were in turn reliant on transmitters who had lived for almost one hundred years under the rule of the Umayyads. Abbasid politics and fervent hatred of the Umayyads could have played a role in choosing or ignoring attributers, as well as altering certain attributions considered pro-Umayyad (Elhadj 2007).

Many hadiths were fabricated to favor the Umayyad caliphs. However, when the Abbasids overthrew the Umayyads, many of the hadiths favoring the Umayyads were nullified, and new ones were composed to favor the Abbasid caliphs (Gilchrist 1986). Yet, while the early Abbasid caliphs presented themselves as transmitters and narrators of hadiths, they seemed to be seeking admission into the ranks of the *ulema* (scholars). As such, some of the hadiths an Abbasid caliph is said to have reported would have an Abbasid family *isnad* (chain of transmission) that does not extend back to Prophet Mohammad but rather stops with Ibn Abbas. Additionally, an Abbasid caliph quotes or narrates a tradition with an isnad comprising well-known hadith transmitters rather than members of the Abbasid family. So as to legitimize their own cause, the Abbasid caliphs created a large number of hadiths in order to remove legitimacy of the Umayyads (Zaman 1997).

Although the Abbasids took power with the slogan of supporting Ahl al-Bayt, they followed the footsteps of the Umayyads. Otherwise, the Abbasids would have no choice but to hand over power to the Imams of Ahl al-Bayt and their followers. Moreover, it wasn't the Abbasids who exclusively started the recording of hadiths in written form but rather the Umayyads, especially narrators such as Abu Hurayra who constructed numerous hadiths with political purposes to please the Umayyad Caliph Muawiyah. However, it was during the reign of the Abbasids that the practice of collecting and recording hadiths flourished. Bear in mind that when the Abbasid caliphs were composing their own hadiths, the six Sunni collectors of *Kutub al-Sittah* were also compiling and recording hadiths. It should be noted that the six Sunni collectors lived during the time of the Umayyad Emirs (not caliphs) of Cordoba and the Abbasid caliphs (appendix 7).

The Abbasid were Arab caliphates that depended on Persians for their victory and to the extent that the Persians influenced the many facets of their lifestyles. Hence, the old Arab influence was slowly replaced by a strong Persian influence that persisted in the court, culture, and government (The Islamic World). Interestingly, the six Sunni scholars themselves were all Persian.

Sunni-Shi'a Relations during the Abbasid Dynasty

During the eighth and ninth centuries, the concept of *mihna* (inquisition) became part of the rule that the Abbasid dynasty enforced on the Islamic religious community. Mihna was instituted to recentralize the political authority of the caliphate to counteract a growing movement of the religious leadership. However, in the eighth century, the role and religious function of Caliph Harun al-Rashid eventually coincided with that of the ulema (religious scholars). Moreover, the mihna only reinforced what the caliphs had already acknowledged, which was that they had to derive their legitimacy from the ulema (Koelliker 2011).

When Caliph al-Ma'mun reigned in the ninth century, he reinstituted mihna by punishing and imprisoning the Sunni ulema until they conceded the doctrine of the createdness of the Qur'an (Zaman 1997). Createdness refers to the doctrinal position that the Qur'an is created. The Mu'tazilite doctrine holds that the Qur'an is the created divine word, while the dominant varieties of Muslim theology consider the Qur'an to be coeternal with Allah and, hence, uncreated (Corbin 1993). The traditional Sunni view is that the Qur'an is an uncreated document. It is eternal and coexistent. The createdness of the Qur'an was in response by the Mu'tazilites to charges by the Christians that making the Qur'an eternal meant that it was coexistent with Allah (Mathews 2010). The objective of al-Ma'mun's mihna was to wrestle authority over religious knowledge from the Sunni ulema—for example, the traditionalist Ahmad ibn Hanbal. Al-Ma'mun imprisoned Ahmad ibn Hanbal because of his belief that the Qur'an was uncreated, and he had him whipped until he was unconscious (*The Encyclopedia of Islam*).

The Sunni custodians of religious knowledge had a vested interest in espousing the doctrine of the Qur'an to be uncreated, as this would increase the importance of their position in the larger Muslim community and government as maintainers and interpreters of the actual, eternal Word of Allah, rather than something, although divine in origin, still space-time contingent (i.e., having both spatial and temporal qualities) (Duderija 2005). Al-Saduq, a prominent Shi'a scholar, said that the Qur'an does not contain in it that it is created, and the reason to refrain from describing it as created is because the created, linguistically, could mean fabricated or false (Al-Saduq 2013). However, the idea of the Imam significantly influenced al-Ma'mun with regards to the potential control the mihna could provide, giving him supreme autonomy over the ummah as well as blood ties to Ahl al-Bayt.

The policy of mihna was in effect for fifteen years, from AD 833 to AD 848, continuing through the reigns of Caliph al-Ma'mun, Caliph al-Mu'tasim, and Caliph al-Wathiq, as well as through two years under Caliph al-Mutawakkil, who reversed it. During that period, the Mu'tazilites also embraced mihna. Caliph al-Ma'mun publicly adopted the principle of createdness, instituting a mihna to ensure acceptance of this doctrine (Nawas 1994). Al-Ma'mun's declaration of the mihna was a reflection of his partiality to Shi'a doctrines, whereas al-Mutawakkil's cancellation of mihna was ingrained in his resentment toward the followers of Imam Ali ibn Abi Talib (Patton 1897). With the elimination of mihna, it brought an end to the Abbasid caliph's pretense to decide on religious matters (Zaman 1997).

The most reliable six Sunni ulema collectors of hadiths lived during the time of the mihna and the caliphs mentioned above (appendix 7). These caliphs were strong and powerful, had extensive knowledge of Islam, and some were scholars and competent to give judgment in Islamic law. Caliph Harun al-Rashid was the first caliph who officially employed the ulema as his personal advisors, urging them to compile the hadiths of the prophet (Yaqub 1969). Under the Umayyads, the Arab nationality had been predominant. Under the Abbasids, the Persian nationality became predominant.

Although the Shi'as allied with the Abbasids to defeat the Umayyads, the Abbasids deceived the Shi'as and commenced to persecute, torture, harass, imprison, and kill them. The Persian Sunnis monopolized all the important and prestigious posts in the government administration. When Harun al-Rashid died, his son, al-Ma'mun, took over the reign. Al-Ma'mun provided freedom for people to pursue knowledge without government interference. The religious conflict between al-Ma'mun and the Sunni ulema during the mihna was primarily one of jurisprudence. Al-Ma'mun's objective was to control the informal circle of the ulema and to structure a uniform code of law.

It is worth noting that *Sahih Bukhari* and *Sahih Muslim* did not narrate any hadiths from al-Shafi'i, not because he was inferior in knowledge, but because he had inclinations toward the school of Ahl al-Bayt. These ulema examined tens of thousands of hadiths; however, they omitted a great number of those pertaining to Imam Ali and Ahl al-Bayt. Nonetheless, the relationship between the Sunni ulema and the caliphs was dominated by the ulema's attempts to assert their authority over all Muslims, including the caliphs, at least on matters of religion. However, the caliphs, responsible for the Muslim community's religious and secular affairs, were in a strong position to demand the ulema's obedience (Elhadj 2007).

By postulating themselves as the deputies of Allah's messenger, the Abbasid caliphs were bound to the *sunnah* (sayings and doings of the prophet and his companions) and what was to become the edited and textualized hadiths (Choueiri 2005). Nonetheless, religious authority was a cooperative enterprise between the caliphs and the Sunni ulema (Zaman 1997). Moreover, the hadiths had to be compiled, edited, and textualized systematically for the purposes of both political power and the evolution of the schools of law. The force of the Sunni ulema, perceived as the only source of religious authority, gave political legitimacy to the Abbasid caliphs (Choueiri 2005).

Although the caliphs were the legitimate bearers of authority within the Sunni Muslim community, the ulema considered themselves as the true successors of the prophet in terms of religious authority. Undeniably,

Sunni scholars contributed to the importance of the Sunni caliphate (Hanne 2007). Once in power, the Abbasids embraced Sunni Islam and disavowed any support of the Shi'a beliefs. While under Abbasid absolutism, the Shi'a attitude was one of denial of legitimacy with a passive patience and abstention from action (Algar 1969).

Undoubtedly, the relationship between Sunni and Shi'a Muslims throughout history has been shaped by the political landscape of that period. The Abbasid caliphs persecuted, imprisoned, tortured, and killed Shi'a Imams and encouraged Sunni ulema to define Sunni orthodoxy and power in order to suppress and contain the appeal of Shi'as (Nasr 2006). The main confrontation of the Shi'as was with the Hanbalis, followers of Ahmad ibn Hanbal. However, they did not have much of a problem with the ulema of the other Sunni schools. Rather, other schools like the Shafi'is even had close ties with the Shi'as. The Hanbalis were opposed to the open propagation of Shi'ism, and this opposition led to confrontation (Ya'ghoubi 2013).

Shi'a Hadiths

The seven most reliable hadiths (appendix 3) accepted by Shi'as are:

- *Al-Kafi* by al-Shaykh Abu Ja'far Muhammad b. Ya'qub b. Ishaq al-Kulayni (died AD 940); 16,099 hadiths
- *Man la Yahduruhu al-Faqih* by al-Shaykh Abu Ja'far Muhammad b. 'Ali b. Husayn b. Babawayh al-Qummi (al-Shaykh al-Saduq) (died AD 991); 5,998 hadiths
- *Tahdhib al-Ahkam* by Shaykh al-Ta'ifah, Abu Ja'far Muhammad b. Hasan al-Tusi (died AD 1067); 1,359 hadiths
- *Al-Istibsar* by al-Shaykh al-Ta'ifah, Abu Ja'far Muhammad b. Hasan al-Tusi (died AD 1067); 5,111 hadiths
- *Wasa'il al-Shi'ah ila Tahsil Masa'il al-Shari'ah* by al-Shaykh Muhammad b. Hasan al-Hurr al-'Amili (died AD 1693); 35,868 hadiths

- *Bihar al-Anwar* by Muhammad Baqir b. Muhammad Taqi al-Majlisi (died AD 1698); 110 volumes
- *Mustadrak al-Wasa'il wa Mustanbat al-Masa'il* by al-Hajj Mirza Husayn al-Nuri al-Tabarsi (died AD 1902); 23,000 hadiths

It was Imam Ali ibn Abi Talib who was the first to record, in writing, the prophet's sayings during the prophet's lifetime. Therefore, it was the Shi'as who first embarked on collecting and recording the hadiths, and they continued to do so throughout the reign of many caliphs. In fact, the twelve Imams of Ahl al-Bayt were the authenticated chain of transmitters, and each of the Imams upheld the same hadiths without any discrepancies. The Shi'a collectors of hadiths are listed above. These Shi'as compiled the hadiths attributed to Prophet Mohammad and his Ahl al-Bayt.

In addition to the hadiths, there are other notable works. For example, *Nahj al-Balagha (Peak of Eloquence)* contains sermons, letters, sayings, and maxims of Imam Ali ibn Abi Talib on a wide variety of topics, including our existence, relationship with Allah, and reflections upon historical events. Furthermore, *al-Sahifa al-Sajjadiyyah al-Kamilah (The Psalms of Islam)* of Imam Ali ibn Imam Hussein is another notable work. Shi'as do not totally reject *Sahih Bukhari* or other Sunni hadiths but, rather, accept many of their hadiths. However, Shi'as take the position that whatever is in *Sahih Bukhari* or other Sunni hadiths is not always true.

Al-Kafi (The Sufficient Book), the most reliable of all Shi'a books on hadiths, is a collection of 16,099 narrations compiled by Mohammad ibn Ya'qub al-Kulayni (AD 864–940). Al-Kulayni lived during the time that the four deputies represented Imam al-Mahdi during his minor occultation (AD 874–941). Therefore, al-Kulayni had access to these four deputies and was in constant contact with them. Moreover, these four deputies who were in constant touch with Imam al-Mahdi confirmed al-Kulayni's collection of hadiths.

Sunni and Shi'a Position on Authenticity of Hadiths

Al-Kulayni is to the Shi'as what *Sahih Bukhari* is to the Sunnis. Since Shi'a scholars believe that there are no hadith books, Sunni and Shi'a, that are completely *sahih* (authentic), they do not make any assumptions relative to authenticity. Rather, Shi'a scholars take the position that since fallible people collected the hadiths, they may contain both strong and weak narrations. As such, before the Shi'a scholars could determine the authenticity of each hadith, they followed certain criteria, such as chains of transmission, to arrive at a decision. This was the method used by Shi'a scholars in the formative period when the hadiths of *Al-Kafi* were first collected.

However, the consensus of Shi'a scholars in contemporary times is that all of *Al-Kafi's* hadiths are reliable, but they cannot substantiate that they are all authentic. If a conflict arises relative to whether or not a hadith is authentic, the Shi'a scholars rely on the chains of transmission or other criteria in their decision. Therefore, a comprehensive process of authentication must be applied, which leaves the understanding of the hadiths in the hands of the learned. Nonetheless, the basis for accepting or rejecting any hadith is determined by whether or not it agrees with the Qur'an.

Sunni scholars who argue that some of the hadiths of *Al-Kafi* prove the Shi'a to be wrong do not understand the Shi'a position. Realistically, Shi'as do not base their faith on the complete authenticity of *Al-Kafi*. Rather, they believe that anything that goes against previously held ideas must not be authentic. The Qur'an is far more important to Islamic belief than any book on hadith, and Shi'a scholars have pointed this out. While the Shi'a scholars hold to the premise that *Al-Kafi* is not 100 percent authentic, they affirm that it is the best collection of hadiths available. Fallible people compile hadith books, and therefore, they unavoidably have a mixture of strong and weak hadiths. Al-Kulayni states: "Whatever (Hadith) agrees with the Book of Allah (Qur'an), accept it. And whatever contradicts it, reject it" (Meri 2005).

Al-Kulayni never intended for *Al-Kafi* to be discussed as infallible traditions. Rather, he compiled it only to give sincere advice based on authentic Islamic law. Additionally, al-Kulayni intended to preserve rare hadiths in an accessible collection for future generations to study.

Great care was taken in cross referencing the hadiths contained in both Sunni and Shi'a books that agreed on a statement or topic relative to members of Ahl al-Bayt (e.g., Imam Ali ibn Abi Talib or Imam Mohammad al-Mahdi). Numerous agreements in support of the Shi'a hadiths were found in the Sunni hadiths. While these agreements are noted in some of the reliable Sunni hadiths (e.g., *Sunan ibn Majah*, *Sunan Abu Dawud*, *Jami al-Tirmidhi*, or *Sunan al-Nasa'i*), they may not have been recorded in *Sahih Bukhari* or *Sahih Muslim*. On the other hand, agreements contained in *Sahih Muslim* may not have been contained in *Sahih Bukhari* or vice versa.

Relative to the *Hadith al-Thaqalayn* (i.e., the two weighty things of the Qur'an and Ahl al-Bayt), Sunni scholars accept its authenticity:

+ *Sahih Bukhari*, al Ta'rikh al Kabir, V3, p. 96
+ *Sahih Muslim*, V6, Book 44, Hadith 6225 (Sahih/Authentic)
+ *Abu Dawud*, Tadhkirat Khawass al-Ummah, 322
+ *Al-Tirmidhi*, V6, Book 46, Hadiths 3786, 3788 (Sahih/Authentic)
+ *Al-Nasa'i*, Al-Khasais, p. 96, Hadith 79
+ *Ahmad ibn Hanbal*, V5, pp. 182, 189, 350, 366, 419

Sunnis and Shi'as disagree as to what constitutes the term sunnah, which means the practice, path, or lifestyle followed by Prophet Mohammad. The word Sunni is believed to derive from the term sunnah, which refers to the sayings and actions of Prophet Mohammad as recorded in the hadiths. Sunnis hold to the premise that the sunnah is a distinct principle in Islam apart from Ahl al-Bayt, therefore, having its own theological and philosophical significance. Shi'as contend that the sunnah is undeniably part and parcel of Ahl al-Bayt, reflecting the lifestyle and behavior of Prophet Mohammad, the Imamat, and Ahl al-Bayt. However, before we can appreciate the significance and importance of the Imamat, we must first understand the concept of Imam itself.

Chapter 4

Concept of Imam

For centuries, there have been countless discussions as to the meaning and significance of the concept of Imam (leader). The term Imamat (to lead) consists of Imams who act as guides for the Muslim community relative to the *ta'wil* (interpretation) of the Qur'an and the teachings of Islam. The concept of Imamat differs between the Shi'a perspective and the Sunni perspective. Shi'as consider Imamat as a fundamental cardinal principle of Islam, and an extension of prophethood in its spiritual dimension. Additionally, Shi'as believe that the Imamat is infallible, free of sin, and perfected in purity.

Although Sunnis do not reject the concept of Imamat totally, they regard it as other than a cardinal principle and do not accept the divine appointment of the Imamat by Allah. Furthermore, Sunnis consider the Imamat as a social leadership position that can be elected by *shura* (council), rather than by divine appointment of Allah. Moreover, Sunnis believe that the Imamat is the same as khalifah (steward or trustee) of the Muslim community and not one of divine appointment (Mutahhari 1990). Today, neither Sunnis nor Shi'as have a khalifah as the leader of the ummah. However, from the Shi'a perspective, the Imamat still continues as the leader of the ummah via Imam Mohammad al-Mahdi, who remains in his major occultation.

Various Forms and Significance of Imam

Ahl al-Bayt (house of the family of Prophet Mohammad) and the Qur'an are linked together by the rope of Allah not to part until they reach the fountain (*kawthar*) in paradise. The significance of this linkage is that the Imamat of Ahl al-Bayt are the leaders and guides of Islam who are entrusted with safeguarding the sanctity and meaning of the Qur'an as well as guiding the ummah.

Basically, there are three levels of people who were chosen by Allah to carry out his divine laws.

Nabi (prophet) is one who receives the divine law, which may be direct or transmitted by an angel. *Rasul* (messenger) is a prophet who receives the divine law that concerns him and others. Every messenger is a prophet, while every prophet is not a messenger. Prophet Mohammad is the last messenger and last prophet. The total number of messengers is 313, of which five are considered Great Messengers, and the total number of prophets, including the messengers, is 124,000 (Majlisi 1983, *Bihar al-Anwar*, Number 11, page 31). The five Great Messengers (Noah, Abraham, Moses, Jesus, and Mohammad) had a universal mission, and each received revelation, either by way of a book or scroll, while other messengers had only a local mission. Even some angels are chosen by Allah to be messengers (Qur'an 22:75). However, angels cannot be prophets, as the latter must be a human being.

Imam (guide) is one who is appointed by Allah as a leader (Qur'an 21:73; 32:24) and is completely obedient to Allah's commands. While a messenger is a warner, an Imam is a guide (Qur'an 13:7). Imam does not receive divine law. However, an Imam may be informed of past and future events. A messenger sees and hears an angel. Talking to angels is not exclusive to prophets and messengers. Mary, mother of Jesus, talked to angels (Qur'an 3:45), as did Sarah, the wife of Abraham (Qur'an 11:69–73).

The term Imam can refer to a destination, book, or person:

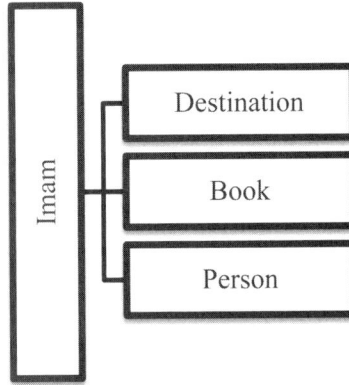

Imam as a Destination

Metaphorically, Imam can indicate a destination or path:

> Verily in this are signs for those who scan heedfully.
> And verily it is on a (high) way that (still) stands. Verily
> in this there is a sign for the believers. And verily the
> inhabitants of El-Aika too were most surely unjust
> ones. We inflicted retribution on them, and indeed they
> were both on an Imam (highway), (still) open. (Qur'an
> 15:75–79)

The opening chapter of the Qur'an is al-Fatiha, and its fifth verse
says, "Guide us on the Straight Path" (*Ihdina-Sirat-al-Mustaqim*).
This verse refers to mankind leading a path of righteousness and
following the example of Prophet Mohammad and the infallible
Imams, beginning with Imam Ali ibn Abi Talib and ending with
Imam Mohammad al-Mahdi. Allah has shown us the permanent
Straight Path and the guide (Imam) for its movement. According to
Imam Ali ibn Abi Talib, every facet of life necessitates that mankind
traverse the Straight Path, which is the middle path of moderation

(Majlisi 1983, *Bihar al-Anwar*, Vol. 87, p. 3). The Straight Path is one in which Allah's books are revelations sent to his messengers as warners and protected by the infallible Imams as guides:

Straight Path
(Sirat al Mustaqim)

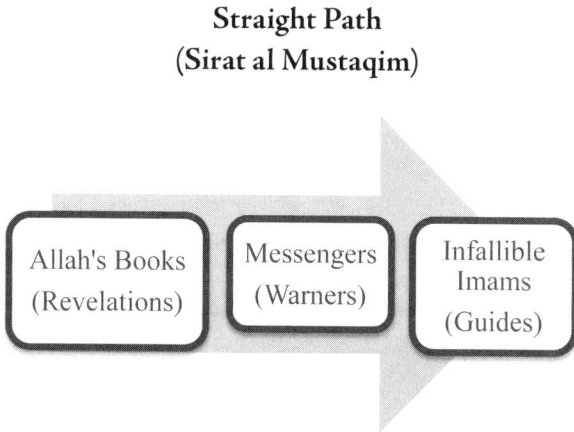

| Allah's Books (Revelations) | Messengers (Warners) | Infallible Imams (Guides) |

The Straight Path is the way of Allah: "Verily, my Lord is on the Straight Path" (Qur'an 11:56). The Straight Path is the very path of the prophets: "Verily thou (O' Mohammad) art of the Apostles (sent by Us), on the Straight Path" (Qur'an 36:3–4). The Straight Path is the path of servitude to Allah: "And ye should worship (only) Me, and this is the (only) Straight Path" (Qur'an 36:61). The Straight Path is the path of trust and reliance on Allah: "Whoever holdeth fast unto Allah, is already guided to the Straight Path" (Qur'an 3:101).

Imam as a Book

Imam is also a book—for example, Allah's books.

Allah's Books as Imams:

As they are guides to mankind, the books of Allah are considered to be Imams. These books are the Scrolls of Abraham, Torah of Moses, Psalms of David, Gospel of Jesus, and Qur'an of Mohammad:

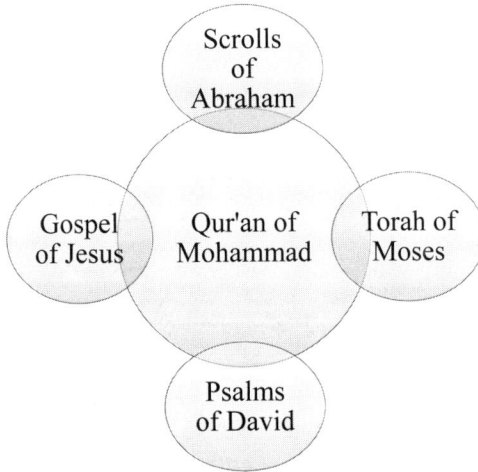

Scrolls
of
Abraham

Gospel
of Jesus

Qur'an of
Mohammad

Torah of
Moses

Psalms
of David

Qur'an

The Qur'an, as a guide, is referred to as Imam or *hadi*:

> This is the Book: there is no doubt in it, (being the word
> of Allah) (it is) a Guidance (Hadi) for the pious (ones)
> who believe in the Unseen, and establish the prayers, and
> of what We have provided them with, they give (in the
> way of their Lord). And who believe in that which hath
> been sent down unto thee (O' Our Apostle Mohammad)
> and that which hath been sent down (unto the other
> Apostles) before thee, and of the hereafter they are sure.
> These are the ones on the Guidance from their Lord,
> and these are the ones who shall be the successful ones.
> (Quran 2:2–5)

The Qur'an has many verses that mention it as a guide, some of
which are 2:185, 7:52, 16:64, 16:89, 16:102, 17:9, 27:76–77, 31:2–5,
and 41:44.

Moreover, the terms Imam and hadi may be used interchangeably
when referring to the term guide. The Qur'an is both a guide and a

mercy (*rahma*). The Qur'an is the sacred book for Muslims. It has also been described as *Al-Kitab* (The Book), *Al-Azeem* (Lofty and Great), *Al-Hakeem* (Wise and Learned), *Al-Majeed* (Glorious and Noble), *Al-Furqan* (Criterion), *Al-Kareem* (Generous and Bountiful), and many others. The Qur'an guides all Muslims. It is a code of rules of proper conduct and behavior in all aspects of life. It enumerates rewards for those who follow and are obedient to Allah's commandments. It also enumerates and warns of punishments to those who transgress and go astray. In the verses of the Qur'an, Muslims find solutions to their problems. In this way, the Qur'an guides the Muslims.

Torah and Gospel (Injil)

The Torah and Gospel (Injil) are also books of guidance (hadi):

> He hath sent down unto thee the Book (Qur'an), with truth confirming what was before it; and He sent down the Torah (of Moses) and the Gospel (of Jesus) aforetime, a Guidance (Hadi) for people and sent down the Criterion (Furqan); Verily for those who disbelieve in the signs of Allah, for them is a severe punishment; Allah is Mighty, Lord of Retribution. (Qur'an 3:3–4)

In addition to being referred to as hadi (guide), the Torah, or Book of Moses, is also referred to as Imam (Guide):

> Verily, We sent down the Torah therein was Guidance (Hadi) and Light ... (Qur'an 5:44)

> Is he then (like unto him) who hath a clear proof from their Lord, and followeth him a witness from Him, and preceded by the Book (Torah) of Moses, a Guide (Imam) and a Mercy (Rahma) (testifying it)? They believe in it; and whosoever of the parties (of the idolaters)

disbelieveth in it, the (Hell) fire is the promised place; so be thou not in doubt about it; verily it (Qur'an) is the truth from thy Lord; but most of the people believe not. (Qur'an 11:17)

And gave We unto Moses the Book (Torah) and made it a Guidance (Hadi) for the children of Israel, (saying) that "Take ye not other than Me (any one as) a guardian." (Qur'an 17:2)

And indeed We gave Moses the Book (Torah) after We had destroyed the generations of yore, (containing) clear arguments for mankind and a Guidance (Hadi) and Mercy (Rahma), that happily they might reflect. (Qur'an 28:43)

And indeed gave We unto Moses the Book (Torah), so be thou not in doubt of receiving this from Him (Allah), and it (Torah) made We a Guidance (Hadi) unto the children of Israel. And of them made We Leaders (Imams) to Guide (Hadi) (the people) by Our command as they were steadfast (in the calamities); and they of Our signs were quite certain. (Qur'an 32:23–24)

And before it the Book of Moses (the Pentateuch) was a Guide (Imam) and Mercy (Rahma): and this (Qur'an) is a Book confirmeth (the previous Scriptures), in the Arabic language that it may warn those who are unjust; and (contains) glad-tidings for the doers of good. (Qur'an 46:12)

The Gospel is referred to as a guide (hadi):

And We caused to follow in their footsteps, Jesus, son of
Mary, confirming the Law (the Torah), which was before
him, and We gave him (Jesus) the Gospel in which was
Guidance (Hadi) and light and confirmation of what was
before it of the Torah, and a Guidance (Hadi) and an
admonition for those who guard (against evil). (Qur'an
5:46)

Scrolls of Abraham and Psalms of David (Zabur)

By deductive reasoning, it can be stated that the Book of Abraham
(scrolls or scriptures) is also an Imam. Since Prophet Abraham rose to
the rank of Imam, then it logically follows that his book is also an Imam.
However, the name of Prophet Abraham's book is not mentioned nor
has it been found:

Or hath he not been told of what is in the Scriptures
of Moses? And of Abraham who fully discharged (his
mission)? (Qur'an 53:36–37)

Verily, this is in the Scriptures earlier, the Scriptures of
Abraham and Moses. (Qur'an 87:18–19)

As for the *Zabur*, or Psalms of David, there is no mention in the
Qur'an as to whether it falls within the category of Imam. However,
Prophet David, a descendant of Prophet Abraham, would have achieved
the status of Imam, according to the Covenant of Abraham. Therefore,
it logically follows that Imam can be attributed to the psalms as well.
Clearly, Allah revealed the inspiration to Prophet David, as he did to
other prophets:

And thy Lord knoweth best (all) those who are in the
Heavens and the Earth; and indeed We have exalted

some Apostles to some (other Apostles): and gave We
unto David, "Zaboor" (the Psalms). (Qur'an 17:55)

As the Qur'an revealed that the Torah is a guide (Imam) and mercy
(rahma), this would also indicate that each of the books of Allah is a
guide and mercy: Scrolls or Scriptures of Abraham, Torah of Moses,
Psalms of David, Injil (Gospel) of Jesus, and the Qur'an of Mohammad.
As Muslims, the Qur'an guides us in every aspect of our lives. The Qur'an
is the final guide and mercy.

Guide as Attribute of Allah (al-Hadi; ar-Rasheed)

Guide is also one of the attributes of Allah:

> And thus We did appoint for every Apostle an enemy
> among the guilty ones; but sufficient is thy Lord as a
> Guide and a Helper (for thee). (Qur'an 25:31)

Allah guides mankind by his creation (Qur'an 20:50, 26:78–81,
27:60–64, 43:27), his messengers (Qur'an 2:213, 3:3–4, 6:84–85, 9:33,
48:28, 61:9), and his divine inspiration (Qur'an 1:6, 7:43, 10:25, 18:13–
14, 19:76, 24:35, 27:63, 28:56, 64:11).

Imam as a Person

A person who is a spiritual leader can be referred to as an Imam. One
who leads a congregational prayer is an Imam. An Imam can also be the
leader of a mosque, institution, or community. Scholars and learned men
in Islam may also be called Imams. A father, as head of his household, is
considered an Imam of his family. The Qur'an mentions that there are
evil Imams (Qur'an 9:12; 28:41–42). For example, Pharaoh Ramses II
(*Fir'awn*), an Imam during the time of Prophet Moses, led his followers to
be doomed to hell. Other evil Imams were Yazid ibn Muawiyah, Genghis
Khan, Adolf Hitler, Joseph Stalin, and Saddam Hussein. However,

the perfectly good Imams are the infallible Imams appointed by Allah. There are a number of verses that refer to the infallible Imams of the Imamat: Qur'an 2:124; 2:207; 3:7; 3:103; 4:59; 5:1–2; 5:3; 5:55; 5:67; 6:97; 11:72–73; 11:124; 13:7; 14:37; 17:71; 21:73; 25:74; 32:24; 33:33; 36:12; 43:28.

Prophet Abraham as Imam

Prophet Abraham was elevated to the position of Imam:

> And remember when his Lord tried Abraham with certain words then he fulfilled them; He said, "Verily I make thee Imam for mankind;" (Abraham) said "And of my offspring?" He said: "My Covenant reacheth not the unjust." (Qur'an 2:124)

Prophet Abraham's descendants are many, which include his sons, Isaac and Ishmael, and their descendants, Moses, Jesus, and Mohammad:

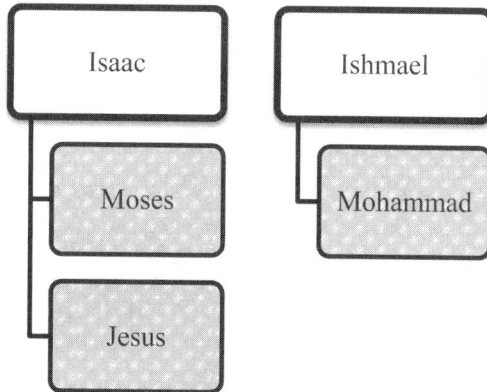

Prophet Abraham held two divinely appointed positions, prophet and Imam. Allah granted Prophet Abraham that he would have Imams from his offspring and the descendants thereafter but not from the unjust descendants. While the Qur'an states that Prophet Mohammad is the final prophet, there are no verses that point to the termination of the Imamat, only its continuation.

As with Prophets, Imams are appointed by Allah and not elected by man. The basis of Imamat is clearly established in the following verse:

> And We gave him (Abraham) Isaac, and Jacob, as a further gift, and made We all of them righteous ones. And We made them Leaders (Imams) Guiding (the people) by Our command, and revealed We unto them the doing of good, and the establishing of prayer, and the giving of alms, and (only) unto Us did they worship. (Qur'an 21:72–73)

Prophet Mohammad as Imam

As with Prophet Abraham, Prophet Mohammad was also a messenger and an Imam:

> O' People of the Book! Indeed hath come unto you Our Apostle (Mohammad) explaining unto you after the break in (the series of) Our Apostles, lest ye say; "There came not onto us any bearer of glad tidings nor a warner"; but now hath come unto you a Bearer of glad tidings and a Warner (Our Apostle Mohammad); and verily, Allah, over all things, hath power. (Qur'an 5:19)

> And say those who disbelieve: "Why hath not a sign been sent down unto him (Mohammad) from his Lord?" Verily thou art a Warner and a Guide (Hadi) unto every people. (Qur'an 13:7)

Prophet Mohammad was also a guide (Imam) and a mercy (rahma). So, as an Imam, Prophet Mohammad was entrusted with safeguarding the Qur'an from distortion and misinterpretation. Therefore, Prophet

Mohammad's hadiths (traditions) were given to explain the meaning of the concepts and verses in the Qur'an. It is important to note that both Prophet Mohammad and the Qur'an have the same characteristics of guide and mercy, not coincidentally but as revealed by Allah. To protect the Qur'an from distortion and misinterpretation required one who had been divinely inspired with these same characteristics as the Qur'an. That person is Prophet Mohammad, who self-actualized in the concept of the Imamat or Islamic leadership.

Prophet Mohammad acquired the titles of all the major prophets, including the titles of Imam and rahma:

> And We sent thee not (O' Our Apostle Mohammad!)
> but a Mercy unto all the worlds. (Qur'an 21:107)

Some of the attributes of Prophet Mohammad are:

+ *Safi Allah* (Allah's sincere friend)
+ *Kalim Allah* (he to whom Allah has talked)
+ *Habib Allah* (Allah's beloved friend)
+ *Khalil* (good friend)

Some of these attributes are also attributed to other prophets. While the English translation of some of these attributes seems to quantify Allah, they are only illustrative, as Allah cannot be quantified. For example, since Allah is not lonely, in need of a friend, then the term friend is regarded as the ideal character or role model favored by Allah. Moreover, Allah bestowed the title of Imam upon Prophet Abraham and Prophet Mohammad, after they had already been messengers of Allah.

This high status is significant, as it underscores the importance of the term Imam. Let us examine this point in the context of the Qur'an. The main function of a messenger is to warn mankind about that which Allah has ordained and commanded. The main function of an Imam is to guide mankind toward understanding the meaning and significance of the verses of the Qur'an. There is a chronology of Islamic events that takes place. It begins with the concepts of *tawhid* (unity of Allah) and *adl* (justice of Allah). The *nabuwwat* (prophecy) is the chain of prophets, which totaled 124,000 and began with Prophet Adam and ended with Prophet Mohammad (Majlisi 2012).

While the Imamat has its historical reference to prophets—for example, Prophet Abraham and Prophet Mohammad—Imam Ali ibn Abi Talib receives full control of the Imamat upon the death of Prophet Mohammad. The concept of the Twelve Infallible Imams begins with Imam Ali ibn Abi Talib and ends with Imam Mohammad al-Mahdi, the latter that is still living in his major occultation. The last state of the chronology is the *Qayyamat* (Day of Judgment). Moreover, the binding tie between Prophet Mohammad and Imam Ali ibn Abi Talib sets the stage for the khalifah succession of the infallible Imams.

Chapter 5

Binding Tie

Never in the history of mankind has there been a closer relationship between two people in faith, righteousness, truth, and patience than that of Prophet Mohammad and Imam Ali ibn Abi Talib. Volumes of books have been written about the binding tie and common linkage between these two luminaries. The rope of Allah bound their virtues, thoughts, spirituality, devotion, loyalty, lifestyle, and myriad other characteristics. Truly, they were together as one light (*nur*):

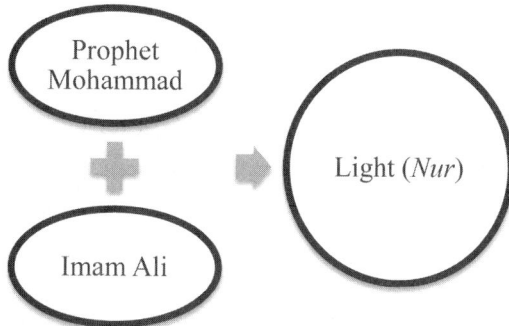

O' People of the Book! Indeed Our Apostle (Mohammad), had come unto you, manifesting unto you much of what ye had been concealing of the Book, and passing over much; Indeed hath come unto you from Allah, Light and a Manifesting Book (Qur'an). (Qur'an 5:15)

The *light* is Prophet Mohammad who leads mankind out of darkness. The *book* is the Qur'an, which cannot be fully understood without the light of Prophet Mohammad. Nothing can be studied without the necessary light. Prophet Mohammad said:

O' Ali, you and I were created from the same light ... (Bihar al-Anwar, 11/5, Hadith 12)

Salman al-Farsi narrated that:

I heard the Messenger of Allah saying: "I myself and Ali were one light ..." (Imam Reza Network [Mizan al-Ei'tidal, by al-Dhahabi, Vol. 1, p. 235; Fada'il al-Sahaba, by Ahmad ibn Hanbal, Vol. 2, p. 663, Tradition #1130; al-Riyadh al-Nadhirah, by al-Muhib al-Tabari, Vol. 2, p. 164, Vol. 3, p. 154])

Prophet Mohammad nurtured and cultivated the upbringing of Imam Ali ibn Abi Talib. He instilled in the mind and heart of Imam Ali the intricacies of understanding the many facets of life. He molded Imam Ali into the perfect personification of all that is virtuous, the standard by which others would aspire to reach self-actualization. Truly, they reinforced each other in brotherhood, solidarity, and self-denial, as they were linked together as one in faith, devotion, and allegiance.

Characteristics of Prophet Mohammad and Imam Ali ibn Abi Talib:

- divinely inspired, one light (nur), safeguarded Qur'an and Islam
- unity of ummah, knowledgeable and wise, charitable, pious, and forgiving
- purity of heart, mind, and soul, moral and ethical, diplomatic
- patient, merciful, and humble, leadership qualities and creative energy
- fought for truth and justice, courage and conviction
- trustworthy and righteous, charismatic and authoritative
- sympathetic and empathetic, never deceived, misled, or betrayed anyone
- polite and honest, led a simple life, sincere and eloquent, truth of certainty

Early Years of Imam Ali

Prophet Mohammad's father, Abdullah, died before he was born, and his mother, Amina, died when he was six years old. Thereafter, the prophet's grandfather, Abdul Mutallib, raised him for a short time. When Abdul Mutallib died, Prophet Mohammad's uncle, Abi Talib, raised and protected the prophet, even during the prophet's pursuit of Islam. Abi Talib was the sheikh of the Bani Hashim clan in the Quraysh tribe as well as the custodian of the Ka'bah. Imam Ali was the son of Abi Talib and Fatima bint Asad. As first cousin to Prophet Mohammad, he married Fatima, and with her had four children: Imam Hassan, Imam Hussein, Lady Zainab, and Umm Kulthum. Allah ordered Prophet Mohammad to perform the marriage of Imam Ali to Fatima (Jafari 2009). From an early age, Imam Ali lived with the prophet. It was there that he spent his adolescence, during which he was a close observer of all the developments that happened in the life of the prophet. Prophet Mohammad was Imam Ali's guide and teacher, as he educated him in the vast dimensions of knowledge and wisdom. Prophet Mohammad named Imam Ali, which means the exalted one.

Imam Ali Embracing Islam

Imam Ali was one of the early followers of Islam, becoming a Muslim as a child. When Prophet Mohammad received a divine revelation, Imam Ali was the first male to accept his message and convert to Islam. Embracing Islam as a child, he never bowed before the idols, while other companions of the prophet did so before they became Muslims. His support and dedication to Prophet Mohammad and Islam were clear at the outset. For example, in a meeting with the leaders of Quraysh, the prophet told his fellow clansmen about the new faith of Islam and asked who would support him. Imam Ali, even though a young boy, stood up and pledged his support (Jafari 2009).

Imam Ali's Loyalty to Prophet Mohammad

Imam Ali's loyalty to the prophet meant risking his life. The most famous example was when the Meccans decided to assassinate the prophet. The Muslims had already begun the *hijra* (migration) to Medina. Imam Ali slept in the prophet's bed waiting for the assassins. Prophet Mohammad gave him the title *Asadullah* (Lion of Allah) for his service to Islam (Bokhari 2012). Imam Ali shared with the prophet his persecutions and hardships. He also defended the prophet against the polytheists and struggled with him against the unbelievers. He protected the prophet with his own life from the enemies of Islam. When the prophet died, it was Imam Ali who made all the arrangements for his funeral.

Agreement between Sunnis and Shi'as Regarding Imam Ali

Despite the differences between Sunnis and Shi'as, both groups have great respect for Imam Ali. A major agreement among the schools of thought is the birth, upbringing, character, leadership, and authority of Imam Ali. He was born in the Sacred House (Ka'bah) in Mecca. No one before or after him has ever been born in the House of Allah (Razwy 2001). Prophet Mohammad raised Imam Ali. Under the delicate care and education of Prophet Mohammad, Imam Ali attained nobility and respect. Imam Ali was the first male whom the prophet summoned to Islam and who answered positively (Shah 2009). He is respected for his courage, wisdom, knowledge, belief, honesty, unbending devotion to Islam, deep loyalty to the prophet, equal treatment to all people, and generosity in forgiving his defeated enemies. For example, he was known for his courage on the battlefield and highly respected as a writer and religious authority.

Sunni and Shi'a scholars agree that: (a) no one can match the loyalty to Prophet Mohammad that Imam Ali displayed; (b) he shared with the prophet the persecutions, abuse, and adversities; (c) he protected and safeguarded the prophet against the polytheists and struggled with him against the unbelievers; and (d) he defended and shielded the prophet with his own life from the enemies of Islam. Furthermore, it is the consensus of Sunni and Shi'a scholars that the following verse is attributed to Imam Ali:

> And among men there is one who selleth his self (soul) seeking the pleasure of Allah; and verily, Allah is affectionate unto His (faithful) servants. (Qur'an 2:207)

This verse relates to the time when Imam Ali slept in the bed of Prophet Mohammad when the prophet had to migrate from Mecca to Medina. Imam Ali offered himself to take the place of the prophet by sleeping in his bed, even though the enemies of Islam came to kill the prophet, thinking he was in the bed. Imam Ali was ready to give his life in order to safeguard the life of the prophet. Here was a man who was willing to risk his own life to save Islam. His will and courage to sleep under the swords of the enemies further illustrates the courage and nobility of this great Imam. He never hesitated to give his life for the protection of Prophet Mohammad and the promotion of Islam.

We find yet another verse, of many verses, in the Qur'an that is attributed to Imam Ali, as confirmed by Sunni scholars (Ahlul-Bayt Islamic Library [*Shawahid al-Tanzeel by Allama Haskani*, Vol. 1, p.

106; *al-Bidahiya wa al-Nihayiah*, Vol. 7, p. 359; *Kanz al-Ummal*, Vol. 6, p. 154; *Asadul-Bilagha*, Vol. 4, p. 22 and Vol. 1, p. 22; *Kitabul Sagheer*, p. 15; *Manaqib Khawarizmi*, p. 49; *Dhakhair al Uqba*, p. 78; *Musnad of Ahmad Hanbal*, Vol. 1, p. 185; and *Maqtal Hussain*, Vol. 1, p. 43]):

> He granteth wisdom to whomsoever He willeth, and he who hath been granted wisdom hath been granted abundant good; and none shall mind it save those endowed with wisdom. (Qur'an 2:269)

In this verse, the word *wisdom* implies the best knowledge in seeking to act with fullness and soundness of one's own conscience. Imam Ali derived his vast knowledge and eloquence by virtue of his long and close relationship with Prophet Mohammad. With divine inspiration, the prophet was the source of all such knowledge and wisdom, and he taught Imam Ali these virtues. These gifts of knowledge and wisdom were bestowed upon the divinely chosen and purified ones, as revealed in the following verse:

> Verily Allah intendeth but to keep off from you (every kind of) uncleanness O' ye the People of the House, and purify you (with) a thorough purification. (Qur'an 33:33)

Sunni scholars are in agreement that this verse was dedicated to Prophet Mohammad and his Ahl al-Bayt, which includes Imam Ali, Fatima, Imam Hassan, and Imam Hussein (Ahlul Bayt Digital Islamic Library Project Team [*Sahih Muslim*, chapter of "Virtues of Companions," section of the "Virtues of Ahl al-Bayt of the Prophet," 1980 edition, published in Saudi Arabia, Arabic version, Vol. 4, p 1883, Tradition 61; *al-Tirmidhi*, Vol. 2, 902; *Manaqib Ahl al-Bayt, Tirmidhi*, Vol. 2, p. 308]).

Sunni scholars unanimously agree that the following verse is also about Imam Ali:

Your guardian is (none else but) Allah and His Apostle (Mohammad) and those who believe, those who establish prayer and pay the poor-rate, while they be (even) bowing down (in prayer). Whoever taketh as his guardian, Allah and His Apostle (Mohammad) and those who believe, verily, (he hath joined) Allah's battalion; they are those that shall (always) be triumphant. (Qur'an 5:55–56)

Sunni scholars agree that Imam Ali gave away his ring while he was kneeling and in a state of prayer (Ahlul Bayt Digital Islamic Library Project Team [*Tafsir al-Kabir*, by Ahmad ibn Muhammad al-Tha'labi; *Tafsir al-Kabir*, by Ibn Jarir al-Tabari, Vol. 6, pp. 186, 288–289; *Tafsir al-Durr al-Manthoor*, by al-Suyuti, Vol. 2, pp. 293–294; *Ahmad ibn Hanbal*, Vol. 5, p. 38]). It was Imam Ali who more than anyone else resembled the prophet with respect to his spiritual qualities, knowledge, devotion, and insight.

Well-known and respected Sunni scholars have been accredited and commended for their collection of hadiths. However, the authenticity of some of these hadiths has been questioned. Since the following hadith is recorded in each of their collections, one can make the argument in favor of its validity:

Ali is with the Qur'an and the Qur'an is with Ali; they will never separate until they reach me (Prophet Mohammad) at the Fountain of Kawthar (Inlagg 2013):

+ *Al-Mustadrak, Ala al-Sahihain,* by Hakim al-Nishaburi, Vol. 3, p. 134, Hadiths 226, 4628 (al-Nishaburi claimed that all the Hadiths in it were authentic according to the conditions of either *Sahih Bukhari* or *Sahih Muslim* or both)
+ *Fayd al Qadir fi Sharh al-Jami' al-Saghir,* by Abd al-Ra'uf Muhammad al-Munawi, Vol. 4, p. 170, Hadith 5594
+ *Kanz al-Ummal fi Sunan al-Aqwal Wa'l Af'al* by Ali Ibn Abd-al-Malik al-Hindi, Vol. 11, p. 603

+ *Al-Mu'jam al-Saghir*, by Abu al-Qasim Sulaiman ibn Ahmad ibn al-Tabarani, Vol. 1, p. 255
+ *Al-Mu'jam al-Awsat*, by Abu al-Qasim Sulaiman ibn Ahmad ibn al-Tabarani, Vol. 5, p. 135
+ *Kitab Al-Manaqib*, by Abu al-Muayyid Khatib al-Khawarizmi, Vol. 1, pp. 176–177, Hadith 214
+ *Al-Sawa'iq al-Muhriqah*, by Ibn Hajar al-Haythami, Vol. 1, p. 175

This hadith underscores the importance of the Imamat, as only they can be entrusted with the protection of the Qur'an that, by the grace of Allah, Prophet Mohammad revealed to mankind. Among the many verses attributed to Imam Ali ibn Abi Talib in the Qur'an is the following verse:

> Verily We (and) We (alone) give life unto the dead, and We write down what they have sent before them and (even) their footprints (which they leave behind them): And everything have We confined (recorded) into an Imamun-Mubeen (Manifesting Guide). (Qur'an 36:12)

According to the Fifth Infallible Imam, Mohammad al-Baqir, he said that when the aforementioned verse was revealed, Abu Bakr and Umar had asked Prophet Mohammad if the *Imamun-Mubeen* was the Torah, the Injil (Gospel), or the Qur'an, and the prophet responded that they were not. Then the prophet turned to Imam Ali ibn Abi Talib and said:

> Verily this is that Imam (Guide) in whom Allah has contained the knowledge of everything. (Majlisi 2003)

Prophet Mohammad also said to Imam Ali:

> You are to me as Aaron was to Moses, but there will be no prophet after me.

+ *Sahih Bukhari*, V5, Book 64, Hadith 4416 (Sahih/Authentic)
+ *Sahih Muslim*, V6, Book 44, Hadith 6218 (Sahih/Authentic)
+ *Ibn Majah*, V1, Book 1, Hadith 121 (Sahih/Authentic)
+ *Al-Tirmidhi*, V6, Book 46, Hadith 3730 (Sahih/Authentic)
+ *Al-Nasa'i*, Al-Khasais, pp. 15–16
+ *Ahmad ibn Hanbal*, V1, p. 174

When Prophet Mohammad assembled his closest family members to obtain their support, he explicitly asked who would support him in his mission so that he might be his brother (*akhi*), successor (*wasiyyi*), and caliph (*khalifati*). Only Imam Ali responded in the affirmative. Imam Ali was just a youngster at the time. Prophet Mohammad then said:

> Verily this is my brother, my successor, and my caliph amongst you. Therefore, listen to him and obey. (Tabarsi 1981; Majlisi 1983, Bihar al-Anwar, Vol. 18, p. 192)

The following hadith is well known among Sunni scholars, and the message is clear that Imam Ali is the path by which to reach Prophet Mohammad:

> I (Mohammad) am the City of Knowledge (House of Wisdom) and Ali is its gate. (Al-Tirmidhi, Vol. 6, Book 46, Hadith 3723)

This hadith is believed to have been authentic but later removed. However, *Jalal al-Din al-Suyuti*, p. 170 (Al-Suyuti 1996), and *al-Naysaburi*, Vol. 3, pp. 126–127 (Al-Naysaburi 1915–1923) allude to Al-Tirmidhi having made the exact quote.

Sahih Bukhari recorded the following hadith:

> He (the Prophet) then said to Ali, "You are from me and I am from you …" (*Sahih Bukhari*, Vol. 5, Book 64, Hadith 4251)

The well-known Sunni scholar Al-Tirmidhi narrated many hadiths on Imam Ali ibn Abi Talib. Following are just a few of these hadiths:

+ Hadith No. 3713: Abu Sariah or Zaid ibn Arqam—Shu'ab had doubt—narrated, from the Prophet: "For whomever I am his Mawla, then Ali is his Mawla."
+ Hadith No. 3716: Al Bara bin Azib narrated that the Prophet said to Ali ibn Abi Talib: "You are from me, and I am from you."
+ Hadith No. 3719: Hubshi bin Junadah narrated that the Messenger of Allah said: "Ali is from me and I am from Ali. And none should represent me except myself or Ali."
+ Hadith No. 3723: Ali narrated that the Messenger of Allah said: "I am the House of Wisdom and Ali is its Door."

In addition, Sunni scholars have recorded the following hadith: "Loving Ali is the sign of belief, and hating Ali is the sign of hypocrisy."

+ *Sahih Muslim*, V1, Book 1, Ch. 33, Hadith 235 (Sahih/Authentic)
+ *Ibn Majah*, V1, Book 1, Hadith 114 (Sahih/Authentic)
+ *Al-Tirmidhi*, V6, Book 46, Hadith 3718 (Hasan/Good)
+ *Al Nasa'i*, V6, Book 47, Hadith 5021(Sahih/Authentic)
+ *Ahmad ibn Hanbal*, V1, pp. 84, 95, 128

Imam Ali as Successor to Prophet Mohammad

As to the claim that Imam Ali ibn Abi Talib was the successor to Prophet Mohammad, there are certain events that transpired that authenticate Imam Ali's authority to take the banner of leadership after Prophet Mohammad:

+ Imam Ali's birth in the Ka'bah
+ Imam Ali's appointment as a young child to succeed Prophet Mohammad
+ Imam Ali's destruction of the idols at the Ka'bah

+ Prophet Mohammad's final sermon at Ghadir Khumm in which he appointed Imam Ali as his successor
+ Imam Ali being the first to compile and codify the Qur'an

All of these events are linked. It was not an accident that Imam Ali was born in the Ka'bah but by the will of Allah. Why? This event was a forerunner, a sign or foreshadowing, of future events to take place. When Prophet Mohammad embarked on his mission to spread the faith of Islam, he asked of his family and clan who would be the first to convert to Islam and be his spiritual heir (*wasi*), vizier, and successor. No one responded in the affirmative except Imam Ali, who was just a youngster at the time.

Another event that later took place was the destruction of the false idols at the Ka'bah. Prophet Mohammad and Imam Ali destroyed the idols at the lower level of the Ka'bah. They then turned to the idols at the higher level of the Ka'bah, including the biggest idol. At first, Prophet Mohammad stood on the shoulders of Imam Ali to destroy the idols. However, Imam Ali could not hold the prophet, as Imam Ali felt that the weight of the whole world rested on him. So Prophet Mohammad stepped down and placed Imam Ali on his shoulders, and the weight of Imam Ali was like that of a feather. So Imam Ali proceeded to destroy the idols (Al-Qurashi 2007 [*Sifat as-Safwah*, Vol. 1, p. 163; *Musnad Ahmad ibn Hanbal*, Vol. 1, p. 84; *Ibn Sa'd*, Vol. 3, p. 13]).

Now we all know that Imam Ali was very strong, so the weight of Prophet Mohammad on his shoulders should not have been a problem. However, it was Allah who intervened and made the weight of Prophet Mohammad extremely heavy. Moreover, Allah demonstrated to the people that Prophet Mohammad is the foundation upon which Imam Ali rises. Just as Prophet Abraham destroyed the false idols of his time, Imam Ali likewise destroyed the false idols of his time. These two occurrences of Prophet Abraham and Imam Ali are linked, as they were done personally to Allah and Allah only. And we are reminded that Prophet Abraham was also an Imam.

The destruction of the false idols at the Ka'bah brings about another important milestone. Allah linked Prophet Mohammad and Imam Ali together to underscore who would be the eventual successor to Prophet Mohammad. Thereafter, the speech at Ghadir Khumm was the climax of the duty that Allah had bestowed on Prophet Mohammad to perform. That duty was to finalize the revelations of the Qur'an while at the same time passing on the successful leadership of the ummah and the Imamat to Imam Ali and his progeny, the infallible Imams. It is this linkage of the completion and perfection of the Qur'an with the Imamat of Ahl al-Bayt that continues to secure the rope of Allah (Qur'an 3:103).

Therefore, the baton of leadership that passed on to Imam Ali was that of the Imamat, as a guide of the Qur'an and the leader of the ummah. Additionally, the Imamat had the major responsibility of conveying to the ummah the true meaning of the verses of the Qur'an. Furthermore, the Imamat was entrusted with protecting the Qur'an from distortion and misinterpretation. Moreover, Imam Ali was the first to compile and codify the Qur'an. Hence, in addition to the khalifah leadership, it was the Imamat leadership that was the pinnacle of Prophet Mohammad's sermon at Ghadir Khumm, in which he proclaimed that, "Whomever I am his master, then Ali is also his master." With this declaration, Allah revealed the following verse:

> This day have I perfected for you, your religion, and have completed My favor on you, and chosen for you Islam (to be) the Religion … (Qur'an 5:3)

The concept of khalifah, or stewardship, is a responsibility for all mankind to protect one another as well as to protect plants, animals, and the environment. Adam was the first khalifah. At the outset, he had no humans to rule or guide, but he was to protect all that was around him at the time. Later, Adam and Eve had children that multiplied to form communities. So khalifah for them was to protect each other, all creatures, and the environment. Likewise, the infallible Imams are also the khalifah or stewards and protectors of mankind, creatures, and the environment.

While Imam Ali spoke of his right as *mawla* (successor) to Prophet Mohammad, his primary objective was to safeguard the unity in Islam, as outside forces continued their quest to destroy Islam. While there was division within the Muslim community, Imam Ali worked toward uniting the community. There were constant arguments and dissentions within the Muslim community, and Imam Ali resolved these differences, thereby restoring order within the Islamic ummah. Imam Ali pursued unity with all his power, intellect, and wisdom, even protecting those who rejected Prophet Mohammad's declaration of Imam Ali as his mawla.

Moreover, Imam Ali, as mawla after Prophet Mohammad, is confirmed in the following Sunni hadiths:

+ *Ibn Majah*, V1, Book 1, Hadith 121(Sahih/Authentic)
+ *Al-Tirmidhi*, V6, Book 46, Hadith 3713 (Sahih/Authentic)
+ *Al-Nasa'i*, Al-Khasais, pp. 4, 21–26, 40
+ *Ahmad ibn Hanbal*, V1, Hadith 641 (Sahih/Authentic)

This was the Straight Path that Imam Ali pursued, but he never accepted any post under the caliphs. It was a Straight Path of his dedication to the genuine objectives of Islam. As Dr. Ali Shariati stated, "the responsibility of an intellectual is to transmit the inequities within society to the self-consciousness of the people of that society. Then society performs its own movement" (Shariati 1980). And that is exactly what Imam Ali and the other infallible Imams did.

After completing his last pilgrimage, Prophet Mohammad declared the tradition of the two weighty things (*Thaqalayn*) in his *Farewell Sermon* (appendix 6) at Ghadir Khumm, March 10, AD 632 (18th Dhu-l-Hijja, AH 10):

> It seems the time approached when I shall be called away (by Allah) and I shall answer that call. I am leaving for you two precious things (thaqalayn) and if you adhere to them both, you will never go astray

after me. They are the Book of Allah (Qur'an) and my Progeny ('itrah), that is, my Ahl al-Bayt (Household). The two shall never separate from each other, until they come to me by the Pool (of Kawthar on the Day of Judgment).

During the same *Farewell Sermon* (appendix 6), Prophet Mohammad said to Imam Ali:

Stand up O' Ali, for I am pleased to announce you Imam and Guide after me. So whomever I was his leader (mawla), then this is his leader (mawla). So be to him supporters in truth and followers …

Sources: *Al-Bidayah wa'l Nihayah*, Vol. V, p. 209 (Ibn Kathir 2009); *Dhakha'ir al-'Uqba*, p. 16 (Tabari 2001); *al-Fusul al –Muhimmah*, p. 22 (Sharaf al-Din 1996); *al-Sawa'iq al-Muhriqah*, p. 147 (Al-Haythami 1965). In *Ghayat al-Maram*, thirty-nine versions of this hadith have been recorded from Sunni sources and eighty-two versions from Shi'a sources (Bahrani 2001).

Although the Qur'an does not mention the name of Imam Ali ibn Abi Talib, it does, however, allude to him in many verses, one of which is the following:

Verily, your guardian is (none else but) Allah and His Apostle (Mohammad) and those who believe, those who establish prayer and pay the poor-rate, while they be (even) bowing down (in prayer). (Qur'an 5:55)

Sunni (*Musnad of Ahmad ibn Hanbal*, Vol. 5, p. 38) and Shi'a (Majlisi 1983, *Bihar al-Anwar*) scholars have reported that this verse was revealed after Imam Ali gave his ring to a poor beggar as charity while he was bowing down in prayer.

And among men there is one who selleth his self (soul) seeking the pleasure of Allah; and verily, Allah is affectionate unto His (faithful) servants. (Qur'an 2:207)

Sunni (*Musnad of Ahmad ibn Hanbal*, Vol. 1, p. 248) and Shi'a (*ibn Shahrashub* 1959, Vol. 2, pp. 68–78) scholars state that this verse was revealed for Imam Ali, who courageously slept in the bed of Prophet Mohammad, who was being pursued by the enemy to murder him. For Imam Ali, the safety of the prophet took precedence over his own safety.

In the following chapters, the concept of Imam and the Straight Path will be further explored relative to the meaning and significance of the Imamat of Ahl al-Bayt.

AHL AL-BAYT

Chapter 6

Imamat of Ahl al-Bayt

Ahl al-Bayt is a designation that literally means the house of the family of Prophet Mohammad. Imamat means to lead, and as leaders, they have absolute command of the Muslims in all religious and secular affairs, in succession to Prophet Mohammad. Shi'as closely identify the Imamat as the infallible Imams whom they regard as the legitimate holders of authority, bearers of sacred knowledge, the personification of wisdom, and they believe in the messianic return of the twelfth Imam at the end of time. The following chronology of the Twelve Infallible Imams of Ahl al-Bayt is derived from the *Brief Timeline of Islamic Events* in appendix 1:

Chronology of the Twelve Infallible Imams of Ahl al-Bayt

Rank	Imam	Birth-Death (AD)	Manner of Death
First	Ali ibn Abi Talib	600–661	Assassinated
Second	Hassan ibn Ali	625–670	Poisoned
Third	Hussein ibn Ali	626–680	Beheaded
Fourth	Ali al-Sajjad ibn Hussein	659–712	Poisoned
Fifth	Mohammad al-Baqir ibn Ali	676–733	Poisoned
Sixth	Ja'far al-Sadiq ibn Mohammad	702–765	Poisoned
Seventh	Musa al-Kazim ibn Ja'far	746–799	Poisoned
Eighth	Ali al-Rida ibn Musa	765–818	Poisoned
Ninth	Mohammad al-Jawad ibn Ali	811–835	Poisoned
Tenth	Ali al-Hadi ibn Mohammad	827–868	Poisoned
Eleventh	Hassan al-Askari ibn Ali	846–874	Poisoned
Twelfth	Mohammad al-Mahdi ibn Hassan	869–Present	Still Living*

*Major Occultation

Sources: Wikipedia and Islamic articles and books.

Qur'anic Verses on Imamat

The Shi'as uphold to the premise that the Imamat are based on verses from the Qur'an. The verse that links the Qur'an with Prophet Mohammad and the infallible Imams is the following:

> Verily We have sent down the Thikr (Reminder) (the Qur'an), and verily We (Ourself) unto it will certainly be the Guardian. (Qur'an 15:9)

This verse answers the pessimists who questioned Prophet Mohammad about the thikr (reminder):

> And say they, O' thou! (Our Apostle Mohammad) on whom hath come down the Thikr (Reminder) (the Qur'an) verily thou art insane. (Qur'an 15:6)

The *We* in the preceding verse refers to Allah, and it is Allah who protects the Qur'an, the Final Word, from being corrupted. Hence, Allah sent the Qur'an, which is the thikr, to Prophet Mohammad to protect it and to ensure its protection through the Twelve Infallible Imams, beginning with Imam Ali ibn Abi Talib and ending with Imam Mohammad al-Mahdi:

Thikr (Reminder)
(Qur'an)

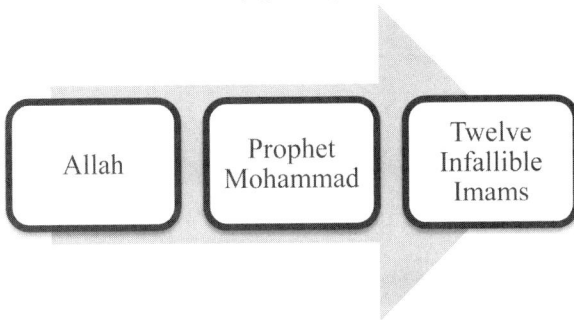

Allah → Prophet Mohammad → Twelve Infallible Imams

> And He it is Who made the stars for you that ye may be (rightly) Guided by (observing) them in the darkness of the land and the sea; indeed have We made plain the Signs for the people who (can) know. (Qur'an 6:97)

The analogy here is that as the stars in the sky are the source of guidance to travelers, so are the Twelve Infallible Imams the source of guidance for mankind. Additionally, just as the stars will remain in the sky until the Day of Judgment, mankind will never be without an infallible Imam from Ahl al-Bayt.

> And of them made We Leaders (Imams) to Guide (Hadi) (the people) by Our Command as they were steadfast (in the calamities); and they of Our Signs were quite certain. (Qur'an 32:24)

The divine appointment of the Twelve Infallible Imams is cemented in the following verse, which references *ulu 'l-amr* as those whose infallibility qualifies them to speak the mind of Prophet Mohammad when they make any command of themselves:

> O' ye who believe! Obey Allah and obey the Apostle (Mohammad) and those vested with authority (ulu 'l-amr) from among you; and then if ye quarrel about anything refer it to Allah and the Apostle (Mohammad) if ye believe in Allah and the Last Day (of Judgment); this is the best and the fairest way of ending (the dispute). (Qur'an 4:59)

Tantamount to the above verse are the following verses that also allude to the Twelve Infallible Imams who would follow Prophet Mohammad and act as guides to mankind:

> And say those who disbelieve: "Why hath not a sign been sent down unto him (Mohammad) from his Lord?" Verily thou art a Warner and a Guide (Hadi) unto every people. (Qur'an 13:7)

> Remember the Day (of Judgment) when We will summon every people with their Imam (Leader); then whosoever is given his book in his right hand, these shall read their books (with pleasure), and they shall not be dealt with (even) a shred unjustly. And whosoever is blind in this (life), he shall in the Hereafter (also) be blind and gone further astray from the (right) way. (Qur'an 17:71–72)

In these verses as well as 25:74–75 of the Qur'an, the Imams are the divinely inspired and purified Imams of Ahl al-Bayt, led by Prophet Mohammad, the best of all the Imams.

The concept of the infallible Imams is cemented in the following verses:

> Verily, Allah intendeth but to keep off from you (every kind of) uncleanness O' ye the People of the House, and purify you (with) a thorough purification. (Qur'an 33:33)

> And hold ye fast by the Rope of Allah all together, and be not divided (among yourselves); and remember the bounty of Allah bestowed upon you … (Qur'an 3:103)

The above verse alludes to Ahl al-Bayt, of which Imam Ali ibn Abi Talib, Fatima, Imam Hassan, and Imam Hussein are members. Well-known Sunni scholars, such as al-Musnad of Ahmad ibn Hanbal (Shakir 1995) and Jami' al-Tirmidhi (Al-Tirmidhi 2007) authenticate the same explanation of this verse.

Throughout the centuries, the ummah needed the leadership of those who would guide the people flawlessly toward self-actualization as Muslims. As such, each Muslim achieves spiritual enlightenment according to his or her capacity to understand, practice, and become absorbed in the tenets of Islam. Toward this end, each Muslim can achieve a higher realization of Islam via the teachings of the divinely appointed Imamat.

The responsibilities of the Imamat are many. Following are just a few of these responsibilities:

- Preserve truth.
- Propagate Islam.
- Protect, defend, and implement divine law.
- Comment on, interpret, and protect the Qur'an.
- Provide inner guidance to mankind.

The central focus of the Imamat is the preservation of truth. Propagation of Islam and expansion of the sphere of its social and governmental influence is a function entrusted to the Imamat. An Imam has to execute all the functions of a ruler and government, including the settlement of legal disputes while maintaining law and order. Imamat is religious leadership as well as political leadership, which entails the management of the affairs of the community and improving the position of the Muslims.

Allah appoints the Imams as trustees to protect, defend, and implement the divine law (shari'ah). Toward this end, the Imam invites the people to Allah by means of logic, argument, and sound advice. As the leader and guide of humanity, the Imamat instills in the minds and hearts of each Muslim the explanation (*tafsir*) of the Qur'an. The Imam provides commentary, interpretation (*ta'wil*), as well as protection of the Qur'an from innovation, distortion, and misinterpretation.

As the Imam provides inner guidance to mankind, he does so with all his purity, piety, knowledge, wisdom, and devotion. As such, all virtues are manifested in the Imam, and he is the role model that sets the practical example and standard of excellence. As he matures mankind's spiritual capacities, he illuminates the hearts of believers.

Man is on a continuous struggle to achieve self-actualization. Without guidance, man is at a loss to achieve a genuine understanding of the tenets of Islam. Allah appointed the Imams to be the guides to lead mankind on the Straight Path. Toward this end, the role of the Imams is to enlighten the ummah on Islam and guide them by teaching and clarifying the creed and doctrinal bases of faith. This applies to all levels of jurisprudence, knowledge, and the proper conduct of ethics and morals. In effect, the Imams are the vehicles of Allah's grace to guide mankind to explain the inner meanings of the divine law (shari'ah), to properly interpret the verses of the Qur'an, to defend the truth, and to develop the Islamic personality of the ummah. Without the Imams, there would be no link between mankind and their efforts to attain self-actualization in Islam.

We have noted that the term Imam is a reference to several entities, some of which are Allah's books, prophets, messengers, and Ahl al-Bayt.

Any discussion relative to the authenticity of the Imamat should refer to the verses in the Qur'an that were detailed earlier. Additionally, the legitimacy of the Imams can also be cited in a number of hadiths. For example, Muslims must recognize their religious authority and know whom they should follow in religious matters. There is a well-known tradition (hadith) by Prophet Mohammad that appears in both Shi'a and Sunni sources, which states that each person should relate to an Imam by recognizing him or obedience to him:

> One who dies without recognizing the Imam of his time dies the death of ignorance. (Majlisi 1983, Bihar al-Anwar, Vol. 51, p. 38)

> Prophet Mohammad said: One who dies without obedience (to an Imam) dies as a pagan and disbeliever. (*Sahih Muslim*, Vol. 12, p. 240 [al-Nawawi's Exposition])

The use of reason can also validate the concept of Imamat. For example, if the Imamat is nonexistent or lost, then the structure of Islam would fragment and eventually dissolve. As stated earlier, Allah made a covenant with Prophet Abraham, promising that his descendants would inherit his legacy and become Imams of great nations (Qur'an 2:124). Likewise, Allah made a covenant with Prophet Mohammad that his descendants, the Twelve Infallible Imams, are leaders and guides (Qur'an 32:24; 4:59).

Straight Path
(Sirat al-Mustaqim)

The diagram is one of a Straight Path (Sirat al-Mustaqim), beginning with the covenant of Abraham that leads to the covenant of Mohammad and ends with the Twelve Infallible Imams of the Imamat. The Imamat is a divine covenant. It is a covenant decreed by Allah, not by the people. Through the Imamat, one can heighten his or her comprehension of

Islam, as the path guided by Ahl al-Bayt is the means by which to reach this level.

For every era, there is a divinely inspired Imam that guides us to facilitate the link between knowledge and action. Presently, that link is the patience of Imam Mohammad al-Mahdi, who has lived through the centuries and whose lineage is the most exalted and honorable. As all Twelve Infallible Imams were appointed by Allah and declared by Prophet Mohammad as his successors, they guide the Muslim ummah in spiritual, religious, social, and political matters. Infallible, most knowledgeable, and noble, the Twelve Infallible Imams possess complete awareness and interpretation of the Qur'an and traditions (hadiths).

There are many characteristics of Imamat, some of which are necessity, infallibility, appointment, authority, and guardianship.

Characteristics of Imamat

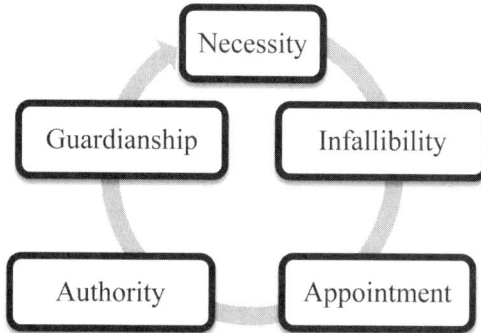

Imamat is one of necessity, as Allah's grace (*lutf*) inspires complete obedience. Another qualification of the Imamat is their infallibility, which protects their purity from sin and error. The designation of Imamat is one of appointment that is granted only by Allah. The authority (ulu 'l-amr) of the Imamat binds them with Prophet Mohammad, as they also provide guidance to the community. As guardians, Prophet Mohammad declared the Imamat to be his successors.

The following chapters will examine each of the characteristics of the Imamat, beginning with necessity.

Chapter 7

Necessity

As they walked the Straight Path, the infallible Imams of the Imamat were nurtured and cultivated by the necessity of succession, leadership, justice, knowledge, and obedience.

I. Necessity of Succession

Allah decreed that the infallible Imams would follow Prophet Mohammad to lead mankind:

> Verily, your guardian is (none else but) Allah and His Apostle (Mohammad) and those who believe, those who establish prayer and pay the poor-rate, while they be (even) bowing down (in prayer). (Qur'an 5:55)

The verse refers to Imam Ali ibn Abi Talib, who gave a poor person his ring while in prayer. As stated earlier, there is unanimous agreement among Sunni and Shi'a scholars that this verse was attributed to Imam Ali. Therefore, we can conclude that Imam Ali is the successor to Prophet

Mohammad as a guardian, and likewise, the infallible Imams follow in succession. Since chapter 5 of the Qur'an is the final chapter revealed to Prophet Mohammad, this verse is sending a clear message of succession to mankind. Moreover, Allah's revelation to Prophet Mohammad to complete his message (declaration of successors) is mandated in the following verse of chapter 5:

> (O' Our Apostle Mohammad!) Deliver thou what hath been sent down unto thee from thy Lord; and if thou does not, then (it will be as if) thou hast not delivered His message (at all); and surely will Allah protect thee from (the mischief) of men; verily, Allah guideth not an infidel people. (Qur'an 5:67)

During his *Farewell Sermon* (appendix 6), Prophet Mohammad said to Imam Ali:

> Stand up O' Ali, for I am pleased to announce you Imam and Guide after me. So whomever I was his leader (mawla), then this is his leader (mawla). So be to him supporters in truth and followers ...

Sources: *Al-Bidayah wa'l Nihayah*, Vol. V, p. 209 (Ibn Kathir 2009); *Dhakha'ir al-'Uqba*, p. 16 (Tabari 2001); *al-Fusul al –Muhimmah*, p. 22 (Sharaf al-Din 1996); *al-Sawa'iq al-Muhriqah*, p. 147 (Al-Haythami 1965). In *Ghayat al-Maram*, thirty-nine versions of this hadith have been recorded from Sunni sources and eighty-two versions from Shi'a sources (Bahrani 2001).

Abu Bakr, Umar, and Uthman congratulated Imam Ali. Umar said:

> Congratulations, congratulations to you, O 'Ali; you have become my leader (mawla) and the leader of every faithful Muslim. (*Ahmad ibn Hanbal*, Vol. 4, pp. 281, 368, 370)

This proclamation by Umar, who became the second caliph, is yet another proof that the Imamat is by divine appointment and not by election. We find additional proof of succession in the following hadith recorded by well-known Sunni scholars:

> You are to me as Aaron was to Moses, except there is no Prophet after me.

+ *Sahih Bukhari*, V5, Book 64, Hadith 4416 (Sahih/Authentic)
+ *Sahih Muslim*, V6, Book 44, Hadith 6218 (Sahih/Authentic)
+ *Ibn Majah*, V1, Book 1, Hadith 121 (Sahih/Authentic)
+ *Al-Tirmidhi*, V6, Book 46, Hadith 3730 (Sahih/Authentic)
+ *Al-Nasa'i*, Al-Khasais, pp. 15–16
+ *Ahmad ibn Hanbal*, V1, p. 174

The necessity of succession is very clear. Aaron succeeded Moses as a prophet, but Ali succeeded Prophet Mohammad (seal and final prophet) as an Imam.

II. Necessity of Leadership

An Imam is essential to represent and lead the Muslim community in every period of time:

> Remember the Day (of Judgment) when We will summon every people with their Imam (Leader); then whosoever is given his book in his right hand, these shall read their books (with pleasure), and they shall not be dealt with (even) a shred unjustly. And whosoever is blind in this (life), he shall in the hereafter (also) be blind and gone further astray from the (right) way. (Qur'an 17:71–72)

Those who accept the leadership of the prophets and messengers are the true believers, while those who follow the leadership of Satan are the disbelievers. This verse is a warning to all mankind that they should pay heed to only the just leaders.

Every society requires leaders who understand what it takes to manage and direct a society. The best of these leaders are guardians who possess the innate and intellectual capacity and purity of mind and heart to lead. Sunni and Shi'a scholars agree on the necessity of an Imam. However, Sunnis believe that the Imamat resides within the jurisdiction of the law, while Shi'as believe it is within the principles of faith (usul al-din).

It is necessary to have an Imam throughout the ages because mankind seeks perfection and needs guidance and leadership in order to progress in life. The evidence of effective and genuine leadership can be ascertained by one's achievements. The Imamat demonstrated that they are the chosen leaders, as evidenced by their key achievements displayed in appendix 2.

III. Necessity of Justice

Leadership in Islam necessitates that the Imams execute justice in all aspects of the community. Toward this end, justice includes many aspects of life, some of which are religious, political, economic, and social between mankind and creatures. Allah enjoins people to perform justice and forbids them from engaging in acts of injustice. Therefore, the Islamic way of life is based on justice, and that justice should be exercised and promoted at all times. Islam commands Muslims to sustain the cause of justice. As justice is the link between peace and prosperity, it becomes the basis of structure within the Islamic society. Justice in Islam is one of equality, as it has no preference for color, creed, race, ethnicity, tribalism, nationalism, or biases. All people are created equally in this regard.

Imam Ali ibn Abi Talib declared freedom and equality, and he urged people to behave fairly toward each other. He recommended that people, especially his officers, be just to everyone. The mention of the name of Imam Ali is linked to the idea of justice. Throughout his life, Imam Ali fought against injustice by spreading the justice in Islam. Even in the arena of social justice, Imam Ali instructed judges to always exercise fairness and righteousness in their judgments.

The opposite of justice is injustice and oppression. Once we fully comprehend the magnitude of oppression, we will understand the mission of Imam Mohammad al-Mahdi, the Twelfth Infallible Imam, relative to justice. He will fill the earth with justice and equality, just as it would be teeming with injustice and oppression. Hence, the vision of justice is based upon the elimination of injustice and oppression.

At Ghadir Khumm, Prophet Mohammad was ordered by Allah to appoint someone who had the power to execute justice in its complete manifestation. The primary purpose of Prophet Mohammad's *Farewell Sermon* (appendix 6) was to appoint a successor and to establish justice. So Prophet Mohammad chose Imam Ali to be his successor. Imam Ali had the extensive knowledge, inspired by Allah, to explain and execute justice. With the establishment and prevalence of justice, under the banner of the Imamat, the society is guided to the Straight Path. Allah commands justice:

> Verily, Allah enjoineth justice and benevolence (to others) … (Qur'an 16:90)

Justice is a main purpose of the Imamat, and it is intended in all dimensions. The Imamat has the divine inspiration to establish justice and rid the society of its impurities:

> And thus have We made you a group of middling stand (Ummat-e-Wasat) that ye may be witnesses over mankind and the Prophet be a witness over you … (Qur'an 2:143)

Wasat infers justice and equity by remaining on the middle point without leaning in either direction. As protector and trustee, the Imam personifies the perfect manifestation of justice. From the Shi'a perspective, the Twelve Infallible Imams represent the best example of *ummat-e-wasat*.

IV. Necessity of Knowledge

Man has limited perception and understanding of the various aspects and depths of knowledge. Therefore, a prerequisite to becoming an infallible Imam is knowledge:

> What! He who is prayerful during the hours of the night, prostrating in obeisance and standing, and he taketh heed of the hereafter and hopeth he for the mercy of his Lord! Say thou (O' Our Apostle Mohammad!) "What! Can those who know be equal to those who know not? Verily only the men of understanding take the warning." (Qur'an 39:9)

This verse refers to the infallible Imams who are endowed with distinctive qualities of knowledge and wisdom. It is necessary to have an Imam in every generation who has the knowledge and perception, inculcated and inspired within them by Allah, so as to convey to the people Islam's true meaning.

As there is a necessity for prophets and messengers to communicate Allah's commandments to mankind, there is also the need for Imams to convey Allah's commandments and protect them. Since Prophet Mohammad is the seal of the prophets and messengers, there is the need to have his teachings continued. Allah created man, but man is in need of guidance to conduct his affairs. That guidance comes from an Imam. Because in every generation there is an Imam, it is the responsibility of the people to know and pay allegiance to him. The importance of necessity comes full circle when following Ahl al-Bayt, which is a duty of every Muslim.

Just as the necessity of sending prophets and messengers to mankind hinges on divine benevolence, so too does the appointment of the infallible

Imams hinge on divine grace (*lutf*). The Imamat is a position of spiritual well-being and leadership within the Muslim society. The infallible Imams are pure and impeccable. The unity of the Muslim community can only be achieved under the Shi'a traditions of the Imamat. From the Shi'a perspective, the necessity of the Imamat can be derived by way of reason. Like the prophet or messenger, an Imam must excel in all virtues, such as bravery, piety, and charity, and must possess complete knowledge of the divine law:

> Allah will exalt (you in) ranks (unto Him), those who believe among you, and those who have been granted knowledge … (Qur'an 58:11)

Those gifted by Allah with knowledge are the infallible Imams who are purified and perfected in every aspect of their being. Necessity of knowledge derives from the grace of Allah, as the infallible Imams are guided by Allah's command. It is necessary for Allah's commands to be conveyed to mankind without error.

V. Necessity of Obedience

The reasoning that proves the necessity of prophets and messengers is the same reasoning that proves the necessity of the Imamat. Relative to the necessity of the Imamat, it can also be stated that prophets and messengers played an important role in the evolution and growth of mankind. Hence, the Imamat are also regarded as necessary factors for maintaining Islam and continuing the mission of Prophet Mohammad. Similarly, the need for obedience to Allah by prophets, messengers, and the Imamat is unconditional and binding:

> O' ye who believe! Obey Allah and obey the Apostle (Mohammad) and those vested with authority from among you … (Qur'an 4:59)

Allah is ordering us to obey him and the messenger (Prophet Mohammad). In other verses, Allah mentioned obedience to himself and to his messengers. In the following verse and hadiths, obedience to the messenger (Prophet Mohammad) is obedience to Allah:

> Whoso obeyeth the Apostle, he indeed obeyeth Allah ...
> (Qur'an 4:80)

> Whoever obeys me (Mohammad) obeys Allah; and whoever disobeys me, disobeys Allah.

- *Sahih Bukhari*, V5, Book 64, Hadith 3951 (Sahih/Authentic)
- *Sahih Muslim*, V2, Book 7, Hadith 2010 (Sahih/Authentic)
- *Ibn Majah*, V1, Book 1, Hadith 3 (Sahih/Authentic)
- *Abu-Dawud*, V1, Book 2, Hadith 1099 (Sahih/Authentic)
- *Al-Tirmidhi*, V3, Book 21, Hadith 1672 (Sahih/Authentic)
- *Al-Nasa'i*, V5, Book 39, Hadith 4198 (Sahih/Authentic)

The necessity of obedience to Prophet Mohammad transfers to the obedience of the infallible Imams. As such, it necessitates us obeying the Imamat, who possess the knowledge to guide mankind to happiness and perfection. It is necessary that there are Imams who preserve Islam and explain the Qur'an and hadiths. While it is not necessary for a prophet or messenger to be continuously present among mankind, it is necessary for an Imam to continue to be present and act as guardian of mankind. Even the renowned Sunni scholars attest to this obedience (appendix 5).

Throughout the course of history, the Twelve Infallible Imams had to endure extreme levels of difficulty. For example, Imam Hussein had to endure agony and affliction from the enemies of Islam. By reason of necessity and determination, Imam Mohammad al-Mahdi will persevere through the centuries to render justice when he emerges from his major occultation.

AHL AL-BAYT

Chapter 8

Infallibility

Steadfast on the Straight Path of purity, piety, and virtue is the Imamat of the infallible Imams. If we examined the Straight Path of the infallible Imams, we would come to the realization that their lives contained numerous lessons for mankind who desires to be close to Allah. Infallibility ('*ismah*) is the inability to error. 'Ismah is Allah's grace (lutf) to protect a person so as to abstain from committing sins (*ma'sum*) by his own free will. Therefore, those who have received the lutf of Allah are called infallible ('ismah) and ma'sum (sinless).

While Allah has protected Prophet Mohammad and the twelve Imams from committing any error ('ismah), the concept of ma'sum prevents them from sinning by their own power and free will. They are ma'sum in that they are, by their own free will, completely righteous, conscious of their love for Allah, and aware of the dire consequences of committing sins.

However, Sunnis maintain that as Prophet Mohammad was sinless and infallible *only* in the delivery of Allah's message, he nonetheless erred in other things. For example, some of the hadiths state that Prophet Mohammad fell asleep during *fajr* prayer time (*Abu Dawud*, Vol. 1, Book

2, Hadith 444), forgot to perform his ablution prior to prayer (*Sahih Bukhari*, Vol. 7, Book 70, Hadith 5390), forgot to sit during the prayer prostration (*Sahih Bukhari*, Vol. 2, Book 22, Hadiths 1228–1230), that he was affected by a magical spell that caused severe episodes of hallucination (*Sahih Bukhari*, Vol. 7, Book 76, Hadiths 5765–5766), and that he was present with Aisha while girls were singing and playing musical instruments (*Sahih Bukhari*, Vol. 2, Book 13, Hadith 949; *Sahih Bukhari*, Vol. 4, Book 56, Hadith 2906).

On the contrary, Shi'as contend that these hadiths are an insult to Allah, because if Allah sends sinful men (i.e., messengers) to deliver his message to lead mankind, then we are claiming that Allah approves of sin. The Qur'an states:

> By the star when it goeth down, erreth not your Companion (Our Apostle Mohammad) nor is he led astray. (Qur'an 53:1–2)

Moreover, the mercy bestowed on Prophet Mohammad precludes him from committing sin. Therefore, he is sinless and infallible, as are those (Imam Ali, Fatima, Imam Hassan, and Imam Hussein) referred to in the Qur'an (33:33) as infallible.

Unlike the term inerrant, which means that there are no errors, infallibility means there can be no errors. It also denotes absolute reliability and trustworthiness as well as flawless interpretation of the Qur'an, which itself is infallible. As with Prophet Mohammad, the twelve Imams are also infallible:

> Verily, Allah intendeth but to keep off from you (every kind of) uncleanness O' ye the People of the House, and purify you (with) a thorough purification. (Qur'an 33:33)

> Aishah said: The Prophet went out one morning wearing a striped Cloak of black camel hair. Al-Hasan bin Ali came and he enfolded him in the Cloak, then Al-Husain

came and he enfolded him in it, then Fatimah came and
he enfolded her in it, then Ali came and he enfolded him
in it, then he said: "Allah wishes only to remove Ar-Rijs
(evil deeds and sins) from you, O members of the family,
and to purify you with a thorough purification." (*Sahih
Muslim*, Vol. 6, Book 44, Hadith 6261)

As stated, the *Cloak* referred to by Aisha, wife of Prophet Mohammad,
is Ahl al-Kisa, which includes Imam Hassan, Imam Hussein, Fatima,
and Imam Ali as well as Prophet Mohammad. The same five people
are also members of Ahl al-Bayt. Ahl al-Kisa (family of the cloak of
Prophet Mohammad) are enfolded and embraced within the Ahl al-Bayt
(house of the family of Prophet Mohammad). The event of al-Kisa is also
recorded in the Sunni hadiths (appendix 5):

+ *Sahih Bukhari*, Tafsir al-Kabir, V1, Part 2, p. 69
+ *Sahih Muslim*, V6, Book 44, Hadith 6261 (Sahih/Authentic)
+ *Al-Tirmidhi*, V5, Book 44, Hadith 3205 (Sahih/Authentic)
+ *Al-Nasa'i*, Al-Khasais, pp. 4, 8
+ *Ahmad ibn Hanbal*, V6, pp. 292, 298, 323

Symbolically, it is Ahl al-Kisa that provides the shelter and
protection for Ahl al-Bayt: Ahl al-Kisa and Ahl al-Bayt are inseparable,
as they reinforce and strengthen each other. The event of Ahl al-Kisa
is a demonstration of Allah's validation of the purity and sinlessness
of the five members of Ahl al-Bayt as well as entrusting them with the
exclusive guardianship of Islam. Many Sunni scholars and historians
(e.g., al-Tabari) remark that the purification verse (Qur'an 33:33)
concerns only five people: Prophet Mohammad, Imam Ali, Fatima,
Imam Hassan, and Imam Hussein. *Sahih Muslim* (Vol. 6, Book 44,
Hadith 6261) and *Musnad Ahmad ibn Hanbal* (Volume 1, p. 185) also
confirm the purification of these members of Ahl al-Bayt. While other
Sunni scholars take the position that this Qur'anic verse also includes the
wives and companions of Prophet Mohammad, Aisha does not mention

her name or others as being included within the Cloak or Ahl al-Bayt. Moreover, *Sahih Muslim* records that Prophet Mohammad stated that his wives are not included in the aforementioned Qur'anic verse (*Sahih Muslim* Vol. 6, Book 44, Hadith 6228). In addition, the word *only* in the hadith narrated by Aisha implies that the blessing is for a single group (i.e., those who are pure and infallible).

Even *Sahih Muslim* confirms the purity (infallibility) of Ahl al-Bayt when it cites verse 33:33 of the Qur'an regarding the "perfect purification" of Ahl al-Bayt (*Sahih Muslim*, chapter of "Virtues of Companions," section of the "Virtues of Ahl al-Bayt of the Prophet," 1980 edition, published in Saudi Arabia, Arabic version, Vol. 4, p 1883, Tradition 61). Our Sunni brothers have a difficult time understanding the meaning of "perfect purification" and thus are unable to equate it with the concept of infallibility. Undeniably, the inclusion of "perfect perfection" in the Qur'an verse does, in fact, imply infallibility. As ma'sum (sinless), Prophet Mohammad and the infallible Imams self-actualized in righteousness and were constantly protected by Allah. By divine inspiration, Allah purified the knowledge and deeds of the Imams of Ahl al-Bayt and made them ma'sum and infallible in every aspect of their lives:

> O' ye who believe! Obey Allah and obey the Apostle (Mohammad) and those vested with authority (ulu 'l-amr) from among you ... (Qur'an 4:59)

The ulu 'l-amr are the Twelve Infallible Imams after Prophet Mohammad. If these Imams were not ma'sum (sinless), then Allah would not be telling us to follow them. However, since Allah revealed that we must follow the ulu 'l-amr unconditionally, then we can conclude that they are, in fact, infallible. A distinguishing feature of the Imamat is their immunity from committing sins. Their infallibility is indisputable. These infallible Imams are responsible for consolidating and securing the rules and principles of Islam as well as protecting the Qur'an from deviation.

Pragmatic Infallibility and Cognitive Infallibility

There are a number of levels of infallibility. The souls of those who possessed this trait were protected by Allah from any provocation or incitement of evil and, therefore, from even the thought of committing a sin. Following is a discussion of pragmatic infallibility and cognitive infallibility as they relate to the Imamat:

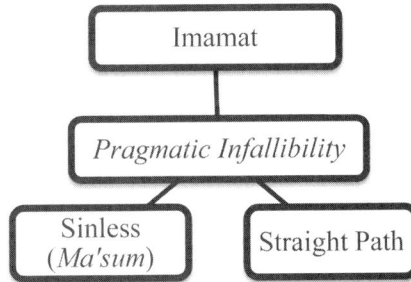

```
                    ┌─────────────────┐
                    │     Imamat      │
                    └─────────────────┘
                             │
                ┌────────────────────────────┐
                │  Pragmatic Infallibility    │
                └────────────────────────────┘
                    │                    │
        ┌──────────────────┐    ┌──────────────────┐
        │     Sinless      │    │   Straight Path  │
        │    (Ma'sum)      │    │                  │
        └──────────────────┘    └──────────────────┘
```

Pragmatic infallibility is the highest degree of piety manifested in behavior and deeds (Ansariyan 2007). It is about value and morality (e.g., ideas and beliefs have value only when they work). Pragmatic leaders focus on the practical, how do to get something done by simply viewing the entire picture to get to the end result. It is a linear approach for the infallible Imams as they trek the Straight Path (Sirat al Mustaqim) and are directly inspired by Allah to carry out their duties and responsibilities. The practical infallibility of the Imams is cemented by 'ismah, as they are immune from ignorance, negligence, arrogance, hypocrisy, doubt, forgetfulness, and fault. The infallibility of Ahl al-Bayt is one of perceiving, executing, and conveying their knowledge and wisdom to mankind. Their pragmatic 'ismah is the result of their devotion to and love for Allah.

While pragmatic infallibility and cognitive infallibility are separate from each other, Prophet Mohammad and the Imams are infallible in the practical stage as well as in the cognitive stage (Mugniyyah 2010). Additionally, the following Sunni hadith implies infallibility for Imam Ali, as he contains attributes of the messengers:

The Messenger of Allah said: He who wants to see Noah in his determination, Adam in his knowledge, Abraham in his clemency, Moses in his intelligence, and Jesus in his religious devotion should look at Ali ibn Abi Talib. (Ahmad ibn Hanbal, V2, p. 449)

As such, Allah inspires prophets and Imams with absolute infallibility. Some examples of pragmatic infallibility are the virtues of boldness, bravery, chastity, generosity, and justice, which are not examples of cognitive infallibility. Cognitive infallibility is one of in-depth knowledge of the world. Cognition encompasses the mental functions, such as the ability to think, reason, and remember. It comprises our thoughts and intelligence as well as our consciousness or awareness (Ansariyan 2007).

Relative to the infallibility of the Imams, it is their cognitive nature that makes them immune to committing sin or error, as the grace of Allah purifies them (Qur'an 33:33). The cognitive infallibility of the Imams is such that they are the receivers of the divine message from Allah who gifts them with pure knowledge (Qur'an 6:124). Prophet Mohammad said:

One who dies without recognizing the Imam of his time dies the death of ignorance. (Majlisi 1983, Bihar al-Anwar, Vol. 51, p. 38)

This proclamation by Prophet Mohammad clearly refers to the cognitive infallibility of the Imams and that it is compulsory for us to follow them. Cognitive infallibility for the Imams is one of inner guidance and inner knowledge:

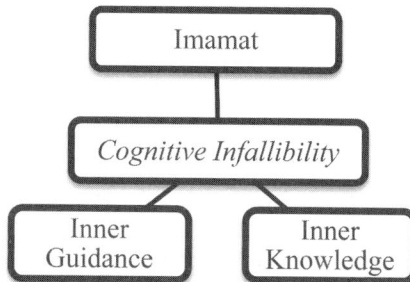

One of the primary functions of the Imamat is to extend inner guidance to mankind by illuminating their hearts with knowledge and wisdom in order to refine and bring their souls to self-fulfillment (Lari 1996). The infallible Imams are entrusted with the responsibility of channeling Allah's commandments to mankind via inner guidance:

> And of them made We Leaders (Imams) to Guide (Hadi) (the people) by Our Command as they were steadfast (in the calamities); and they of Our signs were quite certain. (Qur'an 32:24)

This verse refers to the inner guidance of the Twelve Infallible Imams of Ahl al-Bayt. As custodians and protectors of the Qur'an, they are divinely inspired to provide mankind with the correct interpretations that were revealed by Prophet Mohammad. Hence, inner guidance can be attained only through divine appointment:

> And We made them Leaders (Imams), guiding (the people) by Our command, and revealed We unto them the doing of good, and the establishing of prayer, and the giving of alms, and (only) unto Us did they worship. (Qur'an 21:73)

> Remember the Day (of Judgment) when We will summon every people with their Imam (Leader) ... (Qur'an 17:71)

The inner guidance of the Imams is the channel of divine grace (lutf) that allows them to influence the thoughts and consciousness of mankind so as to refine their souls. This is in contrast to the outer guidance related to issues of the divine law (shari'ah):

> The person upon whose shoulders lies the responsibility for the guidance of a community through Divine Command, in the same way that he is the guide of man's

external life and acts, is also the guide for the spiritual life, and the inner dimension of human life and religious practice depends upon his guidance. (Mavani 2013)

Inner guidance of the infallible Imams is derived from their inner knowledge of Islam. The Imams have inner knowledge of all that was given to the angels and the prophets, including the inner knowledge of the past and the future. While knowledge of the unseen belongs to Allah, he may grant some of this inner knowledge to his servants:

Who is he that can intercede with Him but with His permission; He knoweth what is before them and what is behind them, while they cannot comprehend anything out of His Knowledge save that which He wills ... (Qur'an 2:255)

(He alone is) the Knower of the unseen, and nor doth He reveal His secrets unto any (one else) save unto that one of the Apostles whom He chooseth ... (Qur'an 72:26–27)

This makes it clear that the inner knowledge of the unseen is only with Allah, and Allah may choose to grant this gift to one of his apostles (e.g., Prophet Mohammad). Prophet Mohammad transferred the inner knowledge to Imam Ali ibn Abi Talib, who in turn transferred it to his progeny. The hidden aspects of inner knowledge are referenced in the Qur'an:

He it is Who hath sent down to thee (O' Our Apostle Mohammad) "the Book" of it there are (some) verses decisive these are the basis of the Book and others are ambiguous; But those in whose hearts there is perversity, they are after that which is ambiguous therein seeking to mislead and seeking to interpret (to suit their selfish motives) while none knoweth its (hidden) interpretation except Allah and those firmly rooted in knowledge; say they: "We believe in it, all is from our Lord" but none mindeth save those endowed with (Wisdom). (Qur'an 3:7)

By the grace of Allah, only Prophet Mohammad and the infallible Imams have the light and inspiration (*ilham*) to interpret all of the verses of the Qur'an, including those that have a hidden meaning. Because of its inability to fathom the unseen quality of inner knowledge, society is not qualified to appoint an Imam. Therefore, only Allah can appoint an Imam who not only has the inner knowledge but embraces it as well.

Chapter 9

Appointment

To show us the Straight Path, Allah has been sending prophets and messengers to mankind. Following Prophet Mohammad, Allah appointed twelve successors to lead the people to the Straight Path and to preserve the religion of Islam. Each successor followed the previous successor, and they are known as the Twelve Infallible Imams. There are a number of verses in the Qur'an that prove the appointment of Imam Ali ibn Abi Talib and the infallible Imams of his descendants to succeed Prophet Mohammad as the leaders of the Islamic community. The first verse refers to Imam Ali, who offered his ring, while bowing in prayer, to a poor person:

> Verily, your guardian is (none else but) Allah and His Apostle (Mohammad) and those who believe, those who establish prayer and pay the poor-rate, while they be (even) bowing down (in prayer). (Qur'an 5:55)

The next verse proves that Imam Ali is Prophet Mohammad's successor:

(O' Our Apostle Mohammad!) Deliver thou what hath been sent down unto thee from thy Lord; and if thou dost it not, then (it will be as if) thou hast not delivered His message (at all); and surely will Allah protect thee from (the mischief) of men; verily, Allah guideth not an infidel people. (Qur'an 5:67)

The above verse is in chapter 5 of the Qur'an, and it is the last chapter that was revealed to Prophet Mohammad. Therefore, its content was binding and not subject to change. The verse also ties in the message of succession with the Imamat, as it mandates that the Qur'an is incomplete if the message of Imamat is not enforced. Therefore, Prophet Mohammad appointed Imam Ali as his successor.

Appointment of Prophet Abraham as Imam

We even find the importance of the appointment of an Imam relative to Prophet Abraham:

And remember when his Lord tried Abraham with certain words then he fulfilled them; He said, "Verily I make thee Imam for mankind;" (Abraham) said "And of my offspring?" He said: "My covenant reacheth not the unjust." (Qur'an 2:124)

With the declaration by Allah, the title of Imam came after Abraham was already a prophet, messenger, ummah, and khalil (ideal character/ role model). Therefore, we can conclude that the title of Imam has great importance relative to that of prophet, messenger, or other titles bestowed upon Abraham. Why? Because Allah appointed Abraham as the *Imam for mankind*, irrespective of what geographical location people resided in. As Imam Abraham requested that his offspring also become Imams, Allah concurs but only for the just of Abraham's lineage. Therefore, the concept of Imamat was born. Additionally, this verse proves beyond the shadow of a doubt that only Allah appoints the Imamat. Other verses in the Qur'an substantiate the appointment of the infallible Imams:

> And We made them Leaders (Imams), guiding (the people) by Our command … (Qur'an 21:73)

> And of them made We Leaders (Imams) to guide (the people) by Our command as they were steadfast (in the calamities); and they of Our signs were quite certain. (Qur'an 32:24)

Responsibilities of Messengers and Imams

Messengers are warners and Imams are guides:

> And say those who disbelieve: "Why hath not a sign been sent down unto him (Mohammad) from his Lord?" Verily thou (Mohammad) are a Warner and a Guide unto every people. (Qur'an 13:7)

This verse also bestows upon Prophet Mohammad the title of guide (hadi). When referencing people, the concepts of hadi and Imam are the same, because they both mean to guide. As Imam, Prophet Mohammad is a guide to all mankind, as was Prophet Abraham an Imam and guide to all mankind. Upon the death of Prophet Mohammad, the seal of prophethood was closed, but the door of Imam remained open.

Relative to the infallible Imams that followed Prophet Mohammad, the renowned Sunni scholar al-Shafi'i stated:

> Ali will judge mankind and allot them either Paradise or Hell. He was the leader of men and Jinns, the true Testator of the Holy Prophet. If the followers of Ali are "Rafidhi" (Rejecters) verily I am one of that sect … (*Collection of Imam Shafi'i Poetry* 1993)

The last of the Twelve Infallible Imams is Imam Mohammad al-Mahdi. *Sahih Muslim* authenticates Imam al-Mahdi's importance:

> Jabir bin Abdullah said: I heard the Prophet say: "A group among my Ummah will continue to fight for the truth and will prevail until the Day of Resurrection. And Eisa (Jesus) bin Mariam will descend and their leader will say: Come and lead us in Salat, but he will say: No, you are leaders of one another, as an honor from Allah to this Ummah." (*Sahih Muslim*, V1, Book 1, Hadith 395; *Ahmad ibn Hanbal*, Vol. 3, pp. 45, 384)

Prophet Mohammad Appointed Companions to Various Positions

Relative to the issue of appointment, Prophet Mohammad appointed Usama ibn Zayd as the general of the Islamic Army to lead a military expedition to Syria. The prophet assigned Abu Bakr, Umar, and other companions (except Imam Ali) to be under the leadership of Usama (Ibn Sa'd 1904; al-Haythami 1965).

During the Battle of Tabouk, in which Prophet Mohammad participated, he appointed Imam Ali ibn Abi Talib to remain in Medina to discourage any mischief-makers (*Sahih Bukhari*, Vol. 5, Book 64, Hadith 4416).

Since Prophet Mohammad appointed his companions to act as leaders for different events, then it must be abundantly clear that he also appointed his successor.

After completing his last pilgrimage, Prophet Mohammad declared the tradition of the two weighty things (thaqalayn) in his *Farewell Sermon* (appendix 6) at Ghadir Khumm, March 10, AD 632 (18th Dhu-l-Hijja, AH 10):

> It seems the time approached when I shall be called away (by Allah) and I shall answer that call. I am leaving for

you two precious things (thaqalayn) and if you adhere to them both, you will never go astray after me. They are the Book of Allah (Qur'an) and my Progeny ('itrah), that is, my (Household). The two shall never separate from each other, until they come to me by the Pool (of Kawthar on the Day of Judgment).

During the same *Farewell Sermon*, Prophet Mohammad said to Imam Ali:

Stand up O' Ali, for I am pleased to announce you Imam and Guide after me. So whomever I was his leader (mawla), then this is his leader (mawla). So be to him supporters in truth and followers …

Sources: *Al-Bidayah wa'l Nihayah*, Vol. V, p. 209 (Ibn Kathir 2009); *Dhakha'ir al-'Uqba*, p. 16 (Tabari 2001); *al-Fusul al –Muhimmah*, p. 22 (Sharaf al-Din 1996); *al-Sawa'iq al-Muhriqah*, p. 147 (Al-Haythami 1965). In *Ghayat al-Maram*, thirty-nine versions of this hadith have been recorded from Sunni sources and eighty-two versions from Shi'a sources (Bahrani 2001).

Designation of Appointment of Imam Ali

The question arises as to how Prophet Mohammad appointed Imam Ali to be his successor:

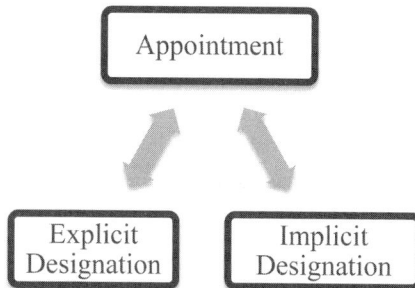

As Allah appoints a prophet, he also appoints an infallible Imam. The Imam is designated by the prophet and not appointed by the people. So it is not merely a question of infallibility of the Imams but also one of designation. Therefore, the explicit designation (*an-nass al-jali*) of Imam Ali marked the beginning of the institution of Imamat. Each infallible Imam has the authority to designate his successor, and it is not from election by the people but solely from the Imam himself, who is inspired by Allah to make the selection.

The concept of *nass* (designation for appointment) is divided into parts: *an-nass al-jali* (explicit designation) and *an-nass al-khafi* (implicit designation) (Lalani 2000). Prophet Mohammad had appointed and designated Imam Ali on many occasions to be his successor. In order to safeguard the election of the first two caliphs, it was falsely based on ambiguity by stating that Prophet Mohammad never explicitly or implicitly announced Imam Ali to be his successor. Prophet Mohammad's *Farewell Sermon* (appendix 6) explicitly and unequivocally announced that Imam Ali would be his successor.

Appointment of Imam Ali as Successor Substantiated by Qur'an and Sunni Hadiths

Let us examine some of the evidence to support that Prophet Mohammad explicitly designated Imam Ali to be his successor:

+ Shortly after he became prophet, Allah revealed the following verse: "And warn thou thy relatives of nearest kin" (Qur'an 26:214). So Prophet Mohammad assembled his closest family members to obtain their support. The prophet explicitly asked who would support him in his mission so that he might be his brother (*akhi*), successor (*wasiyyi*), and caliph (*khalifati*). Only Imam Ali responded in the affirmative. Imam Ali was just a youngster at the time. Prophet Mohammad then said: "Verily this is my brother, my successor, and my caliph amongst you. Therefore, listen to him and obey" (Tabarsi 1981; Majlisi 1983,

Bihar al-Anwar, Vol. 18, p. 192). As we can note, the statement was explicitly clear.

✦ As can be noted from the hadith of the *Farewell Sermon* (appendix 6) discussed above, the following quotes are indications of Prophet Mohammad's explicit designation of Imam Ali and the Imamat:

Hadith Thaqalayn: "I have left among you two heavy things to prevent you being misled: the Book of Allah and my nearest kins." (and) "If you grasp the two heavy things that I leave among you, you will never go astray." (*Jami' al-Tirmidhi*, Vol. 6, Book 46, Hadiths 3786, 3788; *Ahmad ibn Hanbal*, Vol. 5, p. 182)

One day the Messenger of Allah stood and addressed us at a watering place called Khumm ... then he said: "O people ... I am leaving among you two weighty things, the first of which is the Book of Allah ... And the people of my household, I remind you of Allah with regard to the people of my household, I remind you of Allah with regard to the people of my household, I remind you of Allah with regard to the people of my household." Husain said to him ... "Aren't his wives among the people of his household?" He said: "His wives are among the people of his household, but the people of his household are those to whom Zakat is forbidden after he is gone ... They are the family of Ali, the family of Aqil, the family of Ja'far, and the family of Abbas." ... "Was Zakat forbidden to all of these?" He said: "Yes." (*Sahih Muslim*, V6, Book 44, Number 6225)

Hadith Mawla: "Stand up O' Ali, for I am pleased to announce you Imam and Guide after me. So whomever I was his leader (mawla), then this is his leader (mawla). So be to him supporters in truth and followers ..." (Rizvi 2014 [*Al-Bidayah wa'l Nihayah*,

Vol. V, p. 209; *Dhakha'ir al-'Uqba*, p. 16; *al-Fusul al –Muhimmah*, p. 22; *al-Sawa'iq al-Muhriqah*, p. 147])

+ When Prophet Mohammad departed from Medina to head an army of followers to Tabuk (northwestern Saudi Arabia) to engage the Byzantine army, he gave explicit instructions to Imam Ali to remain behind in Medina to administer the state of affairs:

Allah's Messenger set out for Tabuk appointing Ali as his deputy (in Al-Madina). Ali said, "Do you want to leave me with the children and women?" The Prophet said, "Will you not be pleased that you will be to me like Harun (Aaron) to Musa (Moses)? But there will be no Prophet after me." (*Sahih Bukhari*, Vol. 5, Book 64, Hadith 4416)

+ The following hadith is well known among Sunni scholars, and the message is clear that Imam Ali is the path by which to reach Prophet Mohammad:

I (Mohammad) am the City of Knowledge (House of Wisdom) and Ali is its gate. (*Al-Tirmidhi*, V6, Book 46, Hadith 3723)

This hadith is believed to have been authentic but later removed. However, *Jalal al-Din al-Suyuti*, p. 170 (Al-Suyuti 1996), and *al-Naysaburi*, Vol. 3, pp. 126–127 (Al-Naysaburi 1915–1923) allude to *Al-Tirmidhi* having made the exact quote.

+ Statement by Umar: "… our best judge is Ali." (*Sahih Bukhari*, Vol. 6, Book 65, Hadith 4481)

Verse of *Tabligh*:

(O' Our Apostle Mohammad!) Deliver thou what hath been sent down unto thee from thy Lord; and if thou dost not, then (it will

be as if) thou hast not delivered His message (at all); and surely
will Allah protect thee from (the mischief) of men; verily, Allah
guideth not an infidel people. (Qur'an 5:67)

+ Verse of *Wilayah*:

Verily, your guardian is (none else but) Allah and His Apostle
(Mohammad) and those who believe, those who establish prayer
and pay the poor-rate, while they be (even) bowing down (in
prayer). (Qur'an 5:55)

+ Verse of *ulu 'l-amr*:

O' you who believe! Obey Allah and obey the Apostle
(Mohammad) and those vested with authority (ulu 'l-amr) from
among you; and then if ye quarrel about anything refer it to
Allah and the Apostle (Mohammad) if ye believe in Allah and
the Last Day (of Judgment); this is the best and the fairest way
of ending (the dispute). (Qur'an 4:59)

Undoubtedly, Sunnis and Shi'as both agree that Allah alone appoints
Imam Mohammad al-Mahdi to lead mankind. They also agree that the
people cannot appoint or elect Imam Mohammad al-Mahdi. Moreover,
they agree that he will be the Imam for all mankind, and whoever denies
him or opposes him will have deviated from Islam.

Since Sunnis uphold this belief of appointment, then why do they
cling tenaciously to the notion that others can be elected or appointed
by the people (e.g., the caliphs)? Undeniably, there is an inconsistency in
their logic, as the most renowned Sunni scholars agree that the twelve
caliphs of Islam are all from Quraysh and Ahl al-Bayt, and that Imam
Mohammad al-Mahdi is the twelfth and final caliph (appendix 4):

+ *Sahih Bukhari*, V9, Book 93, Hadiths 7222–7223 (Sahih/
Authentic)

+ *Sahih Muslim*, V5, Book 33, Hadith 4705 (Sahih/Authentic)
+ *Abu Dawud*, V4, Book 35, Hadith 4280 (Sahih/Authentic)
+ *Al-Tirmidhi*, V4, Book 31, Hadith 2223 (Sahih/Authentic)
+ *Ahmad ibn Hanbal*, V5, p. 106

Additional hadiths confirm that the caliphs must all come from Quraysh:

> The Prophet said, "authority of ruling will remain with Quraish, even if only two of them remained." (*Sahih Bukhari*, Vol. 4, Book 61, Hadith 3501)

> The Messenger of Allah said: "This matter will remain among the Quraish, even if only two people remain." (*Sahih Muslim*, Vol. 5, Book 33, Hadith 4704)

Therefore, the twelve caliphs of Islam are the Twelve Infallible Imams, and Allah has bestowed upon them complete authority to guide mankind.

Chapter 10

Authority

The Twelve Infallible Imams represent Allah's authority on earth to guide man to the Straight Path. They have the authority that was transferred from Prophet Mohammad to lead, rule, and govern the people to the Straight Path. Authority (ulu 'l-amr) constitutes many categories, some of which are:

- absolute authority of Allah over everything
- divinely granted authority of the angels over creation
- divinely granted authority of Prophet Mohammad and the infallible Imams over mankind, as that authority was also given to other prophets and messengers
- divinely granted authority of mankind over themselves (e.g., parents over their children, judges over the plaintiff and defendant in a court of law, heads of state over the people of their nations, military officers over their troops, scholars over the content of their writings, teachers over their students, and chief executive officers over the management of their companies)

However, to rule the affairs of the Islamic ummah (community), the person should have attained the level of authority (ulu 'l-amr). Allah bestowed upon Prophet Mohammad and the Imamat the designation of ulu 'l-amr.

Criteria for Ulu 'l-Amr (Authority)

Some of the main criteria for one to possess ulu 'l-amr are obedience, purity, and infallibility ('ismah):

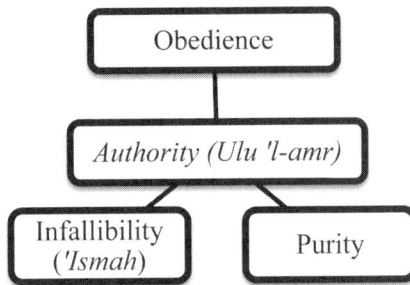

As leaders that guide the Muslims in matters of religious, political, and social aspects, the Imamat is empowered with the authority to do so:

> O' ye who believe! Obey Allah and obey the Apostle (Mohammad) and those vested with authority (ulu 'l-amr) from among you; and then if ye quarrel about anything refer it to Allah and the Apostle (Mohammad) if ye believe in Allah and the Last Day (of Judgment); this is the best and the fairest way of ending (the dispute). (Qur'an 4:59)

Obedience for ulu 'l-amr is unconditional and embodies purity and infallibility ('ismah) (Rizvi 2008). Those who have this quality of ulu 'l-amr are protected by Allah to be sinless (ma'sum) as well as clean from any type of error. Any disagreement with and argument against Prophet Mohammad would render ulu 'l-amr null and void.

Those who disobey Prophet Mohammad are automatically disqualified from ruling the Islamic ummah:

> Whoso obeyeth the Apostle (Prophet Mohammad), he indeed obeyeth Allah; and whoever turns away We have not sent thee upon them to watch. (Qur'an 4:80)

> This because they opposed Allah and His Apostle (Prophet Mohammad), and whosoever opposeth Allah and His Apostle (Prophet Mohammad), then verily Allah is severe in punishment. (Qur'an 8:13)

> Verily, those who disbelieve and hinder (others) from the path of Allah, and oppose the Apostle (Prophet Mohammad) after that the guidance hath been made manifest unto them, can never harm Allah in any way; and He will make null their deeds. O' ye who believe! Obey ye Allah and obey ye the Apostle (Prophet Mohammad), and do not render null your deeds. (Qur'an 47:32–33)

> Whoever obeys Ali obeys me, whoever obeys me obeys Allah, whoever disobeys Ali disobeys me, whoever disobeys me disobeys Allah. (*Superiority of Ali Ibne Abi Talib Over All Others* [*Kanz ul Ummal*, by al-Muttaqi al Hindi, Vol. 11, Hadiths 32973–32976; *Mustadrak al Hakim*, Vol. 3, p. 123, *Riyadh ul Nadira*, Vol. 3, p. 110])

Therefore, the Imamat are the only legitimate rulers of the Islamic ummah, as they were immersed in unconditional agreement and obedience to Allah and Prophet Mohammad as well as Imam Ali. Moreover, when Prophet Mohammad said that he left the ummah with two things (thaqalayn)—i.e., Qur'an and Ahl al-Bayt ('itrah)—it meant that obedience to both the Qur'an and the Imamat are compulsory and cannot be separated from one another. Appendix 5 is replete with many hadiths from Sunni scholars to justify the thaqalayn and obedience to the Imamat of Ahl al-Bayt.

Prophet Mohammad was the religious, political, and social leader of the Muslim community. He passed on this leadership to those vested with authority (ulu 'l-amr) (i.e., the Imamat). Prophets and messengers were entrusted with the religious responsibility of receiving and preaching Allah's commandments as glad tidings and warnings to the society. Although the Imamat did not receive revelations from Allah, they do have similar responsibilities relative to bringing the political aspects and social justice into action. Today, it is the duty of the ulema (religious leaders) to actively participate in the social and political arena on behalf of the Hidden Imam (Imam al-Mahdi) in order to propagate Islam as a total way of life in the society.

While Allah has given the Imamat authority over mankind, their power is contingent upon the power of Allah. For example, Allah granted Prophet Jesus with the power to make a bird out of clay, heal the blind and the lepers, and bring the dead back to life (Qur'an 3:49). As Allah granted permission to Prophet Jesus to perform these miracles, he also gave permission to Prophet Solomon to make the wind and the *jinn* (unseen beings) subservient to him (Qur'an 38:36–38). Prophet Mohammad was vested with authority to travel beyond the dimensions of space and time (e.g., the *Night Journey of the Ascent [Isra' and Mi'raj]*) (Qur'an 17:1; 53:12–18). Therefore, Allah granted permission to the chosen few to have universal authority. Among the chosen few are the pure and infallible Imams of Ahl al-Bayt.

Authority and Power

If leadership of the Imamat is about influencing the community of Muslims, how did they go about developing that influence? In order to understand how the Imamat developed this type of influence, it is critical to understand the difference between authority and power:

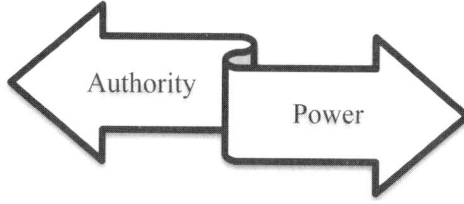

Undoubtedly, there is a fine line between authority and power, especially as bases for leadership. Authority cannot be bought or sold. Authority is the divine, granted right of the Imamat to make decisions, achieve objectives, and obtain obedience. On the other hand, power is the ability of the Imamat to influence the beliefs and actions of others. It is legitimate power, but this type of power comes from the highest authority, which is Allah.

As the power of the Imamat is one of expertise, they possess the requisite knowledge and skills to nurture and encourage the spiritual growth of society. The concept of ulu 'l-amr incorporates both authority and power, which are invested in Prophet Mohammad and the Imamat, as they are the representatives of Allah. As guardians of the purity of their existence, the infallible Imams were entrusted with the authority and power to continue the leadership and mission of Prophet Mohammad.

Chapter 11

Guardianship

The infallible Imams are the guardians toward perfection and advancement on the Straight Path. The Qur'an sets the stage for the Imamat to be the guardians of the Muslim society:

> Verily, your guardian is (none else but) Allah and His Apostle (Mohammad) and those who believe, those who establish prayer and pay the poor-rate, while they be (even) bowing down (in prayer). (Qur'an 5:55)

As stated earlier, Sunni and Shi'a scholars have reported that this verse was revealed after Imam Ali ibn Abi Talib gave his ring to a poor beggar as charity, while he was bowing down in prayer. When Prophet Mohammad died, guardians were needed to continue the intellectual development and perfection of the Islamic society. If it were not for the guardianship of the Imamat, Islam would have come to a screeching halt, thereby opening itself up to distortion and corruption, as evidenced by what Yazid did to try to neutralize Imam Hussein at Karbala. However, Yazid's attempts were futile.

Had it not been for Imam Hussein, the spirit of Islam would have been lost. As guardian, Imam Hussein's uprising was to advise the Muslim community (ummah) to enjoin good and refrain from evil. As guardians, the infallible Imams imparted knowledge to people (e.g., Imam Ja'far as-Sadiq's school of jurisprudence in which the two renowned Sunni scholars, Abu Hanifah and Malik, were his students).

Prophet Mohammad entrusted the guardianship of Islam to Imam Ali ibn Abi Talib, as recorded in the following major Sunni hadiths:

> The Messenger of Allah dispatched an army and he put Ali bin Abi Talib in charge of it. He left on the expedition and he entered upon a female slave. So four of the Companions of the Messenger of Allah scolded him, and they made a pact saying: "If we meet the Messenger of Allah we will inform him of what Ali did." ... So when the expedition arrived, they gave salam to the Prophet, and one of the four stood saying: "O Messenger of Allah! Do you see that Ali bin Abi Talib did such and such?" The Messenger of Allah turned away from him. Then the second one stood and said as he said, and he turned away from him. Then the third stood before him, and said as he said, and he turned away from him. Then the fourth stood and said as they had said. The Messenger of Allah faced him, and the anger was visible on his face, he said: "What do you want from Ali? What do you want from Ali? What do you want from Ali? Indeed, Ali is from me, and I am from him, and he is the guardian (wali) of every believer after me." (Al-Tirmidhi, Vol. 6, Book 46, Hadith 3712, Hadith rating Hasan/Good)

> From the Prophet: "For whomever I am his Mawla (master) then Ali is his Mawla (master)." (Al-Tirmidhi, Vol. 6, Book 46, Hadith 3713, Hadith rating Sahih/ Authentic)

The Messenger of Allah said: "Ali is from me and I am from Ali. And none should represent me except myself or Ali." (*Al-Tirmidhi*, Vol. 6, Book 46, Hadith 3719, Hadith rating Hasan /Good)

Guardianship in Islam is referred to as *wilayat*, and *wilayat-ul-faqih* (guardianship-based political system that relies upon a just and capable jurist) is one who meets all the criteria of expertise in Islamic law (Rizvi 2008). Relative to religious matters, the Muslim community must follow a fully qualified jurist (*marja'a*), a representative of Imam al-Mahdi, who is in his major occultation. The concept of marja'a is not confined to a single individual but rather to those who meet the requirements of wilayat-ul-faqih. Therefore, it is possible that there may be several marja'as engaged in wilayat-ul-faqih at the same time, whether they reside in the same country or different countries.

From the Shi'a perspective, it is incumbent upon every Muslim to be represented by *marja'a al-taqleed*. *Taqleed* means to follow or imitate a *mujtahid* (authority in Islamic law). According to Ayatollah Murtaza Mutahhari, wilayat (guardianship) derives from ulu 'l-amr (authority) inherent in Prophet Mohammad and the Imamat.

Dimensions of Wilayat (Guardianship)

Wilayat is stimulated from the complete authority of ulu 'l-amr, which empowers the prophet and the Imamat to fulfill the revelations of Islam, as they are the obedient representatives of Allah (Mutahhari 1982).

The four dimensions of *wilayat* are:

+ love and devotion (*wila'-e muhabbat*)
+ spiritual guidance (*wila'-e Imamat*)
+ sociopolitical guidance (*wila'-e zi'amat*)
+ universal nature (*wila'-e tasarruf*)

The term Imamat embraces all four dimensions of wilayat, as they are part and parcel of the Islamic faith:

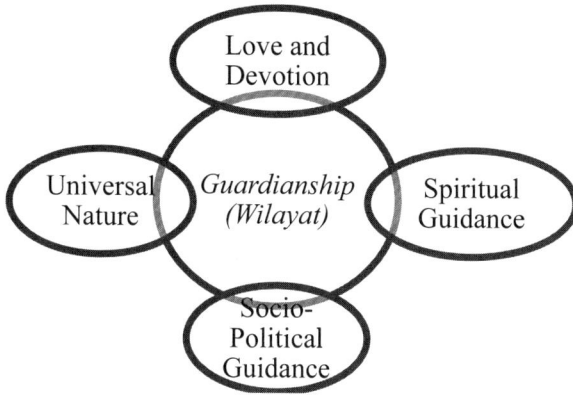

The wilayat of love obligates the Muslims to demonstrate their devotion to Ahl al-Bayt. For example, the inclusion of Ahl al-Bayt in our daily prayers is an indication of our love. It is love that binds the Muslims to Ahl al-Bayt, thereby providing the Muslims the benefit of their knowledge:

> Say thou (O' Our Apostle Mohammad!): "I demand not of you any recompense for it (the toils of the apostleship) save the love of (my) relatives …" (Qur'an 42:23)

The renowned Sunni scholar Al-Shafi'i said:

> O' Family of Allah's Messenger! To love you is an obligation that Allah ordained and revealed in the Qur'an. It is enough proof of your immense glory that whoever invokes not blessing upon you, his prayer is invalid." (*Collection of Imam Shafi'i Poetry* 1993)

The wilayat of the Imamat to guide the followers of Ahl al-Bayt in spiritual matters is a demonstration of their ulu 'l-amr (authority). Here, spiritual wilayat is one of religious wilayat, and Prophet Mohammad and the Imamat are the role models to follow:

> Indeed (there) is for you in the Apostle of Allah (Mohammad) an excellent pattern (of conduct) for him who hopeth in Allah and the latter day and remembereth Allah much. (Qur'an 33:21)

> Say (O' Our Apostle Mohammad!) "If ye do love Allah, then follow me, Allah will love you and forgive you your sins; verily, Allah is Forgiving, Merciful." (Qur'an 3:31)

After completing his last pilgrimage, Prophet Mohammad declared the tradition of the two weighty things (thaqalayn) in his *Farewell Sermon* (appendix 6) at Ghadir Khumm, March 10, AD 632 (18th Dhu-l-Hijja, AH 10):

> It seems the time approached when I shall be called away (by Allah) and I shall answer that call. I am leaving for you two precious things (thaqalayn) and if you adhere to them both, you will never go astray after me. They are the Book of Allah (Qur'an) and my Progeny ('itrah), which is my Ahl al-Bayt (Household). The two shall never separate from each other, until they come to me by the Pool (of Kawthar on the Day of Judgment).

The spiritual wilayat of Ahl al-Bayt is the Imamat who will convey to the Muslim community the true meaning of the Qur'an and all aspects of religion and faith. In this respect, the Imamat will have control over the religious affairs of the Muslims. The Imams are entrusted with the spiritual heritage of Islam. In his uprising at Karbala, Imam Hussein sacrificed his life and those of his family and companions to instill in the mind and conscience of mankind that spiritual wilayat reside with the Imamat.

As guardians, each of the infallible Imams possessed the noble traits of humility, tolerance, kindness, forgiveness, and patience. Imam Ali spoke about the guardianship of the Imamat:

> With us guidance is to be sought and blindness (of misguidance) is to be changed into brightness. Surely Imams (divine leaders) will be from the Quraysh. They have been planted in this line through Hashim. It would not suit others nor would others be suitable as heads of affairs ... (Ibn Abi Talib 1999 [*Sermon 144, Nahjul Balagha*])

> Certainly the Imams are the vicegerents of Allah over His creatures and they make the creatures know Allah. No one will enter Paradise except he who knows them and knows Him, and no one will enter Hell except he who denies them and denies Him ... (Ibn Abi Talib 1999 [*Sermon 152, Nahjul Balagha*])

> The delicacies of the Qur'an are about them (Ahl al-Bayt, the descendants of the Prophet) and they are the treasures of Allah. When they speak they speak the truth, but when they keep quiet no one can speak unless they speak ... (Ibn Abi Talib 1999 [*Sermon 154, Nahjul Balagha*])

> They (Ahl al-Bayt) are life for knowledge and death for ignorance. Their forbearance tells you of their knowledge, and their silence of the wisdom of their speaking. They do not go against right nor do they differ (among themselves) about it. They are the pillars of Islam and the asylums of (its) protection. With them right has returned to its position and wrong has left its place and its tongue is severed from its root. They have understood

the religion attentively and carefully, not by mere heresy or from relaters, because the relaters of knowledge are many but its understanders are few. (Ibn Abi Talib 1999 [*Sermon 238, Nahjul Balagha*])

Just as Prophet Mohammad was permitted to issue jurisprudential commandments from Allah, so too were the infallible Imams permitted to do so from Prophet Mohammad. These commandments were embedded in their guardianship. Therefore, Prophet Mohammad had to declare guardianship commandments in order to address and manage the social affairs of the Islamic community (e.g., taxes, war, peace, and relations with non-Muslim governments). Moreover, when the prophet declared his guardianship commandments, he was empowered to do so by Allah:

> Erreth not your Companion (Our Apostle Mohammad) nor is he led astray; and nor he speaketh of (his own) inclination; it (the wording) is naught but a revelation revealed (unto him), taught him the one intense in power ... (Qur'an 53:2–5)

Imamat Leadership Derived from Obedience and Guardianship

Imamat leadership derives from obedience to Allah and from the guardianship of Prophet Mohammad:

**Straight Path
(Sirat al Mustaqim)**

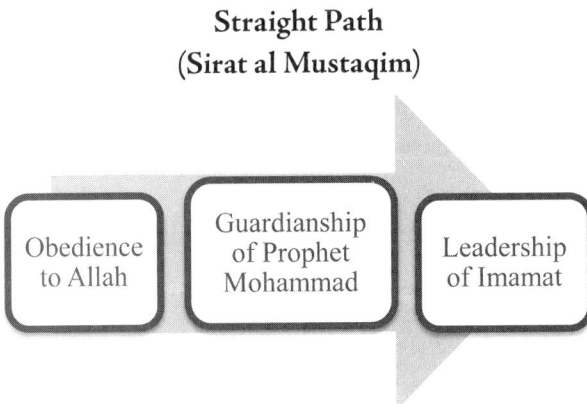

Obedience to Allah → Guardianship of Prophet Mohammad → Leadership of Imamat

Imamat leadership is (a) parallel to the obedience to Allah and (b) parallel to the guardianship of Prophet Mohammad. Aspects of guardianship are jurisprudence and justice.

Relative to jurisprudence, the Muslim society must follow the Imamat who not only guides the truth but knows it as well:

> Say thou (O' Our Apostle Mohammad!) "Of your associates is there any one who can guide unto truth?" Say thou! "It is Allah alone Who guideth unto truth; is then He Who guideth unto truth more worthy to be followed or he who himself goeth not aright unless he is guided? What then has befallen you? How (ill) ye judge?" And follow not most of them (anything) but (their own) conjecture; verily conjecture cannot avail anything against the truth; verily Allah knoweth all what they do. (Qur'an 10: 35–36)

Relative to justice, guardianship belongs to the Imamat and not to a depraved person who does not adhere to Allah's rules regarding what is permitted and what is forbidden:

> And restrain thou thyself with those who call unto their Lord morning and evening seeking His pleasure, and let not thy eyes turn away from them, aspiring the pomp of the life of this world; and obey not him whose heart We have made unmindful of Our remembrance, and he who followeth his inclination, and his case has transgressed the limits. (Qur'an 18:28)

The grace of Allah inspired Prophet Mohammad and the Imamat with the universal authority that made it possible for them to exercise their power over everything that exists. The Imamat guides the truth and knows everything about the divine law's roots and branches as well as the commandments of Islam. As guardians, the infallible Imams knew the complete meaning, explanation, and interpretation of the Qur'an.

Following the death of Prophet Mohammad, the ummah of Islam fell into disorder as to who should be the prophet's successor.

Chapter 12

Caliphate Islam: Dominion of Twelve Infallible Imams

Following the death of Prophet Mohammad, the Straight Path of succession to the caliphate became problematic.

Funeral of Prophet Mohammad

When Prophet Mohammad died, Imam Ali ibn Abi Talib was busy with the funeral preparations of his father-in-law and first cousin. During the time of an honorary bathing (*ghusl*) and shrouding of the prophet conducted by Imam Ali and close relatives, some of the companions, including Abu Bakr, Umar ibn Khattab, and Uthman, decided to attend a meeting in Saqifah in order to elect a caliph. Saqifah was a roofed building used by the tribe called the Banu Sa'idat of the faction of the Banu Khazraj tribe of the city of Medina (Wikipedia). Additionally, the companions wanted to thwart off a challenge for the caliphate by the Muslims of Medina who were mainly of two opposing groups: al-Ansar ('Aws and Khazraj) and al-Muhajirun, the latter from the Quraysh tribe who had migrated from Mecca to Medina. It's a sad commentary when the companions, the Ansar, and al-Muhajirun couldn't wait until after the funeral of the prophet to conduct this meeting.

Most disconcerting is that the companions did not bother to tell Imam Ali or the prophet's uncle, Abbas, about this meeting. What was the underlying purpose of this meeting that neglected to invite members of Bani Hashim, the Quraysh clan of Prophet Muhammad? The prophet's companions took the position that a caliph needed to be elected to safeguard the ummah (community), as the vacuum of leadership would threaten the unity of the Muslims. Hence, as the Muslim community was in grief and an honorary ghusl and shrouding were taking place by the next of kin, an election was taking place to install the new leader. As a result, the pledge of allegiance to Abu Bakr was given at the same time the funeral preparations of the prophet were in process.

According to the Sunni version of the prophet's funeral prayer, Abu Bakr had given instructions to the Muslim men to pray in small groups until they all finished, then the women and thereafter the children, followed by the bondsmen and bondswomen. Therefore, no one led the prayer as an Imam (leader) (*Ibn Majah*, Vol. 2, Book 6, Hadith 1628). However, in the absence of a ruler, the nearest of kin (*wali*) of Prophet Mohammad, Imam Ali or his uncle Abbas, would have this right.

Some Sunni scholars and historians argue that neither the ritual bath nor an Imam leading the prayer was needed, as the prophet was pure by the divine grace of Allah. So why was one (ghusl) applied and the other (Imam leading the prayer) not applied, if the prophet was not in need of either of the two? The reality is that since the Muslim community, including Abu Bakr and other companions, did not contest the ghusl bathing and shrouding, it stands to reason that the Imam of the funeral prayer is also required. If not, then why do we, today, have a funeral prayer for the deceased with an Imam leading the prayer? Can our prophet expect anything less?

Moreover, it was Umar ibn Khattab who led the funeral prayer on Abu Bakr. Why is it right for Umar to lead the funeral prayer on Abu

Bakr but not to have an Imam lead the funeral prayer on the prophet? Since Abu Bakr became caliph, what prevented him from leading the funeral prayer on Prophet Mohammad? If Abu Bakr didn't want to lead the funeral prayer on Prophet Mohammad, then why didn't he have Imam Ali lead that prayer? After all, Imam Ali was the closest of kin to the prophet and the one who bathed and shrouded him!

Abu Bakr and Umar were both Prophet Mohammad's father-in-laws. Uthman was the prophet's second cousin and, according to Sunni historians, his son-in-law married two of the prophet's daughters, and both died during the lifetime of the prophet. Yet they found it more appropriate to attend a meeting at Saqifah at the time of grief and mourning. These three companions of the prophet sacrificed a great deal of their wealth and status in order to support the prophet in the formative and critical stage of the early years of Islam. However, once the prophet died, these three companions took the position that it was necessary to immediately elect a caliph.

Why couldn't these three companions have waited until after the three days of mourning to have the election? Why didn't they wait until Imam Ali could be present? As the prophet was the son-in-law to Abu Bakr and Umar, shouldn't they have been present during the bathing and shrouding in order to stand in line with Imam Ali, Abbas, and other kin to receive the Muslim community at the time of grief and mourning? Does Islam teach us that an election is of a higher priority than the grief and mourning of a family member? After all, this was not just an ordinary person who had died; it was the prophet himself!

Imam Ali Chose the Path of Unity to Protect Islam

In the years following the event of Saqifah, Imam Ali decided not to pursue his right to the caliphate, as it would cause much infighting amongst the early Muslims. Rather, he chose the course of unity in order to protect and defend Islam from the outside forces that wanted to destroy it. Moreover, the first three caliphs relied heavily on the advice of Imam Ali during times of confusion and distress.

Prophet Mohammad's *Farewell Sermon* at Ghadir Khumm (appendix 6) fell on deaf ears, as Abu Bakr and Umar ibn Khattab decided who would be caliph:

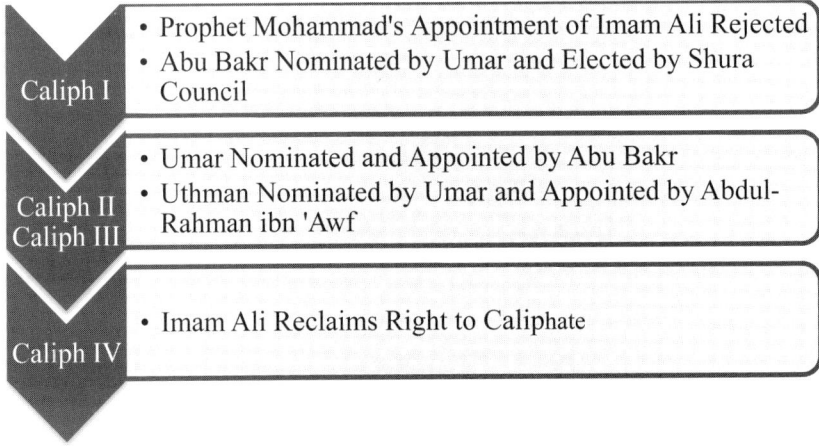

Caliph I
- Prophet Mohammad's Appointment of Imam Ali Rejected
- Abu Bakr Nominated by Umar and Elected by Shura Council

Caliph II
Caliph III
- Umar Nominated and Appointed by Abu Bakr
- Uthman Nominated by Umar and Appointed by Abdul-Rahman ibn 'Awf

Caliph IV
- Imam Ali Reclaims Right to Caliphate

Caliphate Succession

- Why did the Shura Council elect Abu Bakr as caliph in the absence of Imam Ali who at the time was preparing and conducting the funeral services of Prophet Mohammad?
- Why were Umar ibn Khattab and Uthman appointed caliph without election by the Shura Council?
- Why could Abu Bakr and Abdul-Rahman ibn 'Awf appoint a caliph and Prophet Mohammad could not?
- Imam Ali reclaimed his right as caliph by the divine grace of Allah, as the only other contestants, Talha and Zubayr, withdrew and supported him.

Even in the case of Uthman becoming caliph, there was trickery and chicanery perpetrated by Abdul-Rahman ibn 'Awf to ensure that Uthman was selected. After three of the six candidates chosen by Umar had dropped out, only Abdul-Rahman ibn 'Awf, Uthman, and Imam Ali remained. Abdul-Rahman ibn 'Awf withdrew his candidacy, leaving Uthman and

Imam Ali as the final two candidates. Abdul-Rahman ibn 'Awf acted as arbitrator and questioned each of the two remaining candidates as to whether they would act according to the Qur'an, the Sunnah, and the policies of the two previous caliphs. Imam Ali replied that he would act according to the Qur'an and the Sunnah, but he would not follow the opinions of others. However, Uthman replied in the affirmative, and Abdul Rahman ibn 'Awf gave his verdict in favor of Uthman.

An examination of the leadership of Prophet Mohammad discloses that he never failed to appoint a successor when necessary. Whenever he left Medina, he would appoint a governor in his place. Or he would appoint a general to lead his army—for example, Usama. The prophet paid attention to every detail in his leadership and acted accordingly. So the question arises as to how could the prophet be concerned about the minute details regarding diet, hygiene, prayer, fasting, charity, etc. and be silent about the importance of appointing his successor? Unquestionably, many Sunni scholars and historians state that the prophet's appointment of Imam Ali ibn Abi Talib as his successor is supported by the hadiths, some of which are Ghadir, Safinah, Thaqalayn, Haqq, Manzilah, and Da'wat'i 'Ashirah-i-Aqrabin.

If appointment by Prophet Mohammad, as to who would be his successor, is not honored, then any appointments or elections thereafter become null and void. As can be noted, the necessity of appointment by Prophet Mohammad comes full circle. After a period of twenty-four years, Imam Ali ibn Abi Talib finally reclaims his right to become caliph. Not only did Imam Ali reclaim his right to the caliphate, but also, equally important, he set the foundation for the caliphate to pass on to the Imamat of Ahl al-Bayt.

Umayyads Usurp Authority of Caliphate

Unfortunately, with the martyrdom of Imam Ali, evil forces of the Umayyad clan began to manipulate the ummah (community) in order to unjustly take the caliphate away from the Imamat. Moreover, the head of the Umayyad clan, Muawiyah, schemed to take the caliphate away from

Imam Hassan and Ahl al-Bayt by having the Imam's wife poison him. Thereafter, the position of caliph passed on to Muawiyah's son, Yazid. As a result, the Islamic ummah fell into disarray and corruption, and the fear of oppression and persecution followed anyone who defied the unjust leadership of Yazid. Sunnis argue that the succession of the caliphate, based on heredity, from Prophet Mohammad to Imam Ali ibn Abi Talib and his progeny is unacceptable. Yet Sunnis accept the succession of the caliphate, based on heredity, from Muawiyah to his offspring and Bani Umayyah, a clan within the Quraysh tribe.

Sunni Criteria for Selecting a Caliph

Sunnis recognize three principles for selecting a caliph:

1. *Majlis-Ash-Shura* (Consultative Council) whereby selection is done by a group of people who are the most knowledgeable about Islam (not by a general vote of everyone)
2. Nomination by the previous caliph
3. Forceful seizure of power (e.g., military)

A fourth principle for choosing a caliph is *ijma'*, which is consensus of men of power and position on a certain point. As a result, the agreement of all the followers of Prophet Mohammad is not necessary, nor is it essential to secure the consent of all the persons of power and position in the ummah. Additionally, Sunnis consider the following prerequisites in order to be a caliph (Al-Ghamdy 2004):

1. He must be a Muslim.
2. He must be a man.
3. He must be knowledgeable in Islam and be able to make independent decisions, if necessary.
4. He must be just, have good morals, and be trustworthy.
5. He must be physically able (nonhandicapped), spiritually brave, and helpful to protect the ummah against its enemies.

6. He must be politically, militarily, and administratively experienced.
7. He must be from the tribe of Quraysh.

Implications of Sunni Criteria for Caliph

Let us examine the prerequisite of knowledge, which is one of the criteria for becoming a caliph, and determine what the Sunni sources reveal:

"I am the City of Knowledge (House of Wisdom) and Ali is its gate; whoever wishes to attain knowledge (wisdom), let him enter through the gate" (*Al-Tirmidhi*, V6, Book 46, Hadith 3723; Ahlul Bayt Digital Islamic Project Team [*Al- Mustadrak alaa al-Sahihain*, Hakim al-Nishaburi, Vol. 3, pp. 126–127; *Al-Bidaya wa'l-Nihaya*, Tarikh Ibn Kathir, Vol. 7, p. 358]).

Prophet Mohammad said, "The most knowledgeable person in my nation after me is Ali" (Imam Reza Network [*Manaqib al-Imam Ali ibn Abi Talib*, ibn al-Maghazeli al-Shafi'i]).

Imam Ali ibn Abi Talib said about himself:

> Ask me before you lose me. By Allah, if you ask me about anything that could happen up to the Day of Judgment, I will tell you about it. Ask me about the Book of Allah, because by Allah there is no (Qur'anic) verse that I do not know whether it was revealed during the night or the day, or whether it was revealed on a plain or on a mountain. (Jaffer 1998 [*Al-Riyadh al-Nadhirah*, Muhibbuddin al-Tabari, Vol. 2, p. 198; *Tarikh al-Khulafaa*, Jalaluddin al-Suyuti, p. 124; *Al Itqan fi Ulum al-Qur'an*, Jalaluddin al-Suyuti, Vol. 2, p. 319; and *Fath al-Bari*, commentary on *Sahih Bukhari*, Vol. 8, p. 485])

During their tenure as caliph, Abu Bakr and Umar ibn Khattab frequently sought the advice of Imam Ali to solve problems that perplexed them:

> Sa'id al-Musayyib reported: Abu Bakr said: "May Allah
> never put me in a situation where I can not have access
> to Abul Hasan (i.e., Ali) to solve a problem." "Umar ibn
> al-Khattab used to beg Allah to preserve him from a
> perplexing case which the father of al-Hasan was not
> present to decide." Furthermore Umar said: "If there
> were not Ali, Umar would have been ruined." (Ahlul-
> Bayt Islamic Library [*Fadha'il al-Sahaba, Ahmad ibn
> Hanbal*, Vol. 2, p. 647, Hadith 1100; *Al-Isti'ab*, Ibn Abd
> al-Barr, Vol. 3, p. 39; *Manaqib*, al-Khawarizmi, p. 48; *Al-
> Tabaqat*, Ibn Sa'd, Vol. 2, p. 338; *Al-Riyadh al-Nadhirah*,
> Muhibbuddin al-Tabari, Vol. 2., p. 194; and *Tarikh al-
> Khulafaa*, Jalaluddin al-Suyuti, p. 171])

Undoubtedly, Imam Ali ibn Abi Talib was the most knowledgeable authority on Islam after Prophet Mohammad. As for the prerequisite of being a Muslim and male to become caliph, Imam Ali was the first male to convert to Islam after Prophet Mohammad. And as for the prerequisite of being just, again Imam Ali stands far above anyone except Prophet Mohammad:

The prophet said: "Ali is the wisest and superior to all of you. He is the best judge among all" (Tahmasebi 2013 [*Ahmad ibn Hanbal*; *Manaqib*, al-Khawarizmi; *Sunan*, Abu Bakr al-Bayhaqi]).

Umar ibn Khattab said: "Ali is the best in judgment among us ..." (Rizvi 2008 [*Musnad Ahmad ibn Hanbal*]).

Ibn Abbas heard Umar ibn Khattab saying: "The best judge among us is Ali" (*Sahih Bukhari*, Vol. 6, Book 65, Hadith 4481).

Not included in the Sunni prerequisites to becoming caliph is the necessity of never having bowed to idols anytime in his life. Sunnis normally use *Rathi Allahu Anhu* (may Allah be pleased with him) after the name of the companions of Prophet Mohammad. But in many cases, Sunnis use *Karam Allahu* Wajhah (may Allah bless his face) for Imam Ali ibn Abi Talib. For instance, on some tiles of Masjid al Haram, Rathi Allahu Anhu follows the names of the companions. But Karam Allahu

Wajhah follows the name of Imam Ali. Rathi Allahu Anhu may be said when talking about the companions or the mothers of believers. We can say Rathi Allahu Anhu about Imam Ali ibn Abi Talib and also say Karam Allahu Wajhah, as he never bowed to an idol.

> It was narrated that Abu 'Ubaid—the freed slave of Ibn 'Awf—said: "I saw Ali bin Abi Talib—Karam Allahu Wajhah (may Allah honor his face)—on the day of 'Id. He started with the prayer before the Khutbah, then he prayed with no Adhan and no Iqamah." Then he said: "I heard the Messenger of Allah forbidding anyone from keeping anything of his sacrificial animal for more than three days." (Al-Nasa'i, Vol. 5, Book 43, Hadith 4429)

> It was narrated that Ali—Karam Allahu Wajhah (may Allah honor his face)—said: "The Prophet forbade me to use gold rings, Al-Qassi, Al-Mitharah and Al-Ji'ah (a barley drink)." (Al-Nasa'i, Vol. 6, Book 51, Hadith 5614)

> Sa'sa'ah said to Ali bin Abi Talib—Karam Allahu Wajhah (may Allah honor his face)—"Forbid to us, O Commander of the Believers! What the Messenger of Allah forbade to you." He said: "The Messenger of Allah forbade me from using Ad-Dubba' and Al-Hantam." (Al-Nasa'i, Vol. 6, Book 51, Hadith 5615)

Imam Ali never bowed or prostrated to idols, and his mother, Fatima, was also prevented from doing so when she was pregnant with Imam Ali. From the time he was in the womb of his mother, Allah protected him from bowing to idols. While some may argue that the expression Karam Allahu Wajhah could also refer to those born into Islam, the critical point remains that prior to Islam many people were prostrating to idols. Therefore, it makes sense that the leadership of the Islamic ummah is given to those who never bowed to idols at any time in their life. Hence, the logical succession to Prophet Mohammad can only be Imam Ali ibn Abi Talib. Likewise, the heart of Prophet Mohammad was purified when he was a child, which set the stage for him to be a messenger of Allah. Had he prostrated before idols, Allah would not have appointed him as his messenger. The same logic follows with Imam Ali as well, as Allah protected him from the time he was in the womb of his mother.

Furthermore, since Imam Ali ibn Abi Talib is far superior to any other person, based on the seven caliph prerequisites listed earlier, his appointment as successor to Prophet Mohammad should have been honored and fulfilled (appendix 8). Moreover, the Sunni hadiths attest and confirm Imam Ali's superiority.

Sunni and Shi'a Hadiths Substantiate the Leadership of the Twelve Imams

Sunnis take the position that infallibility ('ismah) is not a prerequisite for becoming a caliph. Undoubtedly, we have witnessed the evidence set forth by the Qur'an, Shi'a hadiths, and Sunni hadiths that the Twelve Infallible Imams are the only ones who can claim succession as caliphs of Islam. In support of the Twelve Infallible Imams is a list of major Shi'a books (appendix 3) and hadiths from renowned Sunni scholars (appendix 4):

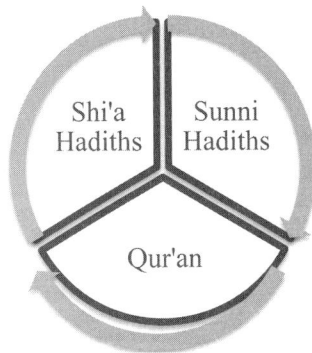

Both Shi'a and Sunni sources are replete with evidence that the rightly guided caliphs can only be from the twelve Imams of Ahl al-Bayt. Since Sunni scholars and their followers adhere to the Sunni hadiths set forth in appendix 4, then they must logically submit to the twelve Imams of Ahl al-Bayt as Prophet Mohammad's successors. Following is a summary of Sunni sources from appendix 4 that authenticate the leadership of the Islamic ummah must be from the twelve caliphs of Ahl al-Bayt:

Leadership of the Islamic Ummah
(Twelve Caliphs of Ahl al-Bayt)
(According to Sunni Sources)

Sunni Sources	Hadith Quotation (appendix 4)
Abu Nu'aym al-Isfahani (*Hilya al-Awliya*)	21, 31, 64
Ahmad ibn Hanbal (*Musnad*)	21, 23, 25, 26, 31, 32
Al-Baghdadi (*Tarikh-i Baghdad*)	29
Al-Bayhaqi (*al-Sunan al-Kubra*)	24
Al-Bayhaqi (*al-Sunan al-Saqir*)	28
Al-Darimi (*Sunan*)	24
Al-Maktab al-Islami (*Itaf al-Sada al-Muttaqin*)	27
Al-Munawi (*Fayd al-Qadir*)	26
Al-Tabarani (*al-Mu'jam al-Kabir*)	24, 28, 30, 31, 32
Al-Tabarani (*al-Mu'jam al-Saghir*)	25
Al-Tahawi (*Mushkil al-Athar*)	25
Al-Tirmidhi (*Sunan; Kitab al-Fitan*)	21, 27, 31, 32
Ali ibn Abd-al-Malik al-Hindi (*Kanz al-Ummal*)	21, 27, 28, 30, 60, 64
Ali ibn Abu-Bakr al Haythami (*Majma' al-Zawa'id*)	23, 26, 35, 37
Hakim al-Nishaburi (*al-Mustadrak ala al-Sahihain*)	25, 29, 31, 61
Ibn Asakir (*Tarikh Madina-Damishq*)	23, 34
Ibn Kuzayma (*Sahih*)	24
Ibn Majah (*Sunan*)	32
Jalaluddin Suyuti (*Durr al-Manthur*)	26, 27, 29
Khatib al-Tabrizi (*Mishkat al-Masabih*)	27
Qadi Ayad ibn Musa (*al-Shifa bi Ta'rif-i Huquq al-Mustafa*)	27
Sahih Muslim (*Kitab-i Fada'il al-Sahaba*)	28

Furthermore, the companions of Prophet Mohammad witnessed how he chose Imam Ali ibn Abi Talib over them for the leadership position. Why would Prophet Mohammad state that Allah loves Imam Ali and that Allah would grant Imam Ali victory unless Allah commanded the prophet to grant the leadership position to Imam Ali?

> The Prophet on the day (of the battle) of Khaibar saying, "I will give the flag to a person at whose hands Allah will grant him victory." So, the Companions of the Prophet got up, wishing eagerly to see to whom the flag will be given, and everyone of them wished to be given the flag. But the Prophet asked for Ali ... (*Sahih Bukhari*, Vol. 4, Book 56, Hadith 2942)

> Allah's Messenger said, "Tomorrow I will give the flag to a man with whose leadership Allah will grant (the Muslims) victory" ... The Prophet said, "Where is Ali bin Abi Talib?" ... The Prophet then gave him the flag ... (*Sahih Bukhari*, Vol. 5, Book 62, Hadith 3701)

> The Messenger of Allah said on the Day of Khaibar: "I shall give this flag to a man who loves Allah and His Messenger and Allah and His Messenger love him, and Allah will grant him victory at his hands." Umar bin al-Khattab said: "I never desired leadership except on that day." He said: "I came before him in the hope that I might be called to it, but the Messenger of Allah called Ali bin Abi Talib. He gave it to him and said: march, and do not turn around until Allah grants you victory." (*Sahih Muslim*, Vol. 6, Book 44, Hadiths 6222–6224)

Obedience to Allah and Prophet Mohammad Cannot Be Compromised

We are further reminded by the following verses from the Qur'an:

> Whoso obeyeth the Apostle (Mohammad), he indeed obeyeth Allah; and whoever turneth away We have not sent thee upon them to watch. (Qur'an 4:80)

> And obey ye Allah and His Apostle (Mohammad) and quarrel ye not, for then ye will be weakened in heart, and will depart your prayer, and be patient; verily Allah is with the patient ones. (Qur'an 8:46)

Therefore, obedience to Prophet Mohammad is also obedience to Allah. This obedience is absolute and not restricted or conditional. When Abu Bakr refused to grant Fatima, the daughter of Prophet Mohammad, her inheritance, was this not disobedience? When Uthman returned Marwan ibn Hakim from the exile that Prophet Mohammad had sent him, was this not disobedience? When Prophet Mohammad demanded a pen and paper to record his statement but was refused by Umar, was this not disobedience?

- *Sahih Bukhari*, V1, Book 3, Hadith 114 (Sahih/Authentic)
- *Sahih Muslim*, V4, Book 25, Hadith 4234 (Sahih/Authentic)

When Abu Bakr, Umar, and Uthman quarreled with Prophet Mohammad as to why he put them under the command of the general, Usama, was this not disobedience? When Imam Ali ibn Abi Talib was refused the caliphate after Prophet Mohammad had declared him to be his successor, was this not disobedience?

The six reliable Sunni books of hadiths confirm this obedience to Allah and Prophet Mohammad:

- *Sahih Bukhari*, V5, Book 64, Hadith 3951 (Sahih/Authentic)
- *Sahih Muslim*, V2, Book 7, Hadith 2010 (Sahih/Authentic)
- *Ibn Majah*, V1, Book 1, Hadith 3 (Sahih/Authentic)
- *Abu-Dawud*, V1, Book 2, Hadith 1099 (Sahih/Authentic)
- *Al-Tirmidhi*, V3, Book 21, Hadith 1672 (Sahih/Authentic)
- *Al-Nasa'i*, V5, Book 39, Hadith 4198 (Sahih/Authentic)

Hence, Allah commands us to obey him unconditionally and furthermore to obey Prophet Mohammad unconditionally, even if the prophet is ill. Moreover, the Sunni hadiths and historical books do not mention a single sin committed by Imam Ali; rather, only praise for his virtues. On the contrary, we find in these same historical references acts of disobedience to Prophet Mohammad committed by Abu Bakr, Umar ibn Khattab, and Uthman. The end result is that we must adhere to the following verse from the Qur'an, which is to obey Allah and Prophet Mohammad as well as his Ahl al-Bayt of the Twelve Infallible Imams:

> O' ye who believe! Obey Allah and obey the Apostle (Mohammad) and those vested with authority from among you, and then if ye quarrel about anything refer it to Allah and the Apostle if ye believe in Allah and in the Last Day (of Judgment); this is the best and the fairest way of ending (the dispute). (Qur'an 4:59)

Hence, there is no dispute because those vested with authority are the Twelve Infallible Imams, as even evidenced by both Shi'a and Sunni hadiths. Moreover, these Imams must also be followed unconditionally! If the foregoing is not enough proof, then let us refer to the following verse from the Qur'an, as well as the Shi'a and Sunni sources, on the matter of the pen and paper that Prophet Mohammad requested but was denied:

> O' ye who believe! Raise ye not your voices above the voice of the Prophet, and speak ye not loud unto him

as speak aloud some of you to the others, lest (all) your (good) deeds become null while ye perceive not. (Qur'an 49:2)

From Shi'a sources:

> From Sulaym ibn Qays Al-Hilali, he said: "I heard Salman saying: I heard Ali saying after that man (Umar) said what he said and made the Messenger of Allah angry and pushed the paper: Do we not ask the Messenger of Allah about that which he wanted to write in the paper, which if he wrote no one would go astray and no two would disagree ..." (Al-Hilali 2014, *Kitab e Sulaym Qays Al-Hilali*, p. 398)

> Sulaym ibn Qays said that Ali said to Talha when the Muhajiroun (Immigrants) and Ansar (Supporters) were boasting about their favors and preference: "O' Talha! were you not present when the Messenger of Allah asked for a paper so that he could write that with which the nation would not go astray nor differ/disagree? At that time your companion said what he said that the Messenger of Allah is hallucinating, so the Messenger of Allah became very angry and left it." So Talha said: "Yes I was present at that time." (Sheikh Muhammad bin Ibrahim Nomani, *Al-Ghaybah al-Nomani*, p. 8, *Bihar al-Anwar*)

From Sunni sources:

> Narrated Ubaidullah ibn Abdullah: Ibn Abbas said, When the ailment of the Prophet became worse, he said, "Bring for me (writing) paper and I will write for you a statement after which you will not go astray." But

Umar said, "The Prophet is seriously ill, and we have got Allah's Book with us and that is sufficient for us." But the companions of the Prophet differed about this and there was a hue and cry. On that, the Prophet said to them, "Go away (and leave me alone). It is not right that you should quarrel in front of me." Ibn Abbas came out saying, "It was most unfortunate (a great disaster) that Allah's Messenger was prevented from writing that statement for them because of their disagreement and noise." (*Sahih Bukhari*, Vol. 1, Book 3, Hadith 114)

It was narrated that Ibn Abbas said: When the Messenger of Allah was dying, there were men in the house among whom was Umar bin Al-Khattab. The Prophet said: "Come, let me dictate for you a document after which you will not go astray." Umar said: "The Messenger of Allah is overcome with pain, and you have the Qur'an; the Book of Allah is sufficient for us." The people in the house disagreed, and they argued. Some of them said: "Come close and let the Messenger of Allah dictate for you a document after which you will not go astray." Others agreed with what Umar said. When their idle talk and argument in the presence of the Messenger of Allah became too much, the Messenger of Allah said: "Get up and leave." Ubaidullah said: Ibn Abbas used to say: "What a calamity it was when the Messenger of Allah was prevented from dictating that document for them because of their disagreement and noise." (*Sahih Muslim*, Vol. 4, Book 25, Hadith 4234)

However, the pessimists would espouse their view that the prophet could have had his statement written by Imam Ali or someone else in the presence of witnesses. Had the prophet done so, those who disagreed with him would have seized the opportunity to further escalate the untruth that his illness overpowered him, thereby rendering him incapacitated. Then the dissidents would have publicized their view that the prophet was not in control of his senses, thereby making the written statement lose its value. Nonetheless, there were those who wanted to atone for their ill treatment of the prophet and offered to bring pen and paper to fulfill his request. The prophet was very disturbed, but he nevertheless responded:

> "After all that has been said, do you want to bring pen and paper? I recommend only that you should behave well with my progeny." Having said that he turned his face from those present and they, too, got up and dispersed. Only Ali, Abbas, and Fadl remained there. (*Bihar al-Anwar*, Vol. XXII, p. 469, quoted from *al-Irshad* by Shaykh Mufid and *A'lamul Wara'* by Tabrisi)

Sunnis unequivocally state that *Sahih Bukhari* and *Sahih Muslim* are considered authentic hadiths of Prophet Mohammad and that these hadiths cannot be disputed! Therefore, let us thank *Sahih Bukhari* and *Sahih Muslim* for making it perfectly clear that Prophet Mohammad was unjustly denied pen and paper to have his statement written.

Is an Elderly Age a Requirement to be Caliph?

Our Sunni brothers and sisters may argue that age was a determining factor in Abu Bakr's claim to the caliphate, as he was fifty-nine years old, and Imam Ali ibn Abi Talib was only thirty-two years old. Prophet Mohammad was forty years old when he became a prophet. Umar Ibn Abdul Aziz, great-grandson of Umar ibn Khattab, was only thirty-five years old when he became a caliph. Usama ibn Zayd was only eighteen years old when Prophet Mohammad appointed him general, as he also commanded Abu Bakr, Umar ibn Khattab, and Uthman under his leadership. Jalaluddin Muhammad Akbar, known as Akbar the Great, ascended the throne of the Mughal Empire in India at the age of thirteen.

Alexander the Great took the throne of Macedon at age twenty and conquered nearly half of the known world at that time. Queen Elizabeth I was queen of England at the age of twenty-five. Queen Victoria took the throne of England at the age of eighteen. Ramses II (*Fir'awn*) became ruler of the Egyptian Empire at age twenty-four (Wikipedia). Bottom line, Imam Ali ibn Abi Talib was only thirteen years old when Prophet Mohammad appointed him to be his successor (Wikipedia), and at age thirty-two, he should immediately have been the caliph following the death of the prophet!

Inability of Sunnis to Name All Twelve Caliphs

For those who wish to hold to the premise that the twelve caliphs mentioned in *Sahih Bukhari* and *Sahih Muslim* are other than the Twelve Infallible Imams, then who would they consider to be the twelve caliphs? Bear in mind that throughout the history of Islam there were over 150 caliphs (Wikipedia). Sunni scholars and historians state that in addition to the Four Rightly Guided Caliphs (Abu Bakr, Umar, Uthman, and Ali), Umar ibn Abdul Aziz would also qualify as a rightly guided caliph. Some of these scholars and historians would also add the name of Imam Hassan ibn Imam Ali as another rightly guided caliph. Of course, both Sunni and Shi'a scholars agree that Imam Mohammad al-Mahdi is a caliph but with different interpretations as to his birth and occultation.

Undoubtedly, the Sunnis are unable to arrive at the twelve names from this huge number of caliphs. An examination of the Sunni hadiths reveals that the twelve names cannot apply to the Umayyad caliphs, as they were more than twelve, and all them, except Umar ibn Abdul Aziz, were tyrants and unjust rulers. Additionally, they were not from the Hashemite clan, a requirement declared by Prophet Mohammad. Furthermore, the Sunni hadiths cannot apply to the Abbasid caliphs, as they were more than twelve, and they too persecuted the descendants of Prophet Mohammad. Moreover, if only six or seven of the caliphs were rightly guided, then there were about 145 caliphs that were not rightly guided. Therefore, the method of selecting a caliph that was implemented by Abu Bakr and Umar ibn Khattab proved ineffective and unjustified.

History is replete with information as to how the majority of the remaining 145 caliphs were anything but rightly guided, as many were malicious, immoral, and violators of the tenets and decrees of Islam and the Qur'an, even though they accomplished great feats in spreading Islam, the sciences, and architecture. Therefore, we can only conclude that the system Abu Bakr and Umar ibn al-Khattab put in place for the succession of the caliphate was doomed from its inception. Otherwise, how can we explain a system that allows succession to be anything but rightly guided?

On the other hand, Shi'as have a system of rightly guided successors that are pure and righteous in all aspects of religion, politics, and the way of life. Shi'as refer to these rightly guided successors of the twelve caliphs as the Twelve Infallible Imams since there are no other twelve pure candidates upon whose righteousness all Muslims agree. A review of the Sunni hadiths does not find any fault or criticism regarding the Twelve Infallible Imams. Hence, we conclude that the six reliable Sunni books of hadiths can only refer to the Twelve Infallible Imams because they were the most knowledgeable, most pious, most virtuous, and most honored by Allah.

While the dominion of the caliphate rests solely with the infallible Imams of Ahl al-Bayt, some of Prophet Mohammad's companions decided otherwise and, as such, committed an injustice against the prophet's chosen successor, Imam Ali ibn Abi Talib.

Chapter 13

Injustice against the Imamat

Immediately following the death of Prophet Mohammad, those who rejected the prophet's declaration that Imam Ali ibn Abi Talib would succeed him as caliph installed their own code of Islamic laws and ethics to correspond to their personal objectives. As such, the ummah was in disarray. During these turbulent times, however, Imam Ali ibn Abi Talib stood firm and resolute. He continued to preach the true message of Prophet Mohammad in order to restore the community to the lifestyle and conduct that Islam was based on. Nevertheless, the newly installed governments ignored Imam Ali's pleas and moved forward with their own plans.

This was the beginning of the trials and tribulations the Imams, their families, and followers would endure in the generations and centuries that followed. Under the most difficult and inhumane conditions, they were determined and tenacious in their quest to bring the ummah back to the Islam of Ahl al-Bayt. However, the caliphs of Islam under the Umayyad, Abbasid, and Ottoman regimes continued their injustice by engaging in the oppression, persecution, and martyrdom of the Imams and their Shi'a followers:

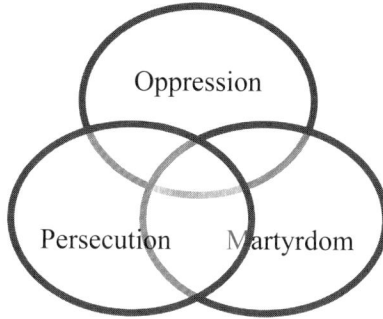

The oppression, persecution, and martyrdom of Shi'as throughout history by despotic rulers of Islam have often been characterized by brutal and genocidal acts. During the Umayyad rule, the oppressors of Ahl al-Bayt appointed Ahl al-Sunnah wal Jama'a to tyrannize Imam Ali ibn Abi Talib and the progeny of Prophet Mohammad. They invented the custom of having preachers in the mosques curse and condemn Imam Ali and the prophet's progeny. This practice continued for eighty years, until in AD 717 the Umayyad's chose as caliph, Umar ibn Abdul Aziz, a great-grandson of the second caliph, Umar ibn Al-Khattab. Much to their surprise, Umar ibn Abdul Aziz issued a decree forbidding insults, harassment, and oppression against members of Ahl al-Bayt by stating that this mistreatment was against Islam and the Qur'an (Ibn Sa'd 2000). Nonetheless, followers of Ahl al-Sunnah wal Jama'a killed him. He was only thirty-eight years old and had served just two years as caliph.

Ahl al-Sunnah wal Jama'a created a diversion by claiming that the members of Ahl al-Bayt were not loyal to the sunnah of Prophet Mohammad but were, in fact, *rafidis* (rejectionists) and people of innovations. The reality is that those who actually excelled in inventing innovations and renouncing the sunnah of Prophet Mohammad and Ahl al-Bayt were Ahl al-Sunnah wal Jama'a. They misled the community by portraying themselves as the only ones who upheld the Prophet's sunnah versus the rafidis of Ahl al-Bayt who rejected it. But, in fact, followers of Ahl al-Sunnah wal Jama'a were the ones who actually rejected the Prophet's sunnah (al-Samawi 1995).

Ahl al-Bayt continued to oppose the unjust and oppressive rule of the Umayyads and later the Abbasids. However, the oppression inflicted on Ahl al-Bayt by the Abbasids was far more devastating than that committed by the Umayyads. The strategic initiatives of Ahl al-Bayt were twofold, as they varied between peace and revolt. Each of the infallible Imams experienced oppression and cruelty from the unjust rulers that wore the crown of caliph. Bear in mind that the extent of the difficulty and suffering that each of these Imams endured was similar, owing to the conditions of the time in which they lived. We do not state that one Imam is greater than another Imam, only that all of the infallible Imams are the continuation of the root of Imam Ali ibn Abi Talib and Fatima as-Zahra.

Psychological Analysis of the Umayyad and Abbasid Caliphs

The pursuit of power and supremacy are primary driving forces of history. As such, people are moved and manipulated by rulers they do not truly understand. For the Umayyad and Abbasid caliphs, it was more preferable to have a community of ignorant people under their control than to have opponents who would oppose and rally against them. Therefore, it was in the interest of these caliphs to nurture deceptions that obscured the true nature of their intent. Their policies were aimed at subjugating the Shi'a Imams of Ahl al-Bayt and their followers who opposed the corrupt caliphs that deviated from the true nature of Islam. The primary objective of these caliphs was to discredit the rival theories of the Imamat. For example, the Umayyad caliphs adopted the title *khalifat Allah* (Allah's deputy) (Crone 1986; Donner 2010) in order to overrule the Imamat's claim that they were Allah's representatives and the leaders of the Islamic community. However, Sunni scholars have frequently reproached the Umayyads for this practice, citing that Abu Bakr had claimed that he was not khalifat Allah but rather *khalifat rasul Allah* (Allah's messenger's successor) (Al-Mawardi 1996). The Umayyad and early Abbasid caliphs upheld the title of khalifat Allah, first attested for the third caliph, Uthman, and regularly used by both the Umayyad and Abbasid dynasties because it conveniently endowed them with all-encompassing religious authority as Allah's representatives on earth (Bennison 2009).

By referring to themselves as khalifat Allah, the Umayyad caliphs believed that they had the exclusive authority to interpret and enforce Islam. As a result, they gained more autocratic power so that no one could challenge their authority on anything, including legal decisions and interpretations of the Qur'an. The end result was that these caliphs engaged in coercive power in order to inflict punishment, persecution, and oppression on Muslims and non-Muslims.

Likewise, the administrative system followed by the Abbasids was in essence the system of the Umayyads (Surur 2001). For the most part, the Abbasid government was one of oppression and tyranny rather than social and political justice. Dictatorial, the Abbasids controlled all judicial and administrative authorities, plundered properties, prevented freedoms, and forced people to do what they hated. The Abbasid caliphs acted according to their personal inclinations and spent the wealth of the Islamic treasury on their immoral desires. The Abbasid caliphs were famous for violence, oppression, and shedding blood. They did not yield to truth and justice. The Islamic community suffered from their oppression and tyranny. As the Abbasid caliphs created Muslim sects to obey their commands, they also forced them to refrain from any contact with the Imams of Ahl al-Bayt. The Abbasid caliphs isolated the Imams of Ahl al-Bayt by preventing the Muslims from communicating with them.

While the Umayyad and Abbasid governments continued their rage of tyranny inflicted upon the innocent, the major concern of the Shi'a Imams of Ahl al-Bayt was to safeguard religious authority and to protect the Qur'an from distortion. On what basis could the political actions and commands of the ruling caliphs be authorized, such that it would become religiously normative for the subjects to obey or cooperate? Who could authorize such judgments? For the Shi'as, that authority would be the Imam of Ahl al-Bayt. For Sunnis, it had been the ummah (Anjum 2012).

As we research the history of the Umayyad and Abbasid caliphs, it becomes clear that power tends to corrupt. Blinded by the lust for power, they would do anything—commit any crime, atrocity, or deception to reach their goal of ultimate control. Undoubtedly, there is a thread that runs through the fabric of this type of sociopathic personality. As the character disorder of these tyrants was associated with the difficulty they had on many levels of interpersonal relationships, they were totally absorbed in satisfying their needs regardless of the cost. Feelings of insecurity and inadequacy, insanity, complete absence of empathy, and an inability to understand cause and effect were characteristics of this character disorder. The only check-and-balance system that emerged during the rule of these tyrannical caliphs was the Imamat. These tyrants were ruthless in their desire for power and motivated by a pathological obsession based on the hate of the Imamat of Ahl al-Bayt. Anyone whom they believed to be their enemy, whether they were or not, was put to death. Each succeeding tyrannical caliph seemed to want to outdo the previous caliph in treachery. They were psychotic and manifested their anger toward their own people and had no hesitation in killing anyone who spoke out against them (Jones 2011).

The antisocial behavior of the tyrannical caliphs included violence, torture, terrorism, oppression, and persecution of the Imamat. They committed evil in ways that demeaned, dehumanized, harmed, destroyed, and killed innocent people. They took pleasure in the infliction of harm on innocent people and in creating political systems of destruction in the Islamic arena. Understanding the motivations and circumstances that contributed to the transformation of the authoritarian personality of these caliphs falls in the realm of social psychology. They engaged in evil deeds that deprived others of their dignity, humanity, and life. Nonetheless, the tyrannical caliphs demanded and received obedience from the Muslims who fell into the mire of complete submission to them. Understanding how the caliphs succeeded in their influence on the Muslim community is tantamount to understanding social order. Toward this end, it was coercive power (i.e., the power to punish) that the caliphs employed in influencing and manipulating the Muslims to obey them.

Muslims who supported the oppressive governments of the Umayyads and Abbasids fell under their evil spell. When the Muslims could not realize their own values and beliefs, they accepted alternatives, however drastic, by embracing these rogue caliphs that gave false promises. Historically, tyrannies have tended to be insecure, and they try to maintain their power by becoming increasingly oppressive (Roland 2000). The caliph's skills in deception, manipulation, and intimidation were an advantage to him in securing power. As Aristotle noted, the tyrant is one who cuts off the heads of those who are too high, undertakes measures to sow discord among subjects, impoverishes people with his exploits, and uses informers and betrayers to undermine trust among his subjects (Simpson 1997; Ferrari 2000). The problem, as Plato recognized in *The Republic* (Ferrari 2000), resides in the tyrant's character and the ways in which he exercises power. Lacking concern for elementary considerations of justice, he needlessly creates enemies and sets himself on a path that leads to increasingly chaotic behavior on his part.

Hence, the Umayyad and Abbasid caliphs sought and exercised power for their own rather than the general interest, and they created a political order based on extreme cruelties and mistrust (Glad 2002). As Machiavelli argued in *The Prince*, the goal of establishing a new regime requires a man with a nature that enables him to be as deceptive and cruel as the situation requires. A newly established ruler, he states, must act as cruelly as necessary to secure himself and establish a reputation for harshness (Machiavelli 1966). Karen Horney noted that the neurotic creates an idealized self-image as a cover for underlying feelings of unworthiness. Whatever the content of his idealized self-portrait, he devotes psychic energies to the self-presentations and the maintenance of the supports that suggest he really is that perfect person. As the idealized self becomes more intensified, he loses contact with his real feelings and thus the capacity for change and growth. The end result is that his efforts are devoted to an unending quest to identify with his ideal self and to win support for it. But even if he reaches some of his goals, he will never be satisfied. At some level, the individual has a dim realization that he does not really live up to his lavish image. To defend the idealized self, he makes claims for recognition and deference and is enraged when it is not forthcoming (Horney 1950).

Oppression and Persecution of Ahl al-Bayt

Let us examine the magnitude of the oppression and persecution inflicted upon Prophet Mohammad and his Ahl al-Bayt as well as the subsequent martyrdom of the infallible Imams. What follows is a summary, derived from a number of sources, of the injustice perpetrated against the prophet and the Imamat.

Prophet Mohammad

The leaders of Quraysh harassed the prophet, who endured both verbal and physical abuse. They first subjected him to verbal attacks and insults. Later, they engaged in physical aggression by throwing spikes, garbage, and dust on him. When the prophet's uncle Abi Talib died, the chief of the clan became Abu Lahab, the prophet's evil uncle. Hence, the prophet lost his tribal protection and fled from Mecca to the city of Taif. The people of Taif became very hostile and began to shout at the prophet while they pelted him with stones. Bloody and battered by the stoning of the street hoodlums, the prophet returned to Mecca. However, the persecution of the followers of Islam intensified to the point that the prophet had his followers flee to Medina. Still, the leaders of Quraysh continued their assault on the prophet and decided to assassinate him while he was asleep in his house in Mecca. The plot was foiled, as Imam Ali ibn Abi Talib took the place of the prophet by sleeping in his bed in order for the prophet to escape.

All through these events, there was violence, persecution, and injustice directed at the prophet and his followers. Even though the people of Mecca, in general, had engaged in the persecution of the prophet and his followers, the prophet granted immunity and mercy to them.

Abu Lahab and his wife continuously persecuted the prophet. Abu Lahab launched a campaign against the prophet by beating, harassing, torturing, and persecuting him and his followers. For example, Abu Lahab would throw stones at the prophet, and his wife would lay wood sprinters on the ground where the prophet would walk so as to cause his feet to bleed. Even when the prophet was in Medina, the Quraysh and other tribes frequently waged battles against him and his followers. Additionally, some of the Jews in Medina, with their devious plots, conspired to murder the prophet. Even the hypocrites in Medina, pretending to be Muslims, waged campaigns against the prophet.

All through his suffering, Prophet Mohammad represented the best example in human potential for hope, goodness, and humility. The lesson learned through the prophet's suffering was that man has the potential to be good or to be evil. Therefore, the prophet's suffering should make us think of how to overcome evil.

Fatima as-Zahra

Fadak was a piece of property willed to Fatima as-Zahra by her father, Prophet Mohammad. From this economic resource, the revenue generated was allocated to the needy families of Medina. Those who wanted to confiscate this property were interested in enhancing their own objectives at the expense of the indigenous people who benefited from this charity. Upon the death of her father, Caliph Abu Bakr ordered Fadak to be taken from Fatima. This action of denying the rights of Fatima would result in her losing outreach support and relevance in the community she was supporting. Additionally, Fatima was angered when the leadership of her husband, Imam Ali, to succeed the prophet was unjustly taken from him.

However, Imam Ali's reasons for not fighting at the time to restore Fadak are the same as why he didn't fight to claim his rightful position as caliph. Had he fought for either his right to be caliph or the restoration of Fadak to Fatima, there would have been many casualties and bloodshed on both sides, weakening the Islamic community and making it vulnerable to the enemies of Islam. Therefore, Imam Ali chose the course of unity in Islam by safeguarding it against its enemies, even at the expense of losing Fadak and his right to be caliph.

The following hadiths relate to Fadak:

> When the Prophet died, Abu Bakr took Fadak from Fatima. Fatima went to him and said, "Restore the land of Fadak to me, as my father the Prophet gave it to me." (ShiaPen Newsletter, *Revealing the Truth*, www.shiapen. com [*Riyadh al Nadira*, Vol. 4, p. 231; *Kitab Mau' jam-al-Buldan*, Vol. 14, p. 238])

> Umar was angry with Abu Bakr and said, "If you give Fadak back to Fatima, where will the expenses for army and defense come from for at present all the Arabs are fighting against you?" He (Abu Bakr) then took the papers of Fadak from Fatima and tore them into shreds. (NationMaster.com, *Insanul Ayun fi Seerah al Halbeeya*, Vol. 3, pp. 487–488)

The following hadiths relate to the malicious treatment of Fatima:

> Who makes her (Fatima) angry makes me (Prophet Mohammad) angry. (*Sahih Bukhari*, Vol. 5, Book 62, Hadith 3714, Sahih/Authentic; *Al-Tirmidhi*, Vol. 6, Book 46, Hadith 3867, Sahih/Authentic)

> Allah becomes wrathful for Fatima's anger, and is pleased at her pleasure. (Administrator 2010 [*Ahmad ibn Hanbal*, Vol. 5, p. 26; *Riyadh al Nadira*, Vol. 2, p. 194])

The merits of Fatima are unmatched by any woman in history, as she had the perfection of all the moral excellence and noble traits. She personified the ideal example of how a daughter, wife, and mother should act, with the utmost purity in character and morality. Supportive of her husband, she was his advisor, assisting him in religious affairs while at the same time maintaining their home as one of peace, modesty, and serenity. She had the distinction of being the daughter of the final prophet, the wife of Amir al-Mu'mineen, the mother of the two leaders of the youth in paradise, and the grandmother of the infallible Imams that followed.

Imam Ali ibn Abi Talib

Imam Ali's right to the caliphate was unjustly taken from him, and a great deal of pressure was exerted on Imam Ali and his supporters to give their allegiance to Abu Bakr as caliph. The governor of Syria, Muawiyah ibn Abu Sufyan, seized the opportunity to inflict his hatred and discrimination against Imam Ali and the Ahl al-Bayt of Bani Hashim. This blazing hatred was inflicted on Imam Ali's descendants and supporters who were violently repressed.

The Ahl al-Bayt family was oppressed not only during their lifetime but after their martyrdom as well. The malevolent offenders seized every opportunity to distort the merits of Imam Ali by fabricating the hadiths of Prophet Mohammad that were attributed to him and his family. In their treachery, they were able to deviate most of the Muslim society from the right path to engage in their oppression and cruelties in order to tarnish and destroy the nobility of Imam Ali and his Ahl al-Bayt. Fabrications against Imam Ali were even perpetrated by Aisha, the wife of the prophet, as she incited her cousins, Talha and Zubair, and others in the Muslim society to take vengeance against Imam Ali by accusing him of the murder of Caliph Uthman. All of these false accusations against Imam Ali were in violation of what Prophet Mohammad had said:

After me, Ali is the best judge and the most knowledgeable individual of my Ummah. (Javed Akbari [Al-Shaykh Al-Saduq, *Al-Amaali*, p. 440, Hadith 20; Muwafiq bin Ahmad Khawarizmi, *Manaqib*, p. 81, Hadith 66])

The Messenger said on the day of the great pilgrimage when he sent Ali with Surat Bara'a instead of Abu Bakr, who came crying and asked, "O Messenger of Allah! Reveal something for me." The Messenger answered, "My Lord ordered me that nobody can discharge my duty except myself or Ali."

- *Ibn Majah*, Vol. 1, Book 1, Hadith 119 (Hasan/Good)
- *Al Tirmidhi*, Vol. 6, Book 46, Hadith 3719) (Hasan/Good)
- *Al-Nasa'i*, al-Khasais, p. 20

Umar had said … our best judge is Ali. (*Sahih Bukhari*, Vol. 6, Book 65, Hadith 4481 [Sahih/Authentic])

These hadiths explain the prophet had absolute confidence that Imam Ali would continue to promote justice in the society by virtue of his complete knowledge of the Qur'an and the hadiths. Even when Imam Ali's claims to be caliph were overlooked, he offered his allegiance in pursuance of the doctrine of preference. Imam Ali chose a logical and reasonable approach to restore the principle of *imamah*, but he never adhered to the motto of "all or none."

As Imam Ali did not fear death, then why didn't he rise up to retrieve his right as caliph? There was nothing more important than martyrdom. Being killed for the cause of the Almighty was his ultimate desire. But in his sound calculations, Imam Ali had reached the conclusion that under the existing conditions, it was in the interest of Islam to foster collaboration and cooperation among the Muslims. He repeatedly stressed this point.

What this means is that Imam Ali was more concerned with the big picture in Islam, which is unity, and he did what he could to safeguard that unity. Since Imam Ali knew that the higher cause was to breed accord and not discord in the Muslim community, he supported the leadership only in the name of unity. He knew that taking the position of the rightful leadership of the Muslim world by waging war would have destroyed Islam. Following the death of Prophet Mohammad, the entire Arabian Peninsula was on the verge of collapse, as turbulence and strife were on the rise on all fronts. People who were rebellious, confused, and disturbed were growing in numbers and posed a threat to Islam.

Imam Ali knew that a civil war at that stage would give opportunities to the Jewish clans of Bani Nazir and Bani Qurayza and the Christian tribes of Najran and Syria supported by the Byzantine armies, and the hypocrites (*munafiqin*) and fresh converts as well as the Persian Empire to simply take advantage of the situation. Imam Ali wanted the enemies of Islam to realize that Islam was powerful enough to defend itself. Therefore, Imam Ali was willing to accept every adversity for the sake of the unity in Islam. As a result, Imam Ali found himself at the crossroads and could not risk a war to claim his right to the caliphate. He was instilled with the noble qualities of vision and action, which taken together transform the ummah and bring about the unity.

Imam Hassan ibn Imam Ali

Influenced by the Umayyad media, Imam Hassan was unjustly portrayed as one who married and divorced excessively, preferred a luxurious and extravagant life, disgraced the believers, and sold his imamah to Muawyiah for these reasons. These false accusations were aimed to distort the Imam's image in the society. Muawiyah succeeded in tempting those who had paid allegiance to Imam Hassan to abandon him, including many of his top commanders. Muawiyah was able to penetrate the ranks of the Imam's army and followers, which inflicted even greater suffering for the Imam. Even the Khawarij spread false rumors about the Imam, creating doubt in the society about him and Ahl al-Bayt.

Muawiyah's main objective was to annihilate the followers of Ahl al-Bayt. He proceeded to crucify them on date palms, bury them alive, terrorize their women, demolish their houses, deprive them of the fixed stipend from *Baitul Maal* (treasury), and many other atrocities. Moreover, Muawiyah also fabricated the hadiths attributed to Ahl al-Bayt, instituted educational programs to teach the youth to hate Ahl al-Bayt, and had the religious scholars at the pulpit curse the prophet's family.

Imam Hassan was forced to accept a peace treaty with Muawiyah in order to save Islam from the ravages of war and, further, because his army had been eaten away by weakness and conflict (Al-Yasin 1998). Imam Hassan's sufferings were further intensified as the oppressors attempted to murder him on several occasions (e.g., being served poison several times). These assassination attempts finally succeeded when his wife poisoned him. Even during his burial, the oppression continued, as arrows were shot into his body, and his coffin was desecrated. The oppression continued in the centuries to follow, as the shrine was destroyed, and when restored, it was destroyed again.

Imam Hussein ibn Imam Ali

Oppression against Ahl al-Bayt continued. Imam Hussein endured the chicanery and insidiousness of the despotic ruler Caliph Yazid ibn Muawiyah until he could tolerate it no more. Yazid was the very essence of oppression and corruption that wreaked havoc throughout the Muslim world. A drunkard, gambler, pervert, tyrant, and oppressor, Yazid had no respect for Islam. He was far worse than his father, who himself was a tyrant and oppressor, and even disavowed the treaty his father made with Imam Hassan. Yazid appointed governors with the major responsibility of terrorizing, oppressing, and torturing anyone who was loyal to Imam Hussein. These governors and officials were influenced by Yazid's corruption, including those in Kufa who reneged on their treaty with Imam Hussein. Therefore, Imam Hussein and his small contingent of less than one hundred followers were all alone on the battlefield of Karbala to face the enemy of over 30,000 soldiers (Shaykh Al-Mufid 2004).

Throughout the centuries, the tragedy of Karbala has been revisited and retold over and over again. Including Imam Hussein, his faithful and courageous Muslims were also martyred at Karbala in their fight against tyranny and oppression. Their memories have not been forgotten, as the annual remembrance and reenactment of the tragedy has become a tradition. The martyrdom of Imam Hussein and his followers is reflected in the phrase, "Every day is Ashura, every place is Karbala, and every month is Muharram." Because Shi'as have experienced so much oppression and persecution throughout history, they interpret their suffering through the suffering of Imam Hussein. As with Imam Hussein, it has been a battle between the innocent and just against the oppressive and unjust (Reis 2013).

Revolution for Imam Hussein was not to enhance his stature in the Islamic world but rather to establish justice and release the community from oppression and tyranny. In essence, Imam Hussein wanted to restore the people to the Straight Path of Islam. His objective was not for glory or for power but to save Islam. Imam Hussein wanted to restore to the people their dignity and self-respect and to instill the true meaning of brotherhood. Imam Hussein did not revolt until all options had been exhausted. He came to the realization that the only way to transform the community back to the Islam his grandfather, Prophet Mohammad, had preached was to sacrifice his own life toward that cause. In essence, Imam Hussein's revolt was a struggle (jihad) only in defense of Islam, as he had to rise against the tyrannical Umayyad regime of Yazid.

Imam Hussein revolted to restore Islamic law. He stepped up to the challenge, and with his bravery and courageous spirit he was victorious. For in this victory he reawakened the consciousness of the people. Following in the footsteps of his father, Imam Ali, he took upon himself the social responsibility of the community (ummah), for that community was the community of his father and grandfather. As such, he fulfilled his responsibility and obligation with determination and sincerity as he sacrificed his life and that of the members of his family and followers so that he could restore freedom, truth, and justice as well as Qur'anic law to the community.

The most important reason Imam Hussein undertook his revolt was to clean up the Islamic caliphate from the Umayyad corruption that they had usurped unjustly. Islam considers the institution of caliphate as an important agency for spreading truth and justice among the people. Therefore, if the caliphate is righteous, the entire ummah shall also be righteous. If the caliphate deviates from its responsibility, the community shall fall into terrible turmoil and calamities. On the basis of this, Imam Hussein rose up so that he could restore to the Islamic caliphate a just and illuminated existence and brilliant future.

The martyrdom of Imam Hussein was the changing point in the history of Muslims and their lives. Suddenly there was a complete change in them, as they became armed with determination and resolve. All the obstacles that had restrained them were removed as the clouds of fear and submission that had imprisoned them changed into ones of revolution and confrontation (Al-Qarashi 2007).

Mahatma Gandhi, the renowned former political and spiritual leader of India, stated: "I learned from Hussein how to achieve victory while being oppressed."

Lady Zainab, Daughter of Imam Ali and Fatima as-Zahra

Perhaps no female in the history of mankind personified the essence of patience (sabr) more than Lady Zainab. Through all the adversities she and her family suffered, she remained steadfast and patient in her worship of Allah. This patience was an act of worship—the highest level of worship—as she exhibited her resolve even though she had been mentally abused and harassed as a captive of the evil, malicious, and illegitimate ruler, Yazid.

We must ask ourselves what would have happened if Lady Zainab were not in Karbala at the time of the tragedy. Most assuredly, 'Ubaydullah Ibn Ziyad, governor of Kufa, would have silenced the tragedy and propagated the incident to the benefit of the ruthless Umayyad regime. As a result, the martyrdom of Imam Hussein and his faithful followers would have withered away in the desert sands of Karbala. Had it not been for Lady Zainab, the tragedy of Karbala would have faded into oblivion.

It was the eloquence of her speech and the aura of holiness that enveloped Lady Zainab as she reproached the enemies of Islam, particularly Ibn Ziyad and Yazid. She confronted her enemies by admonishing and rebuking them for their evil crimes against humanity. Bound with ropes and forced to ride on saddleless, lean camels, the ladies and orphans of Prophet Mohammad's family were taken as captives to Kufa. Her first address of reproach was to the crowds surrounding her caravan as she and her companions were disgracefully paraded through the streets of Kufa. The people of Kufa had earlier reneged on their support for Imam Hussein and deserted him.

Lady Zainab's eloquent speech rebuked the people of Kufa effectively, exposing their false faith in Islam, falsifying their deceitful tears, and introducing them as the most ignoble criminals, as they contributed strongly to the murder of Imam Hussein, his household, and his companions. With the utterance of justice and honesty and the voice of courage and right, Lady Zainab admonished the people of Kufa and pointed to their lowliness and rotten-heartedness. Their forgery and falsehood could not deceive her as she reproached them for their crimes and ascribed to them the meanest characters. Moreover, she commented on their weeping by saying that they should have wept for the big crime of disappointing Imam Hussein and letting him down.

'Ubaydullah Ibn Ziyad, son of the notorious Marjanah, was governor of Kufa. He was whacking the holy head of Imam Hussein with his baton. Lady Zainab's rebuttal to Ibn Ziyad exposed and disgraced him. Ibn Ziyad became inflamed and threatened to cut off the head of Lady Zainab's nephew, Imam Ali al-Sajjad, the son of Imam Hussein. However, Lady Zainab stood firm and said, "If you want to kill him, kill me with him as well." Thanks to Lady Zainab, Imam Ali al-Sajjad was saved from the tyrant.

From Kufa, Lady Zainab and her family and followers were taken to Damascus. At the palace, Yazid was beating Imam Hussein's head with a stick. Yazid rejoiced at the current situation, as the family of Prophet Mohammad was captive and the heads of the prophet's grandsons had been thrown before him. Yazid was overjoyed to have Prophet Mohammad's household killed, as Yazid claimed it was revenge against Prophet Mohammad and Imam Ali for having humiliated his father (Muawiyah) and grandfather (Abu Sufyan) and killing his forefathers during the Battle of Badr some years earlier. Lady Zainab addressed Yazid with one of the most spectacular revolutionary speeches in Islam. Lady Zainab smashed the despotism of Yazid and inflicted disgrace and dishonor on him and on those who caused him to reach such a position. The speech of Lady Zainab was one of the deathblows that snapped the Umayyad State (Shahin 2002).

Lady Zainab played a major role in spreading the account of the tragedy at Karbala. She also protected and supported Imam Ali al-Sajjad. In addition, she was able to convince a whole new generation of Muslims to the way of Ahl al-Bayt. Her powerful and influential sermons in Kufa and Damascus aroused the people who were deceived by the tyranny of Ibn Ziyad and Yazid.

Imam Ali al-Sajjad ibn Imam al-Hussein

After the conclusion of the Karbala event, Imam al-Sajjad was held captive with his aunt, Lady Zainab, and their women and children followers. Although ill at the time, Imam al-Sajjad was put in heavy chains with iron rings around his neck and his ankles, and was made to walk barefooted on the thorny plains from Karbala to Kufa and to Damascus. The humiliation and insults inflicted upon him by Ibn Ziyad and Yazid, both wanting to cut his head off, were far more difficult than if he had been martyred on the field of Karbala. His jihad (struggle) was one of protecting his family and followers as well as to bring the ummah back to the basics of Islam.

With the help of his aunt, Lady Zainab, Imam al-Sajjad confronted Ibn Ziyad and Yazid and exposed their evil intentions and schemes. He eloquently recited verses from the Qur'an as his guide in addressing them and the Umayyad regime. The Imam's life was in danger because his lectures had a positive, huge impact on his listeners. Nonetheless, Lady Zainab came to his rescue by eloquently mesmerizing and captivating the tyrants with her speeches.

Imam al-Sajjad also mesmerized and captivated the mind of Yazid by the power of reason and questions, so much so that Yazid ordered the *muazzin* (one who summons people to prayer) to give *azan* (call to prayer) in order to silence Imam al-Sajjad. When the muazzin uttered the words, "Ash hadu anna Mohammadan Rasulullah" (I bear witness that Mohammad is Allah's messenger), this opened the door for Imam al-Sajjad to stop the muazzin and pursue the questioning of Yazid as to why he would mock Prophet Mohammad and have the family of Prophet Mohammad killed. Yazid was speechless, thereby freeing the enslaved minds of the audience to uncover the crimes of Yazid by blaming him for his atrocities against Prophet Mohammad's household. Fearing for his life, Yazid wanted to conciliate public opinion, so he released Imam al-Sajjad, Lady Zainab, and all their followers, and they proceeded to Medina with full honor and respect (Al-Qarashi 2007).

In Medina, Imam al-Sajjad immediately began to apprise the citizens of the horrid tragedy of Karbala, their unwarranted captivity, and the blasphemy of Ibn Ziyad and Yazid and their Umayyad regime. For the rest of his life, Imam al-Sajjad continued to lecture about the evils of tyranny and oppression. He compiled a list of his supplications, known as *al-Sahifa al-Sajjadiyyah al-Kamilah* (the Psalms of Islam). It consists of sixty-eight *du'as* (supplications), fourteen additional du'as, and fifteen *munajaat* (whispered prayers) (Al-Sajjad 2006).

Imam al-Sajjad continued to live in a society faced with absolute chaos under the Umayyad rule. The rulers struggled to seize the Imam's rightful leadership by snatching the people's economic, political, and social rights through various oppressive measures. For example, they cut pensions and salary, exerted punishments, and fabricated narrations of the hadiths.

As he reawakened the Muslim community by preaching the true Islam in the vicinity of Medina and Mecca, the Imam inspired many people. The Umayyad regime slowly began to realize the dangers that faced them from Imam al-Sajjad's lectures. Years later, the tyrant ruler Walid Ibn Abdul Malik had the governor of Medina poison Imam al-Sajjad (Al-Qarashi 2007). Another chapter in the martyrdom of Prophet Mohammad's household came to an end. However, the legacy that Imam al-Sajjad left with his supplications did not end. His supplications have inspired the minds of Muslims for centuries to follow, and today many Muslims and non-Muslims are genuinely moved by the mastery and eloquence of his writings.

It was Imam al-Sajjad who continued the cause of Islam that his father courageously died for. The Muslim world had to be reawakened to Islam, and it was Imam al-Sajjad who successfully restored and recovered the Muslims back to the Straight Path. He did this by example, and his example was prayer, the root essence of Islam.

His numerous prayers and supplications are recorded in volumes of books, and they are the standard for all Muslims to follow. Two of the special characteristics of Imam al-Sajjad were his piety and self-restraint. Imam al-Sajjad had the same qualities and attributes in his personality that his grandfather, Imam Ali, had. He was the personification of patience, tolerance, forgiveness, and self-sacrifice.

Imam Mohammad al-Baqir ibn Imam Ali

Imam Mohammad al-Baqir was present at Karbala at the time of the horrific tragedy of the massacre of his grandfather Imam Hussein and followers. He also suffered with his father, Imam al-Sajjad, and the women of Ahl al-Bayt the merciless captivity and imprisonment at the hands of the notorious Yazid. After the tragedy of Karbala, Imam Mohammad al-Baqir passed his time peacefully in Medina praying to Allah and guiding the people to the Straight Path. The more the Umayyad government learned about the Imam's prestige and popularity, the more intolerable his existence became.

Despite his dislike for politics, the Umayyad rulers harassed Mohammad al-Baqir for fear of his popularity and influence. During this time, the community questioned who had the right and Islamic authority to rule. The actions of al-Baqir's brother, Zayd ibn Ali, and other followers made the ruling regime distrust him. When Hisham ibn Abd al-Malik became the caliph, he committed many massacres and cruelties, especially with regard to the followers of Bani Hashim.

Zayd ibn Ali, a scholar and pious theologian, met with the caliph to seek redress for the grievances filed against Bani Hashim. Instead of greeting Zayd, the caliph abused and mistreated him with repulsive language. Because of this disgraceful treatment, Zayd left Syria for Kufa, where he raised an army against the caliph. Although he fought bravely, Zayd was killed in battle. Zayd's body was exhumed from his grave, his head was cut off and sent to Caliph Hisham, and his body was placed on the gallows entirely naked for a period of four years. Thereafter, when Walid ibn Yazid ibn Abd al-Malik ibn Marwan became caliph, he ordered that the skeleton be taken down from the gallows, burnt, and the ashes scattered in the wind (Majlisi 2003).

When a number of Shi'as and their delegations made the pilgrimage from Kufa to Medina to perform Haj, they also attended Imam al-Baqir's religious sessions (Lalani 2000). The Imam possessed outstanding merit in traditional knowledge, self-denial, and leadership. When the Umayyad government could no longer tolerate the Imam, he was poisoned by the order of the caliph. The famous Sunni scholar Ibn Hajar al-Haythami said:

> Imam Mohammad al-Baqir has disclosed the secrets of knowledge and wisdom and unfolded the principles of spiritual and religious guidance. Nobody can deny his exalted character, his Allah-given knowledge, his divinely gifted wisdom and his obligation and gratitude towards spreading of knowledge. He was a sacred and highly talented spiritual leader and for this reason he was popularly titled al "Baqir" that means "the expounder of knowledge." Kind heart, spotless in character, sacred by soul and noble by nature, the Imam devoted all his time

in submission to Allah (and advocating the teachings of the Holy Prophet and his descendants). It is beyond the power of a man to count the deep impression of knowledge and guidance left by the Imam on the hearts of the faithful. (*WOFIS* 1984)

Imam Ja'far as-Sadiq ibn Imam Mohammad

Imam Ja'far as-Sadiq lived at a time when the Umayyad regime plunged into a civil war, in AD 743. From that time until AD 750, the Umayyad and Abbasid regimes were at odds. During that time, Imam Ja'far had an opportunity to effectively pursue theology and the sciences, virtually undisturbed. However, the Abbasid regime overthrew the Umayyads in AD 750. The Abbasid caliphs proved to be even more ruthless than their predecessors. During the reign of the Umayyad caliphs, three of the infallible Imams were poisoned (Imam Hassan ibn Imam Ali, Imam Ali al-Sajjad, and Imam Mohammad al-Baqir). During the reign of the Abbasid caliphs, six of the infallible Imams were poisoned (Imam Ja'far, Imam Musa, Imam Ali al-Rida, Imam Mohammad al Jawad, Imam Ali al-Hadi, and Imam Hassan al-Askari).

The second of the Abbasid caliphs, al-Mansur, was displeased and annoyed when Imam Ja'far as-Sadiq spread his belief that the Muslim society could dismiss the cruel rulers from their seat of power and hand over that leadership to those who were capable of following the Islam that was established by Prophet Mohammad. Hence, the caliph set forth to arrest and put a stop to the flow of Imam Ja'far's belief by attempting to refrain the people from joining his school of thought, which is the school of information, consciousness, and movement.

Caliph al-Mansur employed scholars for the implementation of his aims in order to make the people believe in the religion of suppression and constraint. Additionally, the caliph wanted to mold the beliefs of Muslims by getting them to believe that poverty, affliction, oppression, and excesses were all from Allah, and as humans, they could not interfere to reshape it. By accepting the caliph's views, the society would not oppose, revolt, or rise against him. Instead, the community would tolerate the excesses and cruelties of the tyrant ruler and bear the punishments of their criminal masters. As such, rather than object to these cruelties, the people would express their approval and thankfulness.

Imam Ja'far was under severe stress and pressure during the reign of Caliph al-Mansur. At times, the people were stopped from seeing the Imam. The caliph arrested many of the Imam's followers and imprisoned them. The caliph imposed restrictions, thereby exerting numerous pressures on the Imam who was then exiled. There were no limits to the caliph's oppression, as he summoned the Imam from exile several times in order to abuse and take outrageous measures against him. Moreover, the caliph constantly threatened the Imam.

Al-Mansur pursued the act of oppression against Imam Ja'far and his followers with extreme harshness and cruelty. He had only one aim, and that was to kill every descendant of Imam Ali ibn Abi Talib. He proceeded to persecute the Shi'as more brutally than they had been during the reign of the Umayyads. Al-Mansur even inflicted more interference and difficulty in the way of the Imam by forbidding the people to visit him. Additionally, the Imam was forbidden to receive people. This imposed a severe hardship on the community, who was in need of consultation relative to marriage, divorce, and other issues. After a long period of censorship, al-Mansur allowed the Imam to benefit the people with his knowledge. However, spies were present to record his lectures and discussions. Therefore, the Imam had to be extremely cautious in his discourses (Mirza 1997).

Imam Ja'far as-Sadiq lived in an atmosphere filled with animosity, terror, spying, and persecution. But as violent as the political scene was, the Imam succeeded in carrying out his great task of spreading knowledge and teaching, as well as graduating a number of scholars, jurisprudents, and preachers, some of which were Abu Hanifah and Malik ibn Anas, the Imams of two of the four renowned Sunni schools of thought.

Imam Musa al-Kazim ibn Imam Ja'far

Imam Musa al-Kazim lived in the most crucial times under the regimes of the despotic Abbasid caliphs who were known for their tyrannical and cruel administration. He witnessed the reigns of al-Mansur, al-Mahdi (son of al-Mansur), al-Hadi (son of al-Mahdi), and Harun ar-Rashid (son of al-Mahdi). Al-Mansur and Harun ar-Rashid put thousands of innocent descendants of Prophet Mohammad to death, the majority of who were buried alive inside walls or put into ghastly underground prisons. These wicked caliphs knew no pity or justice, and they killed and tortured for the pleasure they derived from human suffering. As for Imam Musa, he fell victim to the ruling caliphs and spent the greater part of his life in prison.

Imprisoned, the Imam was deprived of meeting with his followers. Caliph Harun ar-Rashid was insecure and highly envious of those who had extraordinary personalities, and Imam Musa fell into this category. His distaste for Imam Musa was accentuated by how the society was drawn to the Imam because of his noble personality and other dignified traits. Imam Musa was the most brilliant scholar with the noblest character and personality, and Harun resented it. As a result, he had the Imam imprisoned to veil him from the society.

Harun's oppressive behavior was full of hatred of the Shi'as. He not only buried them alive but also imposed on them house arrest as well as depriving them of their natural rights. Harun was so envious of Imam Musa that his only recourse was to imprison him and deprive the Muslim community of the Imam's knowledge and teachings.

As for those who opposed Harun's policy, it was Imam Musa who undertook that initiative. While the Imam was praying at the tomb of Prophet Mohammad, Harun had the Imam arrested even before he completed his prayer. The Imam was handcuffed and shackled and sent to Basra. While in prison, the Imam fasted by day and spent most of his time performing prayers. Imam Musa's conduct in prison was such that he was able to incline the hearts of his jailors toward him (Al-Qarashi 2005).

KNOW AND FOLLOW THE STRAIGHT PATH

Imam Musa was known for his tolerance, prudence, spirit of forgiveness, and a tight control of his temper, even against those who mistreated him. Understanding human psychology relative to the mind-set, aggressive motives, and aspects of personality, the Imam was able to make friends of his enemies. The Imam was martyred by poison. Even his corpse was not spared humiliation, as it was taken out of prison and left on a bridge in Baghdad.

Imam Ali al-Rida ibn Imam Musa

Caliph al-Ma'mun was filled with envy of Imam Ali al-Rida, who gained the deepest respect of the people because of his virtues and abundant knowledge. It was envy that caused al-Ma'mun to assassinate the Imam and to do away with him. However, the cunning al-Ma'mun took an interim step in that he offered Imam Ali to be his heir apparent to the caliphate, even though the Imam was twenty-one years older than al-Ma'mun. Why? The Abbasid caliphs were afraid of the Imams who were publicly recognized as the true and worthy successors of Prophet Mohammad. The Imams were constantly persecuted and tortured by the ruling caliphs. However, al-Ma'mun thought of finding a new solution for these difficulties that his Abbasid predecessors had not been able to solve.

Al-Ma'mun contrived to invite Imam Ali as heir apparent with the evil intention of making a false friendship with him. Toward this end, the Shi'as would consider al-Ma'mun's government legitimate and would be satisfied with it. Furthermore, the uprisings against al-Ma'mun's government would lose their attraction and legitimacy. Al-Ma'mun strongly felt that once the splendor and glory of the kingdom surrounded Imam Ali, he would fall into the trap of vices.

After being appointed heir apparent to Caliph al-Ma'mun, Imam Ali resisted all attempts of al-Ma'mun to force him into activities of power and draw him into the administrative affairs of the Abbasids. As heir apparent, Imam Ali stipulated his conditions to al-Ma'mun, divesting the heir apparent of its power and political content, which al-Ma'mun had hoped the Imam would exercise so that al-Ma'mun could achieve his strategic aim.

The acceptance of heir apparent by Imam Ali would give him time to realize his objectives: (a) to safeguard Islam and strengthen Ahl al-Bayt; (b) to guide the people by Allah's commands; (c) to protect Islam against the distorted meanings of certain Qur'anic verses; and (d) to protect Islam against the narration of forged and corrupted hadiths ascribed to Prophet Mohammad. Furthermore, the acceptance of heir apparent was only an opportunity for the Imam to expose the chicanery of al-Ma'mun's intentions. Rather than heir apparent, Imam Ali would only act as an advisor and not be involved in the affairs of the government. Moreover, Imam Ali was aware of the evil schemes of al-Ma'mun.

Imam Ali took a stand by educating and making the ummah aware of the political question relative to the principle of nass (designation of an Imam by a previous Imam) as he revealed the fabrications of the Abbasid regime regarding the legitimacy of actual leadership. The Imam disclosed the ambiguity that was exploited in the slogan *al-rida min aal Mohammad* (the chosen from the family of Prophet Mohammad), which was the formula on which the Abbasid regime was politically implemented. In addition, the slogan of *al-rida min aal Mohammad* was the principle of *bay'ah* (oath of allegiance to a leader), which was actually a distortion of the principle of nass aimed to exploit its political potential on one hand, and to escape from its political implication on the other hand (i.e., government by the infallible Imam). All that reawakened the consciousness of the ummah with regard to the principle of nass and the Imamat (Al-Qarashi 2014).

Imam Ali's decision relative to heir apparent was twofold: first, to protect Islam from being distorted, falsified, and misinterpreted; second, to protect the followers of the true Islamic path, the followers of the principle of nass and those close to it, from ignorance, deviation, and liquidation. Imam Ali was aware that the allegiance offered to him was the allegiance of death, whether he accepted to be heir apparent or not.

Imam Ali had to give the impression of accepting to be heir apparent in order to avoid a new wave of oppression, terror, exile, and execution against the followers of Ahl al-Bayt and to prevent the hardline Abbasid faction from taking full control of the regime. Toward this end, Imam Ali was able to get in touch with people who would not have dared to communicate with him. Moreover, it enabled the intellectual leadership to communicate and interact freely and safely with all classes of people, including the upper class. The end result was that the evil schemes of al-Ma'mun backfired, and Imam Ali was victorious. However, the victory of Imam Ali ended in his martyrdom.

Imam Mohammad al-Jawad ibn Imam Ali

After Caliph al-Ma'mun poisoned Imam Ali al-Rida, he then proceeded to have his daughter, Umul Fadhl, married to Imam Ali al-Rida's son, Imam Mohammad al-Jawad. Al-Ma'mun's objective in this marriage was political; he would have his daughter keep vigilance over the Imam. Additionally, by this marriage, al-Ma'mun would be able to get the Imam acquainted with the congregations, partying, and vices, thereby setting a trap for the Imam. Furthermore, if al-Ma'mun's daughter gave birth to a son who would later be appointed an Imam, al-Ma'mun would have gained the honor and pride for himself. But the daughter of al-Ma'mun did not bear a child to the Imam. It was a strained marriage that produced no children, so Imam al-Jawad married Soumaneh, who gave him a son and successor, Imam Ali al-Hadi. Upon al-Ma'mun's death, the baton of the leadership of the caliphate was passed on to his brother, al-Mu'tasim. The new caliph convinced Umul Fadhl to poison Imam al-Jawad, the result of which was his martyrdom at the young age of twenty-five years.

In his short span of a simple life, Imam al-Jawad accomplished a great deal, particularly in the literary field, imparting knowledge and wisdom to the great scholars who would emerge from his teachings. His personality, nature, and character paved the way for him to self-actualize in hospitality and courtesy to everyone, as he rendered equality without discrimination. In addition, he provided for the needy, poor, homeless, and orphans as he guided the people to the Straight Path.

At the young age of nine, the Imam assumed the responsibility of the Imamat. Enriching and expanding the knowledge and understanding of Shari'ah, he defended Islam and opposed obstinate ideas and deviated philosophies and ideologies that existed among the Muslims at that time.

When Imam al-Jawad came to Baghdad, Caliph al-Mu'tasim placed him under house arrest in order to observe and know his affairs and activities. Al-Mu'tasim ordered his men to keep a close vigil over the Imam. Additionally, he prevented the Imam from engaging with his followers and those who believed in his Imamat. However, al-Mu'tasim recognized and engaged the Imam's talents, especially in the field of jurisprudence, much to the chagrin and dismay of other jurisprudents. Consequently, these jurisprudents became envious and angry with the Imam and exhibited harm and malice to him.

The motives of al-Mu'tasim for assassinating the Imam were his envy of the Imam and the high position of honor and admiration the Imam received from the Muslims. Moreover, that envy was further exacerbated by the Imam's high morals, patience, kindness, and charity to those in need. Al-Mu'tasim's heart was full of spite and malice against the Imam. He burst with rage whenever he heard the virtues and exploits of the Imam being mentioned. All these factors led to al-Mu'tasim's decision to assassinate the Imam (Alsamail 2012).

Imam Ali al-Hadi ibn Imam Mohammad

Caliph Mutawakkil's reign of terror exceeded all his predecessors in bearing animosity, malevolence, and hatred toward Ahl al-Bayt. The period of persecution and torture began in full scale for Imam Ali al-Hadi and his family. Imam al-Hadi suffered unyielding misfortunes and agonies from Mutawakkil and his Abbasid associates. No effort was spared in oppressing and harming the Imam. Undoubtedly, Mutawakkil was the most spiteful toward the Imam.

In oppressing the Imam, Mutawakkil confined him to house arrest and surrounded his house with guards to watch his every move. The Imam was deprived of having any friends, religious scholars, jurisprudents, or narrators who could benefit from his knowledge, wisdom, legal opinions, and interpretation of Islamic laws. As Mutawakkil suppressed the dissemination of knowledge, he committed a heinous crime against the teachings of Islam. In addition, Mutawakkil imposed an economic blockade against the Imam by preventing him from taking the legal dues from a number of Islamic countries that would have been used to help the needy, orphans, and other endeavors. In short, the Imam was left in urgent need. Furthermore, Mutawakkil ordered his men to frequently search the Imam's house to see if they could find arms or books that countered the Abbasid rule. Mutawakkil was hoping to find an excuse to kill the Imam, but they found nothing.

To further impose the harshest of torture on the Imam, Mutawakkil transferred him to the custody of Sa'id, a cruel and ruthless man in whose imprisonment the Imam spent twelve years. In spite of all the hardships he had to suffer there, the Imam passed his time in *ibadah* (worship). Later, Mutawakkil ordered that the Imam's imprisonment be changed to house arrest. Even in house arrest, he was not allowed to live peacefully. Again his followers were not allowed to approach him openly to gain the true Islamic knowledge. But the Imam endured all hardships for the sake of giving knowledge to all who sought it from him. Mutawakkil knew that and continued persecuting the followers of the Imam. Mutawakkil had grown tired of people preaching the knowledge and piety of Imam al-Hadi, but mostly he had grown angry hearing the Shi'as talk of how the Imam was more worthy of the caliphate than he was. Hence, Mutawakkil had the Imam poisoned, resulting in his martyrdom. Interestingly, the Imam had told Mutawakkil that his own fate would be realized in three days, at which time Mutawakkil was assassinated, and one of the assassins was his son, al-Muntasir (WOFIS 1984).

Imam Hassan al-Askari ibn Imam Ali

Imam Hassan al-Askari spent his short life of twenty-eight years under the rule of several caliphs who spared no effort in oppressing him. His sufferings and distresses escalated as he was moved from one prison to another. If confinement weren't enough, an economic blockade was imposed on him. During his imprisonment, the Imam was prevented from meeting with his followers, scholars, and narrators. Additionally, religious scholars were prevented from contacting him to benefit from his reservoir of scientific knowledge. The despots often tried to assassinate him, but Allah protected him from their schemes.

During one of these imprisonments, Imam Hassan was put in a cage with wild animals that had not eaten for days. Obviously, these animals were very hungry, waiting to devour anything in sight. His jailors left the prison, leaving the animals in the cage with him. Much to their surprise, when the jailors returned, they saw the Imam praying, surrounded by the wild animals that were all in prostration. The patience (sabr) of Imam Hassan was such that he captivated anyone who came in contact with him. Even some of his jailors succumbed to his patience and were afraid to carry out the death sentence.

Imam Hassan lived most of his life under house arrest or in prison, under the supervision of the Abbasid caliphs. Mutawakkil was the first of these oppressive caliphs. He had strong animosity and malice toward members of Ahl al-Bayt. While under house arrest, Mutawakkil had detectives and guards keep a strong watch on all of the Imam's activities. The Imam was prevented from having anyone contact him. The reign of Mutawakkil came to a screeching halt when his son, al-Muntasir, who had conspired with the Turks, killed him. Unlike his father, al-Muntasir allowed Imam Hassan to have freedom. However, the reign of al-Muntasir did not last long, as he died shortly thereafter.

The succeeding caliph, al-Musta'in, had little political influence and was considered by many to be controlled by the Turks. Nonetheless, al-Musta'in had bitter hatred of Imam Hassan, and he feared that the Imam might rise in a revolt against the Abbasid rule. Eventually, the Turks ended al-Musta'in's rule, and he was forced to hand the position over to al-Mu'tazz. Imam Hassan continued to live under house arrest during the reigns of al-Mu'tazz, al-Muhtadi, and al-Mu'tamid until his death. The cause of his death was poison administered by the last Abbasid caliph, al-Mu'tamid, who like his forefathers was an open enemy of Ahl al-Bayt. He declared that the Imam should be imprisoned with no mercy shown. For example, Mu'tamid engaged Salih bin Wasif to treat Imam Hassan harshly. Salih sent for two of the most evil men he could find to deal with the Imam. By the grace of Allah, these two evil men suddenly became worshippers as they prayed and fasted. When Salih asked these two men why they had a change in character, they responded by saying that the patience (sabr) of the Imam while in prayer just overwhelmed them to the point that they trembled in his presence (Ayleya 2014).

Imam Hassan represented the front of opposition to the Abbasid rule. He criticized the rulers for misappropriating the wealth of the Islamic ummah and extorting the people under their rule. The Abbasid caliphs were considered puppets of the Turks who ruled with terrorism.

Imam Mohammad al-Mahdi ibn Imam Hassan

The theology of the Shi'as is imbedded in the manifestation and return of the Twelfth Infallible Imam, Mohammad al-Mahdi, at a time when the Muslims are oppressed as never before and suffering worse than ever. Emerging from his major occultation, the Imam, in the company of Prophet Jesus, will finally end the horrific persecution of the true believers, taking up arms against their enemies. Among the prominent signs of the reemergence of Imam al-Mahdi is the prevalence of widespread injustice and oppression as well as total absence of peace and security. Violence and terror will have wreaked havoc, fear, corruption, and calamities throughout the world. Mankind will have succumbed to the abyss of their negligence, as ignorance will dominate human society.

While the infallible Imams were oppressed and persecuted, they withstood the agony, harassment, and torment by staying the course of the Straight Path. Notwithstanding the oppression and persecution inflicted on them, the infallible Imams continued to pursue the course of the Straight Path as they reached out to their communities by preaching the true message of Islam. The triumph and success of all of the infallible

Imams was due to their personalities, which were molded by their patience (sabr), energy, and unity:

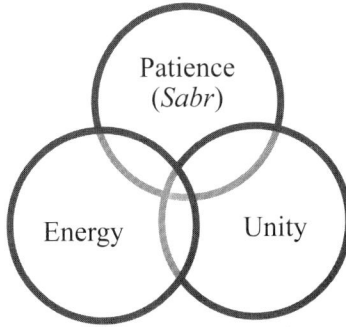

Let us examine how the Imamat of Ahl al-Bayt triumphed in these three virtues.

Chapter 14

Patience (Sabr) of the Imamat

Muslims throughout the world continue to search for knowledge, understanding, and wisdom in order to learn as much as they can about the faith of Islam. From time to time, they fall prey to the desires and evils of this world. A stimulus is needed to assure that their faith is complete and secure. That stimulus needed to bind the ideological aspects (Articles of Faith) and practical aspects (Branches of Faith) of Islam is sabr (patience).

Sabr enables us to fulfill our purpose in life. Without it, we are like nomads in the desert searching for water to quench our thirst but never realizing that the well is just beneath our feet. The essence of sabr is when people restrain themselves from committing evil, obey Allah's orders by holding their hearts firm, and refrain from complaining about anything bad that happens to them.

The best example of sabr is when people who are faced with calamity and adversity hold steadfast in their sabr and place their trust in Allah. Sabr takes on many characteristics, such as patience, endurance, perseverance, and forbearance.

Characteristics of Sabr

The word sabr and its derivatives occur 103 times in ninety-three verses in the Qur'an. The importance of sabr can be understood from the following two passages of the Qur'an and *Nahjul Balagha*:

> O ye who believe! Seek help with patience and prayer; verily Allah is with the patient ones. (Qur'an 2:153)

> Practice endurance (sabr); it is to faith what the head is to the body. There is no good in a body without a head, or in faith without endurance. (*Nahjul Balagha*, Saying #82 of Imam Ali ibn Abi Talib)

Therefore, sabr is the catalyst that brings prayer and faith to self-realization, because without it prayer and faith are weakened. Sabr guards the dignity of the prayer and ensures that our behavior will reflect the true essence and meaning of prayer. Allah stresses the impact and importance of patience (sabr) by linking it with prayer. In the case of faith, sabr is needed to sustain it. A body is useless without a head, since it is the brain that is the chief mechanism for sustaining life. Therefore, the body perishes without the head. Likewise, faith is useless without endurance (sabr), since belief must be sustainable throughout one's life. Moreover, when endurance (sabr) disappears, so does faith. Faith needs endurance (sabr) to become sustainable and actionable.

Prophet Mohammad and his Ahl al-Bayt played a major role in instilling in the minds of mankind the importance of sabr within the Islamic personality. What follows is a summary derived from a number of sources regarding the importance of sabr within each of their lives.

Prophet Mohammad

The prophet endured insults, persecution, and assassination attempts against him. Yet he showed restraint against his enemies. When the Muslims overtook Mecca, the prophet could have acted with impunity against his enemies but instead showed clemency and offered them forgiveness. Prophet Mohammad was the embodiment and personification of patience (sabr). While he endured many years of suffering, hardships, adversities, and calamities, he remained steadfast and patient. He was patient with those who waged war against him as well as with those who killed his companions and family members. He was patient with those who ridiculed, humiliated, demeaned, denigrated, and abased him. During the many years of facing all forms of abuse, boycott, and threats on his life, the prophet remained patient, gentle, and sympathetic even to his enemies. All through these hardships, he was never discouraged by adverse circumstances nor did he ever permit any personal desire to overcome him.

Fatima as-Zahra

Fatima as-Zahra was the personification of sabr, as she persevered relative to those who did her harm and endured self-restraint against that which she loved. Following the death of her father, Prophet Mohammad, she demonstrated steadfast patience. She endured mental anguish and torment from the rulers who denied her the inheritance willed by her father, forcing their way into her home and denying her husband, Imam Ali, of his right to succeed the prophet as the leader of the Islamic ummah. It was her father who taught his daughter the value of patience and forbearance in this life, for she will obtain the eternal reward of paradise. The political indignations suffered by Fatima teach us to have faith and patience.

Imam Ali Ibn Abi Talib

Sabr is not reactive but proactive, and Imam Ali ibn Abi Talib portrayed the best example of patience and endurance. Imam Ali was the first person to declare in public his support of Prophet Mohammad and belief in the message of Islam. During a gathering of family members,

155

Imam Ali was the first to support the prophet as his executor (wasi) and successor (caliph). Imam Ali risked his life by sleeping in the prophet's bed to impersonate him and thwart an assassination plot so that the prophet could escape in safety. During the Battle of the Trench, Imam Ali ibn Abi Talib displayed his patience by restraining his anger as he defeated Amru ibn Abd Wid, the champion of the enemy. Before the migration to Medina, Imam Ali exhibited patience and endurance as he shared with the prophet all the persecutions and bore most of his hardships. When the prophet's appointment of Imam Ali to be his successor as caliph was rejected by some of the companions, Imam Ali patiently endured twenty-four years before he was restored to his right as caliph. His steadfastness and resolve removed any obstacles (e.g., fear) as he faced danger and hardship with the greatest intensity of sabr.

Imam Hassan ibn Imam Ali

The life of Imam Hassan ibn Imam Ali was one of hardships, trials, and deception. Through all of these events, he never wavered from his patience. He remained steadfast even with the tragedies within his family: his mother brutally injured and dying at a young age, martyrdom of his father, substitution of Islam by some for wealth and power, and some of his supporters turning against him. He endured each of these, although sad and distressed. In order to spare bloodshed and war, he signed a treaty with Muawiyah. Nevertheless, Muawiyah did not comply with any of the terms of the treaty and instead nominated his son, Yazid, as his successor and ruler of the Islamic ummah. Muawyiah had Imam Hassan poisoned to clear the path for Yazid.

Imam Hussein ibn Imam Ali

Undoubtedly, the theme of Karbala was sabr, as Imam Hussein stood firm and did not compromise his principles. Can there be a greater example of sabr than what Imam Hussein endured? His children, brothers, and companions were brutally slain before his eyes as they fought off the ruthless and merciless army of Yazid while he himself fell in a hail of enemy arrows, swords, and daggers while prostrating before Allah. Imam Hussein was the essence of sabr, as he was firm in his purpose, maintained his consciousness of Allah, and chose the Straight Path, leading to his ultimate sacrifice to save Islam and monotheism. What he left at Karbala was his example of prayer. His perseverance in prayer at Karbala was the light that drew even some of his enemies to his side. It is important to understand that it was the prayer that Imam Hussein was safeguarding, and it is sabr that ensures the endurance of prayer throughout our lives.

Lady Zainab

Like her mother, Lady Zainab personified the essence of patience. Through all the adversities she and her family suffered, she remained steadfast and patient in her worship of Allah. Her patience was an act of worship—the highest level of worship—as she exhibited her resolve even though she had been mentally abused and harassed as a captive of the evil, malicious, and illegitimate ruler, Yazid. She was proactive in her sabr as she steadfastly supported her brother, Imam Hussein, on the field of Karbala, protected her nephew, Imam al-Sajjad, from being killed, and continued to propagate the tragedy of Karbala in the years that followed. Lady Zainab was able to convince a whole new generation of Muslims to the way of Ahl al-Bayt. Undoubtedly, she was the embodiment of sabr and never showed any negative emotion or negative trait. Truly, she exercised self-restraint in the midst of the most ominous calamity—the tragedy of Karbala. There she demonstrated the practical meaning of sabr, even in the midst of all those painful and heinous scenes at Karbala when members of her family and followers were gruesomely martyred.

Imam Ali al-Sajjad ibn Imam Hussein

Imam Ali al-Sajjad exhibited a great deal of patience relative to his enemies. Following the tragedy of Karbala, he endured very difficult times in the hands of his enemies, but at no time did he display signs of anger or impatience. Rather, he responded to his enemies bravely without showing any wrath or loss of patience. After patiently bearing the tragedies on the plains of Karbala, Imam al-Sajjad continued to endure, as the society was confronted with absolute chaos, and disorder intensified under the rule of the Umayyad regime. The Imam spent the rest of his life giving lectures in the *masjid* of the prophet and patiently wrote his supplications to Allah, which were later compiled in a book and became known as al-Sahifa al-Sajjadiyyah al-Kamilah.

Imam Mohammad al-Baqir ibn Imam Ali al-Sajjad

The life of Imam Mohammad al-Baqir was filled with turmoil and the persecution of the followers of Ahl al-Bayt. Unable to take part in the political movements to oppose the Umayyad regime, he had to endure his silence with pain and distress. Under complete surveillance by the Umayyads, they had secret agents monitor every move and discussion of the Imam. During this time of patience, the Imam made great inroads into the fields of science, jurisprudence, philosophy, theology, and medicine. His contributions in these fields of study were immense and set the template for his son, Imam Ja'far al-Sadiq, to follow. With sabr, he endured the many painful events in order to pursue his achievements in these fields of study. During his life, the society was in complete disarray, and the people were subject to oppression, persecution, imprisonment, torture, and death. The Umayyads took every opportunity to disparage and belittle the Imam's grandfathers by cursing them openly on pulpits and in the mosques. As he had to remain patient, the Imam restrained his anger.

Imam Ja'far as-Sadiq ibn Imam Mohammad al-Baqir

Imam Ja'far as-Sadiq was the most patient and tolerant teacher of his time, as each day he would patiently listen and reply to his students, such as the celebrated Sunni scholars of Abu Hanifa and Malik, on the topic of theology in Islam. His forbearance and fortitude relative to the hardships and difficulties he experienced are a true measure of the extent of his energy and faith. He dealt with these difficulties with patience. No matter how much his enemies harassed, abused, and tormented him, he showed patience and forbearance. Although the Imam would admonish them, he would never curse or use foul language. Regarding his relations with people, the Imam was extraordinarily forbearing and patient. When someone did him wrong, he would pray to Allah to forgive that person.

Imam Musa al-Kazim ibn Imam Ja'far as-Sadiq

Imam Musa al-Kazim had the highest standards of morality and ethical behavior. His patience and forbearance were the virtues that restrained his anger, as he forgave all who inflicted harm on him. He exhibited the highest level of patience in the face of oppression and adversity, right to the very end when he was martyred in prison. He was even kind to those who harassed him. The Imam endured all the atrocities with his perseverance, patience, and courage. It was his sabr that enabled him to contain his sorrow, pain, and suffering. Virtuous and generous, he helped the poor and afflicted in Medina with the necessities of life, such as food, clothing, and shelter. In a complete state of sabr, he devoted his nights to prayer and days to fasting.

Imam Ali al-Rida ibn Imam Musa al-Kazim

The strength of Imam Ali al-Rida's patience is clear when we examine the political persecution he suffered, the degree of agony, and the amount of grief and sorrow that filled his heart. The Imam was aware that the allegiance offered to him by Caliph al-Ma'mun was the allegiance of death. He was under the sentence of death if he did not accept being heir apparent, and he was under the sentence of death if he did accept. His patience was the foundation upon which he could buy time to avoid a new wave of terror, exile, and execution against the followers of Ahl al-Bayt. Additionally, he could get in touch with the intellectual leadership to communicate and interact freely and safely on the basis of the principle of nass (designation of an Imam by a previous Imam).

All during his patience (sabr), the Imam was under surveillance, and his conversations and letters were controlled. He lived in the same painful conditions as Imam Hassan ibn Abi Talib, without being able to explain his ordeal to the people, not even to many of his confidants. He had to suffer martyrdom every day, protecting those whom he loved and defended with his life while they misunderstood and misinterpreted his actions. This was the greatest test of patience he endured, as he was isolated from the people closest to him.

Imam Mohammad al-Jawad ibn Imam Ali al-Rida

When Imam Mohammad al-Jawad moved to Medina with his wife, the daughter of Caliph al-Ma'mun, he restrained his frustration by patiently enduring her constant nagging. As a spoiled princess, she constantly complained about the restrictions imposed on her to live a simple life of humility and self-denial, the same lifestyle that wives of other Imams had lived. She was unable to bear children, which backfired on al-Ma'mun, who wanted a grandson so he could enter through the door of Ahl al-Bayt. Though she was unable to convince her father about the difficult life she had with Imam al-Jawad, she did, however, convince the new Caliph Mu'tasim, who conspired with her to poison the Imam. Caliph Mu'tasim had a deep envy and hatred of the Imam. Imam al-Jawad had taken a second wife who bore him Imam Ali al-Hadi and other children. With patience and perseverance in his spirituality and knowledge, the Imam taught and counseled many students and scholars who benefited a great deal from his teachings in a number of fields.

Imam Ali al-Hadi ibn Imam Mohammad al-Jawad

Imam Ali al-Hadi endured all hardships for the sake of giving knowledge to those who sought it. Caliph Mutawakkil knew that and continued oppressing the Imam's followers. Except for Imam al-Mahdi, Imam Ali al-Hadi's thirty-four years of Imamat was the longest of any other Imam. He had seventeen years of freedom and seventeen years under arrest. In spite of his seventeen years of imprisonment, his patience gave him strength as he passed his time in worship. Steadfast in his patience, he endured six caliphs.

Imam Hassan al-Askari ibn Imam Ali al-Hadi

The oppressive Abbasid government imprisoned Imam Hassan al-Askari. The jailors often found themselves in awe as they witnessed the piety and patience of the Imam. Time after time, the jailors and their reinforcements would find themselves in a state of grace and faith as they witnessed the sabr of the Imam. Enraged, the Abbasids placed a bunch of wild animals that hadn't eaten for days into the cage with the Imam. When the Abbasids came back, they were spellbound, as they found the Imam steadfast in prayer and the wild animals hovered around him in prostration. Imam Hassan was from the most patient people. He suppressed his anger and treated whoever did him wrong with kindness and forgiveness. Even in his imprisonment, he remained steadfast and patient, as he did not complain about his suffering. Rather, his reliance was one of prayer to Allah.

Imam Mohammad al-Mahdi ibn Imam Hassan al-Askari

The minor occultation and major occultation of Imam Mohammad al-Mahdi helped him patiently bear the difficult times throughout the centuries. With patience and endurance, he has witnessed the many tragedies of life, including calamities, famine, pestilence, wars, tyranny, oppression, injustice, genocide, loss of faith, homosexuality, same-sex marriage, and a multitude of other deviations. Upon the awaited arrival of Imam Mohammad al-Mahdi with Prophet Jesus, the triumph of the Imamat culminates in a victory of good over evil, freedom over oppression, and justice over injustice. Unlike the previous infallible Imams that followed up with details relative to the message, Imam al-Mahdi is Allah's decisive victory to make good, freedom, and justice triumph in the world.

Chapter 15

Energy of the Imamat

The miracles for the Imamat were their knowledge, qualifications, and conduct that, by the Grace of Allah, were molded in perfection and inherited from the lineage of Prophet Mohammad. Prophet Mohammad and the Imamat have illuminated our spirits, as their energy flows through every facet of our soul, body, and mind. As inspired by this energy, we must own up to our responsibility to follow the guardianship of Ahl al-Bayt. We must instill this radiant energy within our children so they can carry on the legacy of Islam. Following is a discussion of how Allah enlightened Prophet Mohammad and the Imamat with various forms of energy, such as electromagnetic, creative, charismatic, and spiritual.

Forms of Energy

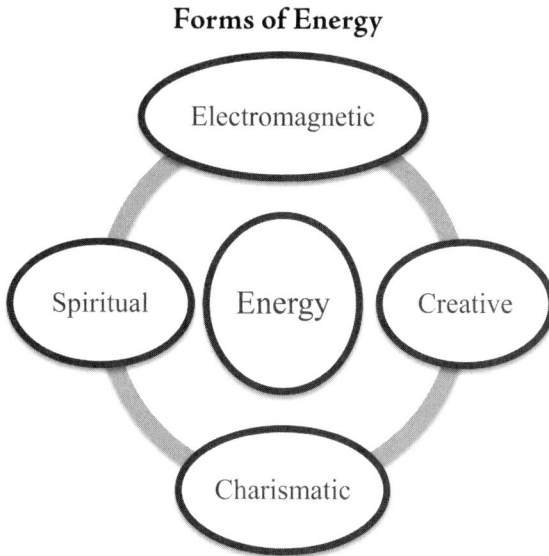

The Twelve Infallible Imams of Ahl al-Bayt expounded upon the concept of free will and volition. They were men of purity and excellence as well as sinless and infallible. They manifested in the divine light of guidance as this light, by the grace of Allah, passed from one Imam to the next. For Shi'as, the twelve Imams are unified strands within the rope of Allah. The following, derived from a number of sources, examines how these forms of energy were instilled within the persona of Prophet Mohammad and the Imamat.

Prophet Mohammad

Never in the history of mankind has the light of divine energy been so completely manifested, demonstrated, and fulfilled than in Prophet Mohammad. He was molded and refined in the spirituality of Islam:

- purification and enlightenment of the soul, body, and mind
- awareness and self-realization of Allah
- revelation of the Qur'an
- Night Journey of the Ascent (Isra' and Mi'raj) following the sequence of experiences

- manifestation of prophet's purpose and resolve
- vision of spiritual and cultural transformation of the society
- establishment of a system of ethics, virtues, and justice
- transfer of power and leadership to the Imamat

Prophet Mohammad was the vehicle by which the universality of divine energy was to be transmitted into the minds of not only the inhabitants of the Arabian Peninsula but to all of mankind. He was the mercy to all humanity, not just the Muslims. The Night Journey of the Ascent (Isra' and Mi'raj) was the crowning touch of divine inspiration, as Prophet Mohammad self-actualized in complete awareness of the Creator and his divine plan. Prophet Mohammad's mission was to awaken the unconscious minds of all humanity. The ascent gave rise to the formation of a new culture, a new order of things, that transcended beyond the provinciality and tribal way of living prevalent at that time.

In order to bring about change in the society, Prophet Mohammad had to be equipped with superhuman energy. The behavior of the community was ingrained in their lifestyles, which were virtually impossible to change. It was a tall order for Prophet Mohammad, but Allah had prepared him well, and the ascent reinforced all the means by which to succeed. He transcended the limitations of the human mind to bring about a code of ethics, justice, and tolerance. It was the ascent that gave Mohammad the conviction, self-assurance, and wisdom to undertake this challenge and change (i.e., the transformation from a pagan society to a faith-driven Islamic community). He was the liaison between heaven and earth, bringing the Qur'an to enlighten mankind.

Even though Albert Einstein's $E=mc^2$ states that there must be variation (mass defect), nothing like that happened to Prophet Mohammad (i.e., no defect was produced). Allah kept Prophet Mohammad safe from every possible defect. Why this happened cannot be explained via physics, because of the many unknown variables that can have an effect on the consequence. No doubt the Night Journey of Prophet Mohammad was truly a miracle, as he was blessed with the light and energy from Allah.

The closer one travels to the speed of light, the heavier his mass becomes, thereby needing more energy to go faster, and therefore the amount of energy needed to go further becomes infinite. In other words, the mass itself will need to undergo a change in state to generate the energy required for travelling faster. Light, however, has a finite speed. During the Isra' and Mi'raj, Prophet Mohammad was supercharged with the light of energy with the transformer generated at full potency, especially since his vehicle was al-Buraq, a steed. During the Night Journey of Prophet Mohammad, the rules of physics stopped, as al-Buraq travelled through the heavens faster than the normal speed of light. Allah made this possible, as he made exceptions for the prophets in order for them to complete their missions (e.g., Prophet Mohammad's Night Journey or the splitting of the Red Sea for Prophet Moses and his followers to cross). Allah has the power to alter the laws of the speed of light and time that differ from our concept of the normal speed of light and time (Turfe 2010).

Fatima as-Zahra

Named by Allah with the title of as-Zahra, Fatima was blessed with the energy of an illuminated spirit, as her light shone among those in heaven. Her birth reflected a radiant halo of light. A marriage ordained by Allah, that light was melded with the light of her husband, Imam Ali ibn Abi Talib. The light of her energy was the reflection of everything that was pure, pious, courageous, generous, and noble. Yet it was her spiritual energy that endured the storm of struggle and difficulties. She tolerated both willingly and happily the poverty of her husband. A short life, she withstood many calamities and severe hardships.

After the death of her father, Prophet Mohammad, Fatima suffered many agonies, yet she persisted in glorifying Allah by praying for long periods and following the Straight Path of her father. When the rights of the caliphate were taken from her husband, she stood up and fought for justice. Standing on the side of truth, she was the example of fighting injustice and oppression.

Fatima was infallible, as Allah purified her from every sin and every defect and endowed her with the virtues that made her an example for all women. Sanctified with the noblest qualities and characteristics, Fatima reached the highest rank of virtue and perfection. As an example of her father's morality and mentality, she resembled him in his deep faith in Allah, his self-discipline, and his abstention from worldly pleasures.

Undoubtedly, her charismatic energy enabled her to be the ideal example of faith, worship, chastity, purity, charity, and kindness to the poor and the deprived. Her Islamic personality, character, and disposition were nurtured and cultivated by various levels of energy that embraced her spirituality and dignified her love for humanity. Even the Sunni scholar *Sahih Bukhari* confirms that Prophet Mohammad had forbidden anyone to hurt or offend Fatima:

> Narrated Miswar bin Makhrama … Fatima is part of me, and he who makes her angry, makes me angry. (*Sahih Bukhari*, Vol. 5, Book 62, Hadith 3714)

Imam Ali ibn Abi Talib

Imam Ali best exemplifies the self-fulfillment of courage, bravery, fortitude, and valor. We will explore how these virtues manifested in the excellence of Imam Ali's personality, attitude, behavior, and dedication to Islam. Courage emanated from Imam Ali's conscience, motivations, and thoughts, which resulted in him protecting Prophet Mohammad, overcoming obstacles, and engaging in heroic feats on the battlefield. Courage was heightened in times of struggles, both in war and peace, as Imam Ali acted upon the heroic spirit of conviction inspired by justice and guided by wisdom.

Courage surfaced from Imam Ali's intention. His courage was a self-affirmation that enabled him to look past the immediate situation to find the strength to self-regulate (i.e., the self that surpasses itself). His courage was the power of the mind to overcome fear. Here, courage was not the absence of fear but rather the ability to act in spite of it. As he feared Allah, he feared nothing else. For Imam Ali, courage was prudent and controlled by a sense of truth and justice that was free of bias and hatred. It was a courage that was humble and nonboastful. His constancy of mind was unshaken as he faced and endured danger. Truly, he had a sense of honor, duty, and piety.

An internal, courage-fueled energy field that magnified his spirit's fulfillment drove Imam Ali. Courage sparked his energy and ignited his leadership. He had not only the courage to win on the battlefield but also the courage to win the peace. Rather than wage war against those who denied him his rightful claim to the caliphate, Imam Ali chose the path of safeguarding Islam against its enemies. For this reason, Imam Ali chose peaceful means by cooperating with the other caliphs. He kept quiet and became patient, even though his right was violated. During that time, the enemies of Islam were awaiting an opportunity to destroy Islam. Imam Ali did not give them that opportunity, because he chose the bigger picture, which was to avoid warfare within the Islamic community.

For many, bravery is impulsive, hurried, stubborn, reckless, blind, and furious. But for Imam Ali, bravery was fearless, steadfast, and resolute. His bravery was the quality of spirit that enabled him to face the danger of pain without showing fear. He did not restrain his fear but rather experienced it. In this respect, he held tenaciously to the good, moderating the fear of which he was fully aware. Bravery is physical, while courage is mental and moral. His courage transcended the noble concept of bravery. One can be brave without courage and courageous without bravery, but Imam Ali possessed both virtues. The basis of his courage was his love of Allah. While his bravery was that of a heroic warrior, his courage was steadfast. This was a case of not only Imam Ali's bravery in the field of battle but also his bravery in the field of patience. Without question, Imam Ali endured all sorts of hardships for the cause of Islam.

Fortitude is a virtue that restrains one's fear and bravery within reason. It strengthens one's mind against the greatest danger, which is that of death. It is this firmness of mind that enables a person to encounter danger with self-confidence. It is a determination to confront danger or to endure difficulty. For Imam Ali, fortitude fastened his will with impregnable reason as he confronted his enemies on the battlefield. His steadfastness and resolve removed any obstacles (e.g., fear) as he met danger. He was willing to sacrifice his life for the cause of Islam. He loved what was larger and more important than him—namely, truth, justice, and the common good. His love for Allah was his priority, and he exposed himself to the danger of death, protecting Prophet Mohammad and Islam.

Valor has all the best qualities of both courage and bravery. It exalts in risking all for a just cause. It looks far ahead and is wise. Men are valiant as they are moved by the higher aims and passions of nature. No man can be valiant for a trifle or a repulsive end. For Imam Ali, what motivated his valor was love of Allah, truth, justice, and everything that is dignified and noble.

The perfection of Imam Ali's virtues was displayed when he slept in the bed of Prophet Mohammad in order to protect the prophet from the enemies who wished to kill him. This act of courage, bravery, fortitude, and valor exhibited his readiness to sacrifice himself for the cause of Islam. To be willing to sacrifice his life while under the swords ready to strike represents the highest sense of piety and loyalty. This heroic act allowed the prophet to safely make his migration to Medina.

During the Battle of the Trench, Imam Ali displayed his power and energy as he defeated Amru Ibn Abd Wid, the champion of the enemy. Amru Ibn Abd Wid, a ferocious and famous warrior, challenged and mocked the Muslims. Imam Ali accepted the challenge and defeated Amru Ibn Abd Wid. As Imam Ali stood to thrust the sword into Amru, the latter spat in Imam Ali's face. Imam Ali was extremely angered by this insult. It took a great deal of self-control for Imam Ali to restrain his anger, so he momentarily postponed killing Amru until his anger was restrained. He waited to kill him because he didn't want his anger or negative energy to be the reason but rather his faith. In other words, Imam Ali wanted to be directed and guided by his positive energy. All present at the Battle of the Trench were in awe as Imam Ali displayed his restraint.

There is a significant difference between the person who is in control of his anger before finishing off his victim and one who is not in control of his anger as he punishes his victim without reflection. Anger simply exists as energy. What one chooses to do with anger determines if it is bad or good. The energy of anger can motivate one to create a better situation, which is the highest purpose for this energy and why we were given the emotion of anger. Imam Ali was a man in control of his emotions, and his electromagnetic energy waves sparked his temperament toward restraint in time of anger. When Imam Ali recognized and acknowledged his anger, it became positive energy that enabled him to change the situation he was angry about. The heroism of Imam Ali was the most decisive factor in the victory. The defeat of Amru Ibn Abd Wid struck terror in the hearts of the enemy, so much that they abandoned the battlefield. This defeat was so devastating for the enemy that the disbelievers gave up their objective to advance to Medina.

In the long history of mankind, there comes a time when someone appears that personifies all that is good and righteous. Such a person stands out as a radiant figure whose presence illuminates the mind, heart, and soul of all who aspire toward perfection in their lives. Such a man was Imam Ali, whose consciousness was manifested in his personality. He was the reflection of the light of Prophet Mohammad's inner reality and reservoir of wisdom.

In his book *Polarization around the Character of 'Ali Ibn Abi Talib*, Ayatollah Murtada Mutahhari, the renowned scholar and martyr, discusses how the creative energy of Imam Ali is demonstrated in the two-powered personality of polar opposites: attraction and repulsion. Mutahhari expounds on a concept called *elixir*, which is a miraculous substance that transforms one material into another—for example, base metals into gold.

For Imam Ali, true elixir is love, and this love is manifested in his power of attraction. Throughout the centuries following his martyrdom, we find many people whose hearts are filled with love and admiration for Imam Ali. As time passes on, this love for Imam Ali becomes more profound and intensified. He was the personification of perfection that transcended beyond his moral virtues of wisdom, eloquence, bravery, and many other characteristics of his soul. Even the corrupt enemies that he punished did not turn away from him, for they knew his act was just. People were attracted to Imam Ali because they felt in their hearts the very soul of his love that emanated from his inseparable unity with truth. Truly, his power of attraction is eternal (Mutahhari 1981).

On the other hand, Imam Ali also had the power of repulsion. There were those who despised him, as he exposed their hypocrisy, deception, ignorance, and deviations. This infuriated his sworn enemies, and they plotted to form false alliances with others against him, ultimately leading to his martyrdom and to the martyrdom of his progeny. By upholding the very sanctity of Islam, Imam Ali had to take steps to uproot the ills in society. As a result, his truthfulness and justice pained his enemies.

Imam Ali's creative energy was characterized by his thoughts, feelings, and emotions that personified the true and ideal essence of Islamic morality. It was an energy that resigned itself in humbleness as he addressed his Lord. His creative energy was relegated toward pleasing Allah in worship, prayers, and obedience. He spent a great deal of his time and energy teaching, informing, and helping others learn about Islam. While he stood in the face of deception, betrayal, trickery, hypocrisy, greed, treachery, and chicanery, he was steadfast in upholding the ideals of Islam. Justice, truth, and freedom of choice were the engines of his creative energy. Imam Ali was pious. For example, as a warrior, while he was brave and courageous, he was also kind, understanding, compassionate, responsive, and affectionate. He devoted a great deal of his energy to tending to the needs of the poor, and his heart was absorbed by his continuous affection and empathy for the afflicted and disadvantaged.

Good and bad are opposite poles, and in any given society there are people who possess both traits: attraction toward the good as well as repulsion from the bad. Imam Ali had both the power of attraction and the power of repulsion. He had very loyal friends as well as wicked enemies who knowingly opposed what was right. We can learn from the experiences of Imam Ali that human nature is very complex and reflects both the complexity of the world and the mind that perceives it. Through our senses, we can experience the external environment and categorize our experiences in terms of polarities—positive and negative, attraction and repulsion, pleasure and pain, calm and agitation, love and hate. Like Imam Ali, as we pursue peace, justice, and happiness, it is our human nature to impulsively desire experiences that our body and mind can translate as positive and to feel aversion to all that is disturbing and negative.

Imam Hassan ibn Imam Ali

One of the most distinguishing attributes of Imam Hassan was his generosity. He devoted his energy to the good that he wanted to do as he contributed his time, energy, and wealth for the well-being of others. His view of generosity was one of helping those in need, whether providing clothing, food, and shelter or paying off one's debts. His generosity was one of ethics, which generated from his deep-rooted sense of piety and faith. His character was profoundly motivated, empathetic, highly energetic, and respectful of the dignity of others. He felt more happiness by bestowing peace and charity upon the community, as that positive and latent inner energy grew within him. The creative source of positive energy within Imam Hassan inspired his charitable undertakings. Contrariwise, Muawiyah partook in negative energy, as he gave enormous sums of money to people in order to entrap and deceive them into carrying out his malevolent plans to persecute and demean Imam Hassan.

Generosity is an expansive energy. Imam Hassan felt the growing sense of abundance that generosity produces, an energy that circulates far and wide. By radiating the energy of generosity and compassion, he caused a shift that left everyone feeling better. What we learn from Imam Hassan's example is that care and warmth enrich our thoughts and actions with generosity, thereby displaying tremendous amounts of positive energy. When we are generous, kind, energetic, or optimistic, we exude energy that attracts others. Imam Hassan's generosity, ethical living, and meditation created great reservoirs of positive energy. Generosity and dedication direct the positive energy to the welfare of all. Imam Hassan's morality and exceptional character were revealed through his generosity and piety.

Imam Hussein ibn Imam Ali

Allah has bestowed upon the most pious individuals the rank of Imam. Relative to mankind, Allah instilled within each of these Imams the power of intellectuality and leadership, as well as the guardian of all matters relative to religion, the laws that govern the society, and the dynamics and dimensions of mankind's existence.

Beginning with Prophet Abraham, the electromagnetic and spiritual energy transferred from one Imam to the next Imam. Like Prophet Abraham, Prophet Mohammad was also an Imam who passed all the tests that Allah gave him. Similarly, Prophet Mohammad's cousin and son-in-law, Imam Ali, was an Imam, as was his progeny who possessed the divine attributes given by Allah.

In a sermon, Imam Ja'far as-Sadiq said the following:

> Allah has illumined ... the Imams from the Household of the Prophet (Mohammad) and made them the abundant spring from which knowledge of religion gushes forth. Whoever recognizes the claims of the Imams, based on sound knowledge and insight will taste the sweetness of faith and come to know the luminous and beautiful visage of Islam. For Allah has appointed the Imams to be His Proof among men and their guide; has placed on their heads the crown of sublimity and leadership; caused the light of His own splendor to shine on their beings; and sustained and supported them with

inexhaustible Heavenly power ... Imam is versed in all the complexities, problems and metaphoric aspects of revelation, and he is chosen by Allah from among the descendants of Hussein ... Allah has chosen all of them to lead the Ummah (community) in order that they should guide the people and judge justly among them. (Lari 1996)

This sermon underscores the connectivity between the Imamat and divinely inspired energy. For example, Imam Hussein possessed this energy within his character, enabling him to make the ultimate sacrifice of his life for the cause of Islam. There is no doubt that Imam Hussein was the catalyst to save Islam. However, without the help of his sister, Lady Zainab, and his son, Imam Ali al-Sajjad, the tragedy would have long been forgotten.

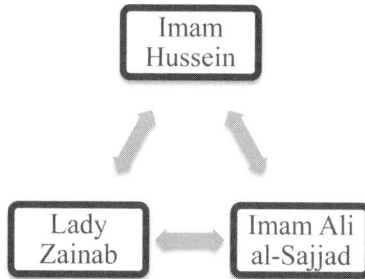

The triad of Imam Hussein, Lady Zainab, and Imam Ali al-Sajjad is the continuation of the root of Imam Ali and Fatima as-Zahra. Divine energy nurtured their bodies, minds, hearts, and souls. Allah kept away all impurities by purifying them thoroughly. It was the light of this energy, which transmitted from generation to generation to Ahl al-Bayt, that guided their every thought and action.

Yazid and his immoral followers polluted their human energy fields. As such, their energy fields were blocked, and the only outcome was depraved and evil acts. Committing vile acts repeatedly made their energy system inert and lifeless.

In analyzing the characteristics of Imam Hussein, it is the bravery and the greatness of his soul that attract attention more than any other of his qualities. Immersed in this energy, Imam Hussein's objective in life and his holy uprising against injustice were far above satisfying his personal needs and interests. His noble soul was and remains unique throughout history. His humility, valor, magnanimity, faith, sincerity, and love for justice are certainly unmatched. With such impeccable personal qualities, he cannot be considered an ordinary person.

Imam Hussein shouldered the tasks of the prophets of the past, and for this reason he is rightly considered as an heir and legatee to such prophets as Adam, Noah, Abraham, Moses, Jesus, and Mohammad. Imam Hussein is a symbol of bravery, patience, and resistance in the face of the worst systems of injustice. Prophet Mohammad's grandson triumphed in martyrdom, and he continues to be symbolic of the values of freedom and justice and the need to confront oppression and tyranny (World Service 2000).

According to the First Law of Thermodynamics, energy cannot be created or destroyed. So where does the energy of Imam Hussein come from? He was endowed with certain genetic characteristics that have the potential to manifest super abilities. However, we know from science that these genes by themselves do not generate super abilities. Imam Hussein had a great source of positive energy, which was transmitted to him genetically from his parents, Imam Ali and Fatima. He was able to pull energy from the spiritual world into the physical world through the transmission of energy from his parents and the lineage before them. This is the energy that Imam Hussein used to manifest his abilities. This source of energy from the spiritual world was nurtured and transmitted to Imam Hussein by the grace of Allah.

The energy that Imam Hussein emitted in the form of radiation had to come from somewhere. He drew energy from the spiritual world, which he emitted as radiation. In other words, when Imam Hussein spoke or counseled or conducted his daily affairs, he radiated and illuminated those in his presence. People who came in contact with Imam Hussein were in awe of his presence, which was one of purity and righteousness.

With Imam Hussein, he had the perfect balance of physical, emotional, mental, and spiritual energies. This balance resulted in the perfect self (i.e., he vibrated at a higher level so he had unmistakable clarity). The electromagnetic energy that emanated from Imam Hussein's thoughts and actions transformed the community (ummah). When super-energized, the electrical wavelengths and magnetic currents of Imam Hussein enlightened the Muslims to regain the Islam of his grandfather, Prophet Mohammad.

Lady Zainab

Women were not expected to engage in jihad (struggle) in defense of Islam, but Lady Zainab stepped up to the challenge and most willingly offered herself in the defense of Islam and Ahl al-Bayt. With courage and determination, Lady Zainab hurried to the battlefield of Karbala. She stood over the mortal remains of her brother, Imam Hussein. The enemies watched and observed her patience as she stood in the face of the dreadful sight of her brother's martyrdom. With serenity and the passion of her faith and belief, she steadfastly looked to the heavens and said, "O' Allah, please accept this sacrifice from us." Rather than Lady Zainab being the "captive," the enemies were captivated and mesmerized by the radiance of her persona and the eloquence of her speech. This display of electromagnetic energy that emanated from deep within her soul was the spark of revolution against Yazid and his Umayyad regime. Following is a snapshot of the virtues of Lady Zainab that she acquired from her parents and which together formed a powerful energy force:

Virtues as a Source of Energy
Characteristics of Lady Zainab

+ sincere, trustworthy, loyal, self-denial, supportive, self-discipline
+ pious, judicious, eloquent, pure, righteous, humble
+ self-control, patient, tolerant, courageous, admirable, heroic

Briefly, she admonished Yazid by exposing his false elation as victorious in the encounter at Karbala. She uncovered the truth that his military superiority was transient and that Allah let the unbelievers enjoy bliss in this world so that their sins would increase and, thus, they will have a painful chastisement on the Day of Resurrection. She reproached Yazid for taking Prophet Mohammad's family as captives. The speech of Lady Zainab was one of the deathblows that snapped the Umayyad State. Having seen the collapse of his pride and arrogance, Yazid could not find any words to answer, except a poetic verse not at all related to the subject.

Lady Zainab was surrounded by a concentration of energy that interacted and was immersed with energy fields of Prophet Mohammad's Ahl al-Bayt. In fact, all of the energy fields of Prophet Mohammad's Ahl al-Bayt interacted with each other and brought about a potent force.

Lady Zainab's energy radiation was expressed in different ways. For example, the energy that is produced by thoughts and emotions generated her magnetism and charisma. This produced a vibration in her energy field that had the power to win over and influence people. Lady Zainab exhibited positive energy. Ibn Ziyad and Yazid both exhibited negative energy that deformed the flow of their thoughts and emotions— for example, their anger, weakness, confusion, and distress. It was in this light that Lady Zainab was able to exploit their negative energy to expose their malevolence and evil schemes.

Lady Zainab, with her charisma and eloquence, was able to influence the thoughts and emotions of the many people who surrounded her caravan as it was disgracefully paraded through the streets of Kufa. Her words radiated each spectator to the point that they began to weep. In effect, she was able to change their mood from one of jeers to one of remorse, sorrow, and guilt.

Even today, Lady Zainab's energy field is able to attract millions of visitors to her shrines as they pay their respect to Her Eminence. These visitors are both Shi'a and Sunni Muslims who are united in their respect and admiration for Lady Zainab. At these shrines, the first thing that becomes perceptible is a change in atmosphere. This change imposes a silence in the mind so that we receive the messages that the shrines radiate.

For Lady Zainab, the operation of her mind is a manifestation of energy known as electricity, magnetism, and light, which emanate from the underlying force of vibration. Thought vibrations and waves reproduce and send similar vibrations so that others may feel the thoughts. Witness how Hind, the wife of Yazid, was impacted by these vibrations and quickly came to the rescue of Lady Zainab. Even this type of vibration energy enveloped Hurr as he left the camp of the enemy to join forces with Imam Hussein. No doubt, Imam Hussein's energy field was so strong that it sent vibration waves to the mind of Hurr, who then regained his Islamic self.

It was through the medium of vibrating sound waves that Lady Zainab was able to convince her audience. In other words, Lady Zainab's mind, in the manifestation of thoughts in her brain, generated a form of energy of intensely high vibratory waves to the brains of others within her field of influence. Truly, this was manifested within the phenomena of electric energy and magnetic energy as well as mental energy.

Kinetic energy is the energy of motion. Lady Zainab was a leader who demonstrated her kinetic energy in a positive and effective manner. She had a compelling vision to restore the great name of Ahl al-Bayt. Her inspiring vision was focused on direction and purpose. A leader, she exhibited her kinetic energy to not only capture the audience with her eloquent communication but also to catch them emotionally. As her transparent life was authentic and had the power to attract people, she set the example for others to follow. Through transparency, Lady Zainab's actions were believable and gained the respect of not only her followers but her enemies as well.

With all the potential energy (stored energy) of knowledge she acquired from her father and grandfather, she skillfully put it into motion (kinetic energy) to win over the Muslim and non-Muslim communities. She was not only an eloquent speaker but a teacher as well, as she educated, encouraged, demonstrated, and counseled the

Muslim community to be more vigilant and actionable regarding their Islamic obligations.

As a kinetic leader, she had definable, measurable standards of performance, and she encouraged the Muslim community to be responsible and accountable in upholding the duties and obligations of Islam. She was discontent with the status quo in which the Muslim community sat idly by, allowing Yazid to oppress and terrorize them. Consequently, she took the leadership into her own hands to expose the evil machinations of Yazid and his cohorts. Most importantly, Lady Zainab knew that her stand against the transgressors was not a destination but rather a continuous, lifelong journey for all Muslims to follow. Lady Zainab knew that her reproach was not short term but one of consistency and discipline, executing her grievances against tyranny.

Lady Zainab inspired trust and knew how to lead. She demonstrated her leadership by being an advocate for the people she represented. She created an environment where her followers took pride as Muslims and displayed positive energy in restoring the ummah back to the morals, ethics, and ideals of Islam. With a reservoir of ideas (potential energy) inherited from Prophet Mohammad's Ahl al-Bayt, she confronted the transgressors by putting these ideas into motion (kinetic energy). Remarkably, she was able to have the Muslim community overcome their inertia energy (resistance to change) and convert it to kinetic energy. She possessed qualities that enabled her to successfully bring about this change.

Effective leadership is characterized by the ability to facilitate positive changes, and Lady Zainab was a true leader. Her well-developed sense of self enabled her to lead with equality, trust, empathy, and integrity. Self-efficacy refers to what Lady Zainab believes about her own ability and her confidence in performing and achieving her goal. In other words, she believed in her ability and knew her leadership potential. Self-efficacy is future-oriented and about motivation and the need for self-determination and accepting responsibility. Lady Zainab's self was dynamic and encompassed forward-moving energy based on her experience and self-efficacy, which transcended into meeting future challenges. Consequently, she carried out her Islamic responsibility by leading the Muslim community back to Islam.

Imam Ali al-Sajjad ibn Imam Hussein

As he was very ill during the tragedy at Karbala, he was unable to participate as a warrior in the battle. After the conclusion of the Karbala massacre, Imam al-Sajjad was held captive with his aunt, Lady Zainab, and their women and children followers. They were dragged through the desert in chains from Karbala to Kufa and then to Damascus. The humiliation and insults inflicted upon him by Ibn Ziyad and Yazid, both wanting to cut his head off, were far more difficult than had he been martyred on the field of Karbala. His jihad was of a different nature; it was to protect his family and followers as well as to bring the ummah back to the basics of Islam.

While the prayers and speeches of Imam al-Sajjad exhibited his kinetic energy, they also exhibited his potential energy because his writings and supplications were stored and contained in volumes of books for all to read and reflect on. Potential energy can be thought of as energy stored within a physical system, such as a book. It is called potential energy because it has the potential to be converted into another state of energy, such as kinetic energy, and to do work in the process. Once the books are being read, potential energy converts to kinetic energy. *An-nur* (light) inspired Imam al-Sajjad to constantly radiate energy of his self (*nafs*). His self had a high intensity of light frequency that radiated clarity of thoughts and actions in his prayers, supplications, and speeches.

Imam al-Sajjad had all the potential energy within him to teach the Muslim community. However, he had to bring the community back to the basics in Islam because a great deal of the religious doctrines had not been observed, owing to the tyrannical regime of Yazid. Muslims were lost and had gone astray during the turbulent times of oppression. They had tainted the very sanctity of the practical obligations of Islam: prayer, fasting, charity, pilgrimage, and jihad (struggle). They needed to be guided and reprogrammed to the Islamic way of life. This was not an easy task. Had it not been for Imam al-Sajjad, Islam most certainly would have been a discarded tenet of the past. Imam al-Sajjad had to spend long hours and sleepless nights trying to remedy the irresponsive and inattentive behavior of the Muslim community.

The intensity and devotion of Imam al-Sajjad's prayers and supplications led to him being admired and followed by the Muslim community, who had to come to grips with their inner selves. They needed to understand how the physical, emotional, mental, and spiritual aspects operated within their human energy fields. Imam al-Sajjad had to instill in their minds and hearts the importance of concentration to replace the negative energy with positive energy. Their stresses, anxieties, depression, and lack of will were all issues that blocked their energy fields. Clearing these blockages through activation of a vibrant life-force energy flow into their systems would help bring about positive changes in their lives and ultimately set them up for success with Allah.

Imam al-Sajjad instilled in the Muslims the importance of bringing the physical, emotional, mental, and spiritual energies into equilibrium and balance with each other. Toward this end, the optimum flow of energy through the entire human system empowers a person with more energy as well as providing a healthy Islamic life.

At the time of the illegitimate Umayyad regime, the ummah was victim to the tyranny of Yazid, and as such, the people were distracted from their obligations to Islam. Their spiritual state was disconnected from the rest of their energy field. Imam al-Sajjad embarked on the road to recovery (i.e., to help reduce these distractions and to return their bodies and minds to a balanced state of equilibrium). Meditation helped reduce these distractions, although it took time, commitment, and patience to achieve a higher level of consciousness. Reconnecting to their positive energy field helped them find the truth about who they truly were, and at the same time it helped them achieve peace and tranquility. Nonetheless, it took many years for the Muslim community to overcome the tyrannical Umayyad and Abbasid regimes. However, thanks to Imam al-Sajjad, the spark of recovery and resurgence was well underway.

Prophet Mohammad based the Islamic government on Islamic laws and principles. It was necessary for each Imam to fulfill this obligation and to ensure that these Islamic laws and principles were practiced and upheld. While each Imam struggled to uphold the Islamic system of justice, their lives were always in danger, resulting in their martyrdom. Only Imam al-Mahdi, the twelfth Imam, survived the ages. Imam al-Sajjad lived in very difficult times, as he had to survive the tragic event of Karbala and bear the imprisonment and mistreatment of Yazid from the moment his Imamat began. Then he had to work secretly to spread the true meaning of Islam, and he did with his supplications and whispered prayers.

The triad of Imam Hussein, Lady Zainab, and Imam al-Sajjad truly protected Islam and upheld the Islamic system of justice. Their sacrifices paved the way for Islam to survive and flourish. These three heroes of Islam, who were the continuation of the root of their forefathers, reinforced one another and kept the hopes and prayers of all who espoused freedom and justice alive. We are indebted to their sacrifices, for today we have the freedom to act and practice our faith of Islam. We can raise our heads high, as our hearts and minds are filled with happiness and gratitude for having such leaders as these three heroes to protect us. The tragedy of Karbala instills in us the energy that transcends time itself. As we commemorate the event each year to embrace the energy of Imam Hussein, Lady Zainab, and Imam al-Sajjad, we heighten our awareness of the sacrifices that we need to be make in order to protect and sustain Islam.

Imam Mohammad al-Baqir ibn Imam Ali al-Sajjad

Imam al-Baqir was known for his widespread knowledge of Islamic science and the meaning of the verses of the Qur'an. The word *baqir* implies "to split open knowledge" or the "expounder of knowledge." His deep thought and superiority over other scholars in the fields of jurisprudence, Qur'anic explanations, traditions, and sciences made his contemporaries hold him in high esteem. His creative energy enabled him to enter into the very root of knowledge and to convey that knowledge to the people. He was known not only for his vast knowledge but also for the immense amount of time he spent in worship. Endowed with the depths of knowledge, he spent his time and energy exploring the science of the self. Additionally, he was gifted with the ability to uncover the mysteries of other sciences.

Imam al-Baqir disclosed the secrets of knowledge and wisdom and unfolded the principles of spiritual and religious guidance. Under the Imam's instruction and guidance, his students compiled books on different branches of the sciences and arts. He taught his students the disciplines of philosophy, physics, chemistry, mathematics, and geography and the importance of scientific research. For example, Imam al-Baqir discovered the presence of hydrogen in water. Additionally, as hydrogen was a highly flammable gas, he demonstrated that water could be turned into fire. He could not have identified this gas and found out its properties without separating it from water through the process of hydrolysis, which was impossible without a strong current of electricity. Furthermore, he discovered that since air contains a combustible energy, if it is isolated in it its purest form, it could even melt away iron.

Imam Ja'far as-Sadiq ibn Imam Mohammad al-Baqir

Imam Ja'far as-Sadiq made many contributions to understanding the concept of energy and its relationship to philosophy and science. Divinely inspired, Imam as-Sadiq exhibited perfection in many areas, some of which were medicine, theology, philosophy, mathematics, and science. A thesis conducted by the Research Committee at Strasbourg, France, was based on the life of Imam Ja'far as-Sadiq (Mirza 1997). This thesis, written in French, was published by the Research Committee and later translated into Persian by Maghze Mutafakkir Jehan Shia in Tehran, Iran, under the title of *Contribution of Imam Ja'far as-Sadiq to Science and Philosophy*. Kaukab Ali Mirza translated the Persian text into English, under the title of *The Great Muslim Scientist and Philosopher Imam Jafar ibn Mohammed As-Sadiq.*

The research committee included twenty-five world-renown scholars and scientists—mostly non-Muslims—who collaborated to unanimously confirm the many scientific discoveries made by Imam Ja'far as Sadiq. These scholars were from universities, such as the University of Brussels, University of Paris, University of Strasbourg, University of London, University of Tehran, University of Chicago, University of Lyon, and the University of Freiburg. Among these scholars and scientists was the 1997 Nobel Prize winner in physics, Claude Cohen Tannoudji of the University of Paris, and Francesco Gabrieli, Professor of Arabic Languages and Literature of the University of Rome. Sayed Musa al-Sadr, the renowned Islamic scholar from Lebanon, was also a member of this research committee.

From the research committee are excerpts of some of the discoveries made by Imam as-Sadiq some thirteen centuries ago, which were translated into English by Kaukab Ali Mirza:

- *Discovery of Hydrogen in Water.* His father, Imam Mohammad al-Baqir, discovered the presence of hydrogen in water and found that it was a highly inflammable gas and that water could be turned into fire. They could not have identified hydrogen without separating it from water through the process of hydrolysis, which is impossible without a strong current of electricity. It was not until AD 1766 that the English scientist Henry Cavendish was able to hydrolyze water, obtain hydrogen, and prove that hydrogen is highly flammable. It's interesting that during Imam as-Sadiq's time, electricity was not available. Today, the pollution of air rising from excessive use of fossil fuels for producing energy has caused us to consider using hydrogen as an alternative source of energy.

- *Theory of Light.* Imam as-Sadiq said that light reflected by different objects comes to us, but only a part of the rays enters our eyes. That is why we do not see distant objects clearly. If all the rays of light that came from them entered our eyes, objects would appear near to us. It was this theory that helped Lippershey of Flanker's to make his first field glasses or binoculars in AD 1608. Galileo made use of these binoculars and invented his telescope in AD 1610. If Imam as-Sadiq had not formulated his theory of light, binoculars and telescopes would not have been invented, and Galileo could not have confirmed through visual observation the theories of Copernicus and Kepler that all planets, including the Earth, rotate around the sun.

+ *Matter and Anti-Matter.* One of the theories of Imam as-Sadiq is that everything except Allah has its opposite, but this does not result in a conflict, otherwise the whole universe would be destroyed. The difference between matter and anti-matter is that in matter the electrons are negatively charged, and protons are positively charged. But in anti-matter, the electrons are positively charged, and protons are negatively charged. Scientists are of the opinion that if one kilogram of matter collides with one kilogram of anti-matter, so much energy will be released that the whole world would be destroyed. Although electrons, protons, and neutrons were not discovered before Imam as-Sadiq arrived, they were still of interest to scientists and philosophers. Even the Qur'an alludes to electrons, protons, and neutrons, and that is what led Imam as-Sadiq to discover them.

+ *Light of the Stars.* Imam as-Sadiq said that among the clusters of stars we see at night, some are so bright that our sun, in comparison, is quite insignificant. During his time and in centuries that followed, many scientists considered his theory to be unacceptable. They could not believe that these small specs of light (stars) could have more light than the light of the sun. About thirteen centuries after the death of Imam as-Sadiq, it was proved that what he had said was correct. It was discovered that there are stars in the universe that are billions of times brighter than the sun. They are called quasars.

• *Theory of Perpetual Motion.* Imam as-Sadiq said that everything in the universe, including inanimate objects, is always in motion, although we may not see it. There is nothing that is without motion. This theory, which was unacceptable in his time, is a scientific fact today. Motion is the essence of being. If there is no motion, there is no existence. He said that it seems to us that when a person dies, his actions and movements come to an end. It is not so. They will continue in another form. Even if the smallest particles of the human body are converted from matter into energy, they will continue to move in the form of energy until the end of time. He added that we feel the passing of time because of our internal movement. Similarly, our sense of space is due to this movement. Without it, we cannot feel the passage of time and have a sense of space. There are two kinds of motion in every object—motion inside the atoms and perpetual vibration within the molecules.

• *Theory of Four Elements.* At age eleven, Imam as-Sadiq attacked the theory of rotation of the sun around the Earth. At age twelve, he rejected the Theory of Four Elements of Aristotle and proved that it was wrong. For a thousand years, Aristotle's Theory of Four Elements remained the cornerstone of physics. No scholar expressed his doubts in accuracy. Imam as-Sadiq said, "I wonder how a man like Aristotle could say that in the world there are only four elements of earth, water, fire, and air. The air is not an element. It contains many elements. Each metal, which is in the earth, is an element." He said that there are many elements in the air and that all of them are essential for breathing. It was not until the eighteenth century, when the father of modern chemistry, Lavoisier, separated oxygen from air and demonstrated the important role it plays in breathing and combustion, that scientists accepted that air is not an element.

- ◆ *Rotation of the Earth on its Axis.* Imam as-Sadiq stated that the Earth rotates on its own axis. When astronauts landed on the moon, they directed their telescopes toward the Earth and observed that it was, in fact, rotating slowly on its axis. Amazingly, only by knowing the laws of mechanics of stars, which was discovered centuries later, did Imam as-Sadiq make this discovery.

Imam Ja'far as-Sadiq recognized the importance of electromagnetic energy on the human system. He stated:

> There are some lights which, if thrown from a sick person to a healthy person, can possibly make that healthy person sick. (The Minister 1984)

We can conclude from this quote that Imam as-Sadiq was explaining the importance of vibrations in the healing process. Electromagnetic energy generated the vibrations, and the electrical impulses are "lights."

In Islam, it is believed that placing one's hands on parts of the body of another person, while at the same time reciting prayers or supplications, may result in healing via electrical vibrations. As the hands are on the same frequency as the brain, they can also act as receptors and sensors of electromagnetism. It takes deep meditation by both the healer and the one being healed for the healing process to work. The end result is one of turning negative frequencies into positive frequencies.

Truly, Imam Ja'far as-Sadiq was ahead of his time, and today the recipients of his knowledge and discoveries are beginning to realize the genius of this great person in the history of mankind. Only the will and grace of Allah could have accomplished the Imam's contributions to mankind. By consensus, the father of chemistry, Abu Musa Jabir Ibn

Hayyan al Azdi, also known as Geber, was a student of Imam Ja'far as-Sadiq (Wikipedia).

Imam Musa al-Kazim ibn Imam Ja'far as-Sadiq

The energy of Imam Musa was electromagnetic, and he drew many scholars and religious leaders to his unique character. They referred to Imam Musa with many titles. For example, he was known as Abd al-Salih for his perfect character and manners and Zain al-Mujtahideen for his lengthy worship and supplication. He was also known as al-Kazim for holding his temper, restraining his anger, and being kind to those who harassed him. Exhibiting tolerance when he faced persecution and harm, Imam Musa was still good and charitable to those who mistreated him. He dealt with them in the best and kindest manner, hoping to lead them to the Straight Path. The period during which he became the Imam was the most ruthless and problematic period for Ahl al-Bayt and the oppressed. However, Imam Musa contained his sorrow, pain, and suffering and endured all atrocities with patience and courage.

By studying the mind-set, personality, weak and strong characteristics, and motives of his enemies, he was able to change their behavior from one of aggression to one of friendship. This was a great attribute of Imam Musa, as he knew the art and science of entering the mind and heart of his enemies in order to change their negative energy into positive energy. His success was derived from his great noble characteristics and the virtues of ethics, tolerance, and prudence and the spirit of forgiveness.

Moreover, Imam Musa was widely known for his kindness, self-sacrifice, and helping the poor and distressed, as he solved their problems, freed the slaves, retired their debts, and kept good relations with them. Toward this end, he lightened the burden of their ordeals and misfortunes. Among the qualities of his noble personality was that of generosity, as he showered those in need with money and gifts in order to rescue them from their bitterness of poverty, deprivation, and misery. A role model in humanitarian care, his spiritual energy was that of humility and empathy, as he felt the pains and problems of the poor. Everyone who believes in ideals and honorable humanity sanctifies and emulates Imam Musa's virtues of knowledge, mercy, kindness, and steadfastness and other noble tendencies.

The secret of Imam Musa's success was his devotion to Allah and the humility that embraced his heart with regard to his feelings, desires, and aspirations. Spending his days and nights in worship and meditation, he gave of himself and his wealth so as to win Allah's pleasure, working hard to save humanity and guiding it to the Straight Path.

Imam Ali al-Rida ibn Imam Musa

Immersed in spiritual energy, Imam Ali al-Rida had to undertake a twofold objective in combatting the evil schemes and negative energy of Caliph al-Ma'mun. Simultaneously, Imam Ali pursued the objective of peace of Imam Hassan and the objective of revolution of Imam Hussein, the children of Imam Ali ibn Abi Talib. The objective of peace was necessary in order for Imam Ali al-Rida to:

+ safeguard Islam and Ahl al-Bayt;
+ guide the people by Allah's commands;
+ protect Islam against the distorted meanings of certain Qur'anic verses;
+ protect Islam against the narration of forged and corrupted hadiths (traditions) ascribed to Prophet Mohammad;
+ protect the followers of the authentic Islamic path from ignorance, deviation, and the danger of physical liquidation;
+ strike a balance resulting in working with the existing system on an administrative level, insofar as it would preserve the general order of the society and provide an atmosphere conducive to safety and freedom of movement for Ahl al-Bayt and its followers;
+ carry out the Imam's duties of supreme leadership in the ummah;
+ meet with the foremost writers and intellectual thinkers promoting his views; and

- continue the *majalis* (meetings) depicting the Karbala tragedy and
  the martyrdom of Imam Hussein, his relatives, and companions.

On the other hand, nurtured by Imam Hussein's objective of revolution, Imam Ali al-Rida took a stand, educating and making the ummah aware of the political question relative to the principle of nass (designation of an Imam by a previous Imam), as he revealed the fabrications of the Abbasid regime regarding the legitimacy of actual leadership. The Imam disclosed the ambiguity that was exploited in the slogan *al-rida min aal Mohammad* (the chosen from the family of Prophet Mohammad). All that reawakened the consciousness of the ummah with regard to the principle of nass and the Imamat.

Hence, Imam Ali al-Rida pursued a strategy of instilling positive energy in the minds and hearts of the ummah in order to protect Islam and Ahl al-Bayt and to protect the followers of the true Islamic path, the followers of the principle of nass and those close to it. The Imam was aware that the allegiance offered by Caliph al-Ma'mun to be his heir apparent was the allegiance of death. He was aware of the schemes of al-Ma'mun, the negative aims of al-Ma'mun offering him to be heir apparent, and the Imam's own dilemma in this offer, which held the danger of acknowledging the legitimacy of al-Ma'mun's rule and thus acknowledging the legitimacy of the Abbasid khalifah. He was aware of the traps that would be set in his way, not the least dangerous of which would be to attempt to involve him in the apparatus of a government and an administration that he had not himself set up, and which were not in keeping with his views, his policies, and his character.

Imam Ali al-Rida's position strongly resembled that of Imam Hassan. The difference between the two was that Imam Hassan faced an immediate or deferred death sentence by withholding what was in his power to give. Imam Ali al-Rida faced immediate or deferred sentence on the basis of the false offer that he would gain his usurped rights in the future. But in order to negate the legitimacy of this right, he chose deferment—like Imam Hassan. Imam Ali al-Rida lived in the same painful conditions as Imam Hassan, without being able to explain his ordeal to the people, not even to many of his confidants. He had to suffer martyrdom every day while he still lived, protecting those whom he loved and defended with his life while they misunderstood and misinterpreted his actions. This and other similar situations reveal to us how sad the responsibility of leadership was, with the Imam isolated from the people closest to him. How many agonies and pains did the Imam suffer because of that?

On the other hand, Imam Ali al-Rida's position strongly resembled that of Imam Hussein. Imam Hussein chose immediate death since it was more in keeping with his circumstances and the circumstances of the ummah of his time, more closely connected to the firm aim of the infallible Imams, and more destructive of his enemy, Yazid and the Umayyad regime. Likewise, Imam Ali al-Rida's objective was revolutionary, as it was with Imam Hussein.

Imam Mohammad al-Jawad ibn Imam Ali al-Rida

During his short life, which lasted only twenty-four years, Imam Mohammad al-Jawad accomplished a great deal, particularly in the realm of academia where he imparted knowledge to his students. Strengthened by his charismatic energy, he self-actualized in the understanding of the human persona with regard to the virtues of gallantry, boldness, charity, forgiveness, and tolerance. Immersed in equality for all, Imam al-Jawad was the personification of hospitality and courtesy to everyone, without bias or discrimination. Toward this end, he helped the poor, orphans, and homeless. Moreover, he guided the ummah to the Straight Path.

At the age of six, Imam al-Jawad took over the Imamat, following the death of his father, Imam Ali al-Rida. However, with regard to the Imamat, age is not a prerequisite for that position, as Allah has already entrusted the leadership to whomever he chooses. At the age of seven, scientists, philosophers, and theologians met with the young Imam only to discover that he possessed a very high level of knowledge that was far beyond their ability to define or describe. Many questions were asked, and the Imam replied to the satisfaction of all. The Imam's deep understanding of sciences, philosophy, and theology amazed them.

Imam al-Jawad's method of teaching was to urge his students and scholars to harness their creative energy to write, record, classify, and publish their works. As a result, these religious scholars wrote many books in different fields of science, philosophy, and theology, and they proliferated by enriching others with original research and thoughts. The hallmark of Imam al-Jawad's intellectuality was his creative energy, inspired by the grace of Allah.

Imam Ali al-Hadi ibn Imam Mohammad al-Jawad

Imam al-Hadi took over the Imamat at the age of eight. His lifestyle and noble qualities were the same as the preceding Imams. He led an extremely simple life and worked laboriously on a farm to sustain his family. Irrespective of the persecution and harassment inflicted on him, the intensified spiritual energy of Imam al-Hadi enabled him to overcome these injustices as he remained absorbed in worship to Allah. Firm and resolute, he was unperturbed by the despair and distress that surrounded him, and he confronted his enemies with kindness and tolerance. The noble qualities and characteristics of Imam al-Hadi were those of humility, generosity, and forbearance to the needy, friends, and adversaries.

Wherever Imam al-Hadi resided, he made sure that his grave would be dug. This act proved to his enemies that he had reached the highest level of spiritual energy and was not afraid of death. Caliph Mutawakkil ordered the mausoleum of Imam Hussein in Karbala to be desecrated and his tomb buried elsewhere, leaving no trace of its whereabouts. Still Imam al-Hadi was not intimidated or frightened by the caliph who was persistent in his acts of negative energy. Rather, Imam al-Hadi utilized all his energies to remain steadfast and concentrated on saving the oppressed and restoring their rights.

Scholars of that time lauded Imam al-Hadi for his knowledge of science, jurisprudence, theology, and philosophy. They often referred to the Imam for his opinions on complicated questions dealing with Islamic Shari'ah with regards to its verdicts, teachings, and principles. The Imam expounded on the correct wording and meaning of the hadiths of Prophet Mohammad as well as the narrations from other infallible Imams. Toward this end, Imam al-Hadi instructed his followers to understand the contents of these hadiths and narrations and act accordingly. He understood the importance of the teachings of Prophet Mohammad, and he made them available so the people could find guidance with regards to morals, disciplines, intellectual issues, and social issues. Imam al-Hadi was so versed in jurisprudence that even the malevolent Caliph Mutawakkil referred to him with complicated questions and preferred his decrees to those of other jurisprudents. As some scholars misunderstood the theology in Islam (e.g., whether one can see and determine the existence of Allah), the Imam disproved these misconceptions. Furthermore, the supplications of Imam al-Hadi were the enlightenment and reflection of his spiritual energy that formed the bases of his behavior and morality.

Imam Hassan al-Askari ibn Imam Ali

Imam al-Askari's brief life of twenty-eight years was mostly spent in prison. As such, he had to reach the people via deputies that he appointed to be the liaisons between his imprisonment and the community. In turn, the Imam taught and gave instructions to these deputies who carried out the duties of guiding the people during his absence. Of course, the deputies could not always reach the Imam, as they were subjected to numerous restrictions and were under the constant surveillance of the caliph's spies.

Imam al-Askari was the personification of human perfection and moral excellence. He exhibited various levels of positive energy in the arena of spirituality, charisma, and creativity with regards to his knowledge, generosity, patience, forgiveness, sacrifice, and piety. Imam al-Askari's jailors were so drawn to his electromagnetic energy that they would freeze in his presence, particularly when he was in the state of grace in prayer. Reinforcement jailors would experience the same feeling and begin to empathize with the Imam.

In spite of his short life, he was able to connect with some of the notable scholars who benefitted immensely from his knowledge and wisdom. Additionally, he curtailed the movement of the philosophers who had been preaching atheism at that time. Scholars gravitated to the Imam, as they were in need of his reservoir of knowledge. Most respected in religious verdicts and affairs, he stood tall in intellectuality and scientific knowledge as well. Moreover, he rebelled against the corrupted Abbasid regime by opposing their oppressive and tyrannical rule as he pursued the course of truth and justice among people.

Imam Mohammad al-Mahdi ibn Imam Hassan al-Askari

Like Prophet Jesus, Imam al-Mahdi has been given divinely inspired energy that has kept him alive for centuries. Both Sunni and Shi'a scholars confirm that Imam al-Mahdi will arrive at some point in the future, along with Prophet Jesus, to put an end to injustice and tyranny and to mankind's immoral and depraved lifestyles. There are skeptics who question how a five-year-old can become an Imam and live for over eleven hundred years. Allah chooses whom he wants to be a prophet or an Imam, at whatever age, and keeps them alive for as long as he decides. For example, Jesus spoke from the cradle, stating that Allah assigned him as a prophet:

> But she (Mary) pointed unto him. They said: "How can we speak unto one who is (yet) a child in the cradle?" He (Jesus miraculously) said: "Verily I am a servant of Allah; He hath given me a Book (Injil) and made me a Prophet!" "And He hath made me blessed wherever I be and He hath enjoined on me prayer and poor-rate so long as I live!" "And (to be) duteous to my mother, and He hath not made me insolent unblest!" "And peace be

on me the day I was born, and the day I die, and the day I am raised alive!" (Qur'an 19:29–33)

And Jesus is still alive since his birth over two thousand years ago. Imam al-Mahdi is also still alive, although we cannot recognize him.

Shi'a sources confirm that Imam al-Mahdi is from the lineage of Ahl al-Bayt:

> The Holy Prophet said: "The world will not come to an end until a man from my family (Ahl al-Bayt), who will be called al-Mahdi, emerges to rule upon my community." (*Bihar al-Anwar*, Vol. 51, p. 75)

> Rasullullah said: "The world will not come to an end until a man from the descendants of Hussain takes charge of the affairs of the world and fills it with justice and equity as it is filled with injustice and tyranny." (*Bihar al-Anwar*, Vol. 51, p. 66)

Sunni sources also confirm that Imam al-Mahdi is from the lineage of Ahl al-Bayt:

- *Ibn Majah*, V5, Book 36, Hadith 4085 (Hasan/Good)
- *Abu Dawud*, V4, Book 35, Hadith 4284 (Hasan/Good)
- *Al-Tirmidhi*, V4, Book 31, Hadith 2230 (Hasan/Good)

The following Sunni hadiths confirm that Imam al-Mahdi is from Ahl al-Bayt:

> The Prophet said: "Even if the entire duration of the world's existence has already been exhausted and only one day is left before Doomsday (Day of Judgment), Allah will expand that day to such a length of time, as to accommodate the kingdom of a person out of my

Ahl al-Bayt who will be called by my name. He will then fill out the Earth with peace and justice as it will have been full of injustice and tyranny before then." (*Al-Tirmidhi*, Vol. 4, Book 31, Hadiths 2230–2231; *Sunan Abu Dawud*, Vol. 4, Book 35, Hadith 4282)

It was narrated from Ali that the Messenger of Allah said: "Mahdi is one of us, the people of the Household. Allah rectifying him in a single night." (*Ibn Majah*, Vol. 5, Book 36, Hadith 4085; *Abu Dawud*, Vol. 4, Book 35, Hadith 4284)

Allah will bring out from concealment Mahdi from my Family and Progeny before the Day of Judgment, even if only one day were to remain in the life of the world, and he will spread on this Earth justice and equity and eradicate tyranny and oppression. (*Ahmad ibn Hanbal*, Vol. 1, p. 99)

Though the clouds may temporarily hide the light of the sun, it will reemerge to provide sustenance with its rays of energy. Likewise, al Imam al-Mahdi, now hidden by his major occultation, will reemerge with an energy that will illuminate the world.

Chapter 16

Unity of the Imamat

Islam is a universal concept that comprehends man and the cosmos. Islam is based from beginning to the end on tawhid (oneness), for Allah is One. Unity is a process of synthesis, a means of becoming whole and comprehending the absolute oneness of all existence. Every facet of Islam revolves around the principle of unity. The basic faith that lies behind the ideal of unity is that the existence of life and humanity has meaning. Islam is essentially a way of knowledge that integrates our being and makes us know who we are and our purpose in life.

Since man is not self-sufficient to guide himself in terms of faith and religious doctrines, the necessity for Imam arises. While patients may be able to read a book on medicine, they still need a physician to help diagnose and administer a cure for their ailment. Similarly, Imams are needed to continue the work of Prophet Mohammad in explaining what the many verses in the Qur'an mean. In short, the Imam's role was to guide mankind in all aspects of their existence. In spite of being harassed, persecuted, and humiliated, the infallible Imams stayed the course of preaching and practicing unity in all of its manifestations. The following will focus on unity as it relates to Prophet Mohammad and the Imamat.

Prophet Mohammad

Prophet Mohammad united the people of Medina with protected privileges for Jews, Christians, and Muslims who lived there. The Charter of Medina was written and signed by members of the three faiths: Jews, Christians, and Muslims (Yildirim 2005). It became the first interfaith constitution ever to be written and enacted. The prophet's policy of tolerance for Jews, Christians, and other faiths played an important role in the expansion of Islam during his lifetime and after his death.

Not only did Prophet Mohammad preach the faith of Islam; he also tended to the economic well-being of the community. He unified the community by making treaties and alliances with many tribes in the Arabian Peninsula, which helped Islam find acceptance and spread over his lifetime. The success of his unifying these tribes was molded in his sincerity, honor, diplomacy, and concern for all people. The hallmark of this unity was built on teaching people the virtues of morality and honesty.

The prophet did not just preach Islam but also showed mankind how to achieve success. He established a religious and social framework for the life of many races. After the conquest of Mecca, he broke the tribal system, setting the stage for a new era of a unified community, ordered his harshest opponents to go free, and implemented social change gradually, which resulted in them willingly and immediately accepting Islam. Allah gave the prophet the special gift to resolve conflicts and disputes. He always emphasized peace and harmonious relations. He united the Arab Bedouin tribesmen who had been, until then, disunited and pitted against each other in internal quarrels.

Throughout the twenty-three years of his mission, Prophet Mohammad emphasized the unity of his ummah. He enforced the concept of ummah as he integrated Muslims of different races, ethnic groups, and social classes into one brotherhood. As Islam expanded, the ummah absorbed a mixture of people from diverse cultures, integrating them into a collective union. It engendered an open society for all to excel. Based on Quran'ic commands, Prophet Mohammad stressed the significance of unity and authorized harsh admonishments and reprimands for those who intentionally assailed the unity of the ummah. Long before the establishment of the United Nations, Prophet Mohammad embarked on uniting many communities, and he succeeded!

Necessity of Imamat

Unity for the Imamat was built around a common purpose, which was harmony of values that created a shared identity. The unified duty of the Twelve Infallible Imams was to lead the ummah in accordance with the Qur'an and sunnah in spiritual, religious, social, and political matters. For the Shi'a, the Imams are divinely appointed leaders whose main objective is to lead the ummah on the Straight Path. Additionally, the Imams remain steadfast to what Prophet Mohammad taught, as there is no new set of rules or laws revealed to them. By the grace of Allah, the Imams possessed complete knowledge of Islam.

If the Islamic society cannot attain contentment and happiness without divine supervision and leadership, then a sinless leader, educator, and guide must be appointed. Moreover, ordinary people may incorrectly interpret the Qur'an and the sunnah, thereby deviating from the truth. Therefore, it necessitated the prophet himself appointing those who have a spiritual link with what is beyond the external world. Those who have that link are the Twelve Infallible Imams. The Imams performed their duties with utmost care, as they espoused the truth of what the prophet taught. As they were unable to openly oppose the tyrant rulers of the time, they were obliged to remain reticent and restrained in order to protect the line of the Imamat and safeguard Ahl al-Bayt.

Over the course of history, there existed a great deal of unanimity and uniformity between the Twelve Infallible Imams. During each period, these Imams preached unity and sacrificed a great deal to preserve that unity. Throughout the 280 years from the time of Imam Ali ibn Abi Talib's caliphate until the onset of the major occultation of Imam Mohammad al-Mahdi, the twelve Imams faced difficult hardships, harassment, oppression, tyranny, and torture. However, each of the Imams stayed the course of the Straight Path and weathered the storm.

Straight Path of the Twelve Infallible Imams (Sirat al Mustaqim)

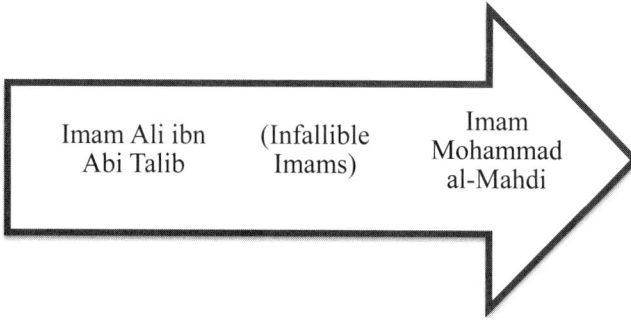

Imam Ali ibn Abi Talib   (Infallible Imams)   Imam Mohammad al-Mahdi

The Twelve Infallible Imams patiently adhered to Prophet Mohammad's policy of safeguarding the *Usul-al-Din* (theoretical and fundamental principles of beliefs) and the *Furu' al-Din* (practical principles of beliefs) by educating the Islamic society. Additionally, they protected the theoretical and practical principles of Islam, the Qur'an, and the sunnah from deviation, corruption, changes, and transformations. However, the ruling governments did everything in their power to crush Ahl al-Bayt, utilizing every method to extinguish the light of their guidance. In spite of this torment and persecution, the Imams continued to follow the unity of Islam as Allah had ordained.

The unity between Prophet Mohammad and his Ahl al-Bayt is cemented not just by offspring but also by spirit. It is a unity that is inspired and symbolized by the *Ahl al-Kisa* (family of the cloak of Prophet Mohammad) event in which Prophet Mohammad wrapped his cloak around Imam Hassan, Imam Hussein, Fatima, and Imam Ali, stating that they were from his Ahl al-Bayt.

All of the infallible Imams endeavored to unite the Islamic ummah, in spite of the oppression and persecution perpetrated against them. A review of just two of these Imams—Imam Hussein and Imam al-Mahdi—will demonstrate how they pursued the course of unity among the ummah. As the Islamic ummah was in disarray under the illegitimate and tyrannical rule of Caliph Yazid, Imam Hussein had to pursue the course of uniting the Muslim ummah in order to safeguard Islam. The tribal leaders of Kufa, Iraq, as well as their warriors, sent numerous letters to Imam Hussein indicating their support for him. The Imam sent his cousin, Moslem ibn Aqil, to go to Kufa to determine if the Kufans were serious about joining forces with the Imam for the cause of unity and guidance. Moslem found the Kufans genuinely united and awaiting the Imam's acceptance to join them. Moslem was so overwhelmed by the support of the Kufans that he advised the Imam to immediately come to Kufa.

However, the situation in Kufa took a turn for the worse, as Yazid replaced its governor with the malicious Ubaydullah Ibn Ziyad who immediately intimidated the tribal leaders, resulting in a breach of support for Imam Hussein. Ubaydullah had Moslem beheaded and his body thrown to the crowd. Ubaydullah also beheaded the Imam's messenger to Basra, Iraq, where the Imam was attempting to unite the leaders of the Basran tribes that were divided over administrative matters. The end result was the tragedy at Karbala, Iraq. Nonetheless, this tragedy was the beacon that set in place the pursuit of unity for the Shi'as by creating a spirit of cooperation and brotherly love among them. Imam Hussein sacrificed his life for the purpose of unity in faith and commitment to Allah and the truth.

When Imam Mohammad al-Mahdi reappears from his major occultation, oppression and injustice will have wreaked havoc throughout the world unlike any other time in the history of mankind. Along with Prophet Jesus, Imam al-Mahdi will fight the oppressors, unite the Muslims, and bring peace and justice to the world. Both Sunnis and Shi'as confirm the emergence of Imam al-Mahdi and his mission to unite humanity by abandoning all forms of idolatry, tyranny, oppression, and injustice. He will bring together people who have different ideas and thoughts and unify them into a singular goal and purpose, thereby restoring their lives to the highest level of morality. The oppressed will unite, permanently defeat the forces of tyranny and injustice, and become victorious. As Mahdi, he will guide people to that which they have been separated from. As Qa'im, he will be commanded to establish the truth. He will unite the Muslims and establish Islam as the dominant religion of the world. By uniting the ummah, he will revolutionize the world according to the ideology of Islam and guide them to the Straight Path.

Both Sunnis and Shi'as agree regarding the Qur'an and Prophet Mohammad. So if unity is to be achieved within the Islamic ummah, the solution has to come from elsewhere. That solution is Imam Ali ibn Abi Talib who is accepted by both Sunnis and Shi'as, though with different levels of importance. Let us examine why Imam Ali is the panacea to the disunity that plagues the Islamic society.

Imam Ali ibn Abi Talib

All over the world, societies are undergoing transformation more rapidly than ever. In the process, the role of Islam in public and private life is being questioned. Some Muslims promote the secularization of society. Others, alarmed at the pace and scope of change, are reemphasizing basic Islamic values and practices. And still discord exists in the Muslim world. Why? The fragmentation between Sunnis and Shi'as is primarily the result of how each views the position of Imam Ali ibn Abi Talib and his progeny. Therefore, the solution to bringing about the unity between Sunnis and Shi'as must come about through an accurate understanding of Imam Ali's principles and practices. The common linkage for Sunnis and Shi'as is Imam Ali, who was not only a symbol of truth but a manifestation of it as well. And who taught Imam Ali these virtues and instilled in his mind the infinite knowledge of Islam? None other than Prophet Mohammad!

Regardless of whether Imam Ali actually felt that he should have been the khalifah, the fact remains that he was more concerned about safeguarding the unity. The issue of the khalifah in regard to Imam Ali and Abu Bakr was not the inherent reason for the divide. This did not become an issue until much later. Imam Ali supported Abu Bakr for the sake of unity. In fact, Imam Ali was well respected and trusted by

Abu Bakr, Umar, and Uthman, as they often came to Imam Ali for his opinion on difficult cases.

During the reign of each of the three caliphs, Abu Bakr, Umar, and Uthman, they became confused and perplexed on issues they were not able to judge and therefore would consult with Imam Ali and agree with his decision. Although there were many times when they needed Imam Ali's help, let us just look at one issue for Abu Bakr and Umar.

When considering whether to wage war against the Romans, Abu Bakr first consulted with a number of his companions. They hesitated, giving no decisive guidance. Abu Bakr then sought Imam Ali's counsel. Imam Ali said, "If you embark on this work, you will succeed." Abu Bakr happily responded, "May you receive good tidings," and thereafter he ordered the expedition under the leadership of Khalid bin Sa'id (Shirazi 2008 [*Tarikh al-Ya'qubi*, Vol. 2, pp. 132–133]).

After the Muslims conquered Persia's Sassanid dynasty, Umar consulted with Imam Ali on how to spend its immense wealth. Imam Ali said, "Once every year, distribute the riches among all people and leave none remaining in the treasury" (Shirazi 2008 [Al-Mawirdi, *Al-Ahkam al-Sultaniyyah*, p. 199]).

To reconnect to the ideal Islamic community, we follow the example of Imam Ali. We need to cling to the attitude and behavior of Imam Ali, who sacrificed a great deal for the sanctity and unity of the Islamic community. For example:

+ Imam Ali supported Abu Bakr, Umar, and Uthman, even though he believed they erred in assuming the position of caliph. He supported them for the sake of unity, for to wage war against them would have surely led to the destruction of Islam.
+ Imam Ali placed his sons, Imam Hassan and Imam Hussein, at the door of the house of the Caliph Uthman to protect him from being killed.
+ When Abu Bakr died, Imam Ali married his wife and raised his son, Mohammad. Why would Imam Ali raise Abu Bakr's son if he did not have respect for Abu Bakr? Imam Ali appointed

Abu Bakr's son, Mohammad, to the position of governor of Egypt. When Mohammad, the son of Abu Bakr, was martyred and his body desecrated, Imam Ali was extremely saddened by his death.

- Imam Ali named three of his sons Abu Bakr, Umar, and Uthman. Abu Bakr and Uthman were martyred on the field of Karbala, along with their brother, Imam Hussein. Even Imam Hassan named two of his children, Abu Bakr and Umar. Abu Bakr was also martyred at Karbala with his uncle Imam Hussein. Imam Ali al-Sajjad named one of his children Umar, and Imam Musa al-Kazim had a daughter, Aisha (Al-Mufid 2004).
- Imam Ali said: "The best man with regard to me is he who is in the middle course. So be with him and be with the great majority (of Muslims) because Allah's hand (of protection) is on keeping unity" (Sermon 126, *Nahjul Balagha*).

The authority of Imam Ali is well accepted by all Islamic schools of thought but with different interpretations as to the declaration made by Prophet Mohammad at Ghadir Khumm that Imam Ali was his successor. Rather than cause division among the Muslims during his time, Imam Ali supported the leadership in the name of unity. Imam Ali knew that the higher cause was to breed accord and not discord. He knew that taking the position of the rightful leadership of the Muslim world by waging war after the death of Prophet Mohammad would have destroyed Islam. Imam Ali was instilled with the noble qualities of vision and action, which taken together transform the ummah and bring about unity.

Even though Imam Ali supported the caliphs in the name of unity, this did not prevent him from openly speaking about his claim and right to have been the first caliph after Prophet Mohammad. While his numerous sermons in *Nahjul Balagha* voiced his disappointment with those who usurped his right to the caliphate, he still supported them in the struggle against the enemies of Islam. Undeniably, he always gave sincere counsel to the caliphs.

Common Ground—Common Principle

Muslims must find the common link to unity by keeping the doors open between the adherents of the different schools of thought. While there will be differences in opinion and interpretations of Islam, we need to avoid discord within the Muslim community. When dialogue on Islamic issues takes place, all parties in the discussion should proceed from the point of harmony. There is commonality among issues within the Muslim world, and we should build our alliance as we strive to understand one another. We are all part of the great Islamic culture and civilization, and we should strive to keep ourselves within the circle of Islam. Only by achieving unity within the Muslim world can we thwart the evils of oppression and colonialism.

"Divided we fall, united we stand." We need to unify and rescue ourselves. We must support and sacrifice for each other and live as brothers and sisters in Islam. Islam is a religion of balance. We should not go from one extreme to another extreme. We must respect all schools, Sunni and Shi'a, whether we agree with them or not. Instead of dividing on small issues, we should unite on common ground and common principle. Muslims need to educate themselves on the views of all the schools, just as we would educate ourselves to understand the views of Judaism and Christianity. Muslims need to peacefully sit down together and have dialogue and get everyone back on the right track … without borders and without prejudices.

It is well documented that both Sheikh Mahmood Shaltoot, head of al-Azhar University in Egypt, and Ayatollah Khomeini, Iran's head of state, did their best to minimize the differences between Sunnis and Shi'as in order to bring home the unity. Sheikh Shaltoot recognized the Ja'far school of thought (Shaltoot 1959). Ayatollah Khomeini condemned Salman Rushdie's book called *Satanic Verses* because Rushdie not only committed blasphemy but also demeaned and denigrated Aisha, the wife of the prophet. Witness the price that Ayatollah Khomeini, a Shi'a, paid to defend Aisha while all the Sunni governments were silent.

There is more common ground between the schools of thought than there is division. All schools of thought accept the concepts of Ahl al-Bayt and sunnah but with different interpretations. All agree that Fatimah, Imam Ali, Imam Hassan, and Imam Hussein are members of Ahl al-Bayt.

When a Muslim begins to emphasize that he is either a Sunni or Shi'a as a separate sect, then he is contributing to fragmentation. Rather, it is best for a Muslim to say that he belongs to a particular school of thought. Therefore, the concepts of Sunni and Shi'a should never lead to fragmentation and should not be confused with the objectives and interpretations of the various schools of thought. From a historical perspective, it was the sixth Imam, Ja'far as-Sadiq, who was the teacher of both Abu Hanifah and Malik Ibn Anas, two of the renowned scholars of the major Sunni schools of thought. Even al-Shafi'i, the leader of one of the four Sunni schools of thought, preached his love for Imam Ali and Ahl al-Bayt.

Our pure objective in achieving unity is the establishment of the *deen* of Allah, rather than the domination of one sect by another. Unless this present dominant mood is removed, and until total adherence to pure Islam through appropriate methods of Islamic debate is achieved, it will be difficult to envision a united and cohesive ummah. It is worth noting that while constructive debates among scholars from the different schools of thought are occurring, they need to also occur at the senior levels in order to have a significant impact on unity.

We should not lose faith or hope if unity is not established today, but we must work and be determined toward the future. Moreover, we must not be drawn into the trap of the opponents of Islamic unity who constantly hide the true nature of Islamic alliance and falsely claim that a unified Islamic ummah is impractical and is bound to fail.

We cannot overemphasize the importance of achieving a complete state of cohesion and unity in the Muslim ummah. We must bear this in mind in every dialogue that we enter and in every action we perform. As we have witnessed the desecration of our holy places, the oppression and tyranny in our Muslim societies, and the threats from outside and inside the Muslim world, we need to restore the ummah to a healthy and vital state of cohesiveness.

When the Muslim community becomes aware of its Islamic responsibilities, it will win back the unity and ward off extremists who misrepresent Islam. Each Muslim must search his or her awareness and bring it into harmony with the consciousness of other Muslims. This will bring about the unity, and the ummah will once again prosper and flourish as it did during the days of Prophet Mohammad.

Let us engage in dialogue to better understand each other so we can overcome our prejudices and preconceived notions. Let us learn to respect one another by recognizing the good in each other. Let us care and love each other and work together toward the common goal of unity. Trying to change each other does not achieve the unity. Trying to understand each other gives us a better chance of achieving not only the unity but also the fulfillment of our obligations. Our goal should be to cling steadfastly to each strand of the rope of Allah. We are what we have—the Qur'an and the sunnah of Prophet Mohammad and his Ahl al-Bayt. As Prophet Mohammad was a mercy to all mankind, including Muslims and non-Muslims, we must follow his example of tolerance and engage in dialogue to bring about harmony and cooperation not only in Islam but with other faiths as well.

Agreement among Muslims

To achieve a just and lasting unity does not mean that all schools of thought should adhere to just one school. It does not mean that unity should be based only on similarities and not differences. To pursue such a course of action is neither logical nor practical. For the sake of unity, there is no need for Muslims to make any compromise on the primary or secondary principles of their school of thought. By Islamic unity, we mean that Muslims should unite, if for anything else, to safeguard themselves against a common foe—those who wish to tarnish and destroy Islam. To bring about unity, Muslims must be committed in spirit and mind and heart. There is a common denominator between Sunnis and Shi'as.

Just to mention a few beliefs and practices, Sunnis and Shi'as agree on the following:

+ They believe in the tawhid (oneness of Allah) and Prophet Mohammad as the final messenger.
+ They believe in the angels, prophets, books of Allah, and the hereafter.
+ They believe in the core fundamentals of Islam, such as the declaration of faith, prayer, fasting, pilgrimage, and charity.
+ The Ka'bah is their *qiblah* (direction of prayer).
+ They read the same Qur'an, and they basically worship the same.
+ They have similar ways of rearing their children and burying their dead.

In addition, Sunnis and Shi'as agree on the following:

+ The ummah is a single community of many countries with diverse cultures and different languages.
+ The ummah is of numerous nationalities and tribes that share the same kind of civilization and follow the one faith of Islam.
+ The ummah adheres to the shari'ah (divine law) that does not change over time, although jurisprudence within that structure is subject to interpretation by the various schools of thought.

Muslims need to avoid insulting and accusing one another. In addition, they need to forego ridiculing the logic of one another, and they should abstain from hurting each other. Furthermore, saying repulsive things about the prophet's companions should cease and desist.

Achieving the Unity

One of the greatest gifts that Allah has bestowed upon us is the affection in our hearts:

Caused He affection between their hearts; had thou spent all that is in the Earth, thou couldest not have caused that affection between their hearts, but Allah caused affection between them; verily He is All-Mighty, All-Wise. (Qur'an 8:63)

The thikr (remembrance) of Allah and sabr (patience) will guide our hearts to be humble and open for knowledge to enter and solidify our faith. Although it is one's right to believe that his *madhhab* (school of thought) is the best one, it is not the right to ridicule and debase the followers of another madhhab. Here we should not put a barrier between the followers of different madhhabs. However, we should guard against fragmenting Islam:

Verily those who divided their religion and became parties, thou hast no concern with anything of them; their affair is with Allah only, then will He inform them of what they did. (Qur'an 6:159)

As fragmenting Islam is forbidden, then how can Sunnis and Shi'as maintain their own views without sacrificing their desire for unity? Some may say that their insistence on truth is a prerequisite for unity and that they cannot and will not compromise the truth. To become united will necessitate the humility to rethink some things that have been very important to us.

Our challenge is to sustain and intensify the unity in light of the complexity of issues causing problems in the Muslim world. In unity there is strength. While we need to address the issues we face from non-Muslims, we also need to address our own social problems, such as divorce, unwed mothers, crime, alcoholism, drugs, and suicide.

If it is vital for all Muslims to unite in the spirit of brotherhood, then why is it not a reality? There are many reasons, and some of these are the result of hatred, suspicion, intolerance, and deficiencies in control and collaboration. The underlying cause of these deficiencies is *jahil murakkab* (closed-minded ignorance) that impedes learning and understanding. The danger is that those afflicted with this ignorance will render views and analyses even though they lack the knowledge to do so.

By seeking knowledge, we are enlightened. Knowledge is the lamp that illuminates the soul and brings about happiness. Winning the struggle against ignorance requires leaders with knowledge and wisdom who understand the dilemma we face. The issues we face are far more difficult and complex than they have ever been. Yet to participate requires that we understand the relevant issues before us.

It is not sufficient to simply make our intention to unify and then forget about it. Bringing discipline into our intention requires a shift in our awareness. We have intention not just of the mind but also of the heart. Rather than searching for our intention, we simply become that intention. Our intention to engage in effective dialogue must adhere to the following:

- atmosphere of mutual respect and trust;
- free expression of ideas and thoughts;
- advancing scholarly questioning and methodical decision making;
- promoting open-mindedness and regard for different points of view; and
- deciding on an outcome after carefully considering alternatives.

However, at the center of many dialogues are obstacles, such as:

- preconception and narrow-mindedness;
- opposition and antagonism;
- absence of constructive criticism; and
- disrespect for others.

Conflict resolution can help overcome these obstacles, as it encourages us to be proactive and face conflict, not avoid it. There needs to be a transformation of the inner self in order to resolve deep-rooted conflicts.

Empathy allows us to understand the needs and concerns of others. Tolerance is the vehicle by which empathy can manifest itself.

Tolerance acknowledges self-respect and equality. It is through the spirit of detachment that we experience the meaning of tolerance to help influence change for the sake of unity. This does not mean that we should forego our differences. These differences should lead to enrichment rather than provocation.

To reconcile necessitates an understanding that all parties in a conflict are hurt, and their wounds are deep. We heal the wounds by having a compassionate understanding of the conflict. Reconciliation requires being good listeners and being noncritical and nondivergent in the exchange of discussion. The listener does not decide in advance who is right and who is wrong and then seek to rectify it.

We must be cautious about the pessimists and cynics who say that reconciliation is not possible. These skeptics believe that reconciliation is dreadfully culture bound, unattainable, and unrealistic. Reconciliation does not mean giving up one's individuality or sacrificing one's principles, but it does mean engaging in diversity to normalize relationships.

Diversity is the awareness that divergent issues do exist and that these issues are fomented by distinctly different views. We have been marked more by discord than by cooperation, more by hostility than by kindness, more by doubt than by trust, and more by lack of knowledge than by truth.

Moreover, we do not take the time to comprehend the issues but are simply satisfied to pass along unnecessary insults in the place of frank and insightful reflection. It is not that disparities between us do not or should not matter. The issue is whether these disparities should be allowed to restrain us from dealing with a greater common enemy: disunity.

To respect diversity, we must be willing to listen to the views of others. To value diversity requires a sense of well-being that is based on ethics and ideals. To manage diversity necessitates being strategically driven and synergistic. Unity in diversity requires leadership. As leaders, we must demonstrate a genuine passion by embracing the religious and cultural values of others.

To achieve the unity, we must cooperate with each other and be willing to recognize the following:

+ diversity is the mechanism by which we can understand each other;
+ intellectual development and cross-fertilization of ideas can be the vehicle by which to better understand the perspectives of each other;
+ divergent issues and contemporary issues are to be approached collaboratively; and
+ brotherhood and solidarity must be preserved.

Are we up to the task? Are we clear about where we want to go and how to get there? Do we understand our responsibilities? We need a positive vision about what we are trying to do. We need to guard ourselves against complacency.

We need to manage our own anger and hostility—to express feelings without hurting others, to communicate in ways that deescalate conflict, to establish limits and comprehend what is negotiable. Can we create a future in which we live peacefully and in harmony with each other? We need to understand from where our own unresolved feelings of frustration and despair arise and resolve them.

For unity to emerge, children of the future must be the leaders and advocates of that vision. As we spend time with children and truly open our hearts, we will find that they have something to teach us … their innocence … their trust. Children come into the world carrying the light of unity within them. As we open ourselves to their teaching, they can show us how to be unified … how to be absorbed in the present. While children can help us rediscover unity, they need to see us working for unity.

Today, there is great demand for eyes that see, ears that hear, minds that think, and hearts that feel. We can no longer be too content in our own respectability nor too complex and too difficult to please because of our own self-importance. As disunity has been unfolded in our presence, we must open our eyes to its disease, open our ears to the call for brotherhood, broaden our minds by being tolerant, and soften our hearts by self-restraint. We must live the life that is compassionate and self-denying.

We must have the will and courage to stand against the multitude, to follow our own light, and to take the ridicule visited upon us. We must take an active part in the quest for tolerance and cooperation not just to get something out of it but, more importantly, to put something into it. We need to unify with all our power so that peace and brotherhood shall no longer be the rhetoric of the platform but dominant, sovereign facts of life.

Here is an optimism that can be attained by all. It is founded not so much on thought as on action. We must be nurtured in the ideals of true brotherhood. Real love for Islam, not hatred; universal knowledge, not ignorance; respect for each other, not envy—these are the virtues of truth. These are the true standards of equality and justice. These spell the end of jealousy. These bring in the day of promise. These usher in the brotherhood of man. In the progress of unity, the dream of yesterday becomes the confident hope of today and the realized fact of tomorrow.

Each of us owes an obligation to winning the unity. It is not going to be won without great sacrifice. If we have good sense, if we have courage, and if we have integrity, we will succeed in our quest for unity. The challenge for us is to join together—hand to hand, heart to heart, in unity. Let us begin—right now!

Let it be our prayer that our generation will see the dawn and sunrise of permanent unity. Today is a sunrise of hope, a unique and wonderful opportunity for us to work together in unity. Let us embrace the twelfth Imam, Mohammad al-Mahdi, as we await his return to unify mankind.

> And hold ye fast by the Rope of Allah all together, and
> be not divided (among yourselves) … (Qur'an 3:103)

Chapter 17

The Hidden Imam

Central to Shi'a philosophy regarding the Hidden Imam, Imam Mohammad al-Mahdi, are the doctrines of *ghayba* (occultation) and *raj'a* (return). Relative to occultation, the Shi'a believe that Allah hid Imam al-Mahdi in order to safeguard and preserve his life. The occultation has two phases, the minor occultation (*ghaybat-us-sughra*) and the major occultation (*ghaybat-ul-kubra*). During the minor occultation, the Imam was able to communicate with mankind via his representatives, while in the major occultation he remains the spiritual guardian to mankind without any representatives. Eventually, the Imam will return (raj'a) and appear to the people of the world. Just as previous prophets foretold the coming of Prophet Mohammad, the prophet of Islam foretold the birth of Imam Mohammad al-Mahdi. He is the son of the eleventh Imam, Hassan al-Askari. Often referred to as *al-Mahdi* (the Guided One), *al-Imam al-Asr* (the Imam of the Period), *al-Qa'im* (the One to Arise), *Bagiyyat Allah* (Remnant of Allah), *Imam al-Muntazar* (The Awaited Imam), and *Sahib al-Zaman* (Master of the Age), the life of the twelfth Imam, Imam al-Mahdi, consists of four periods:

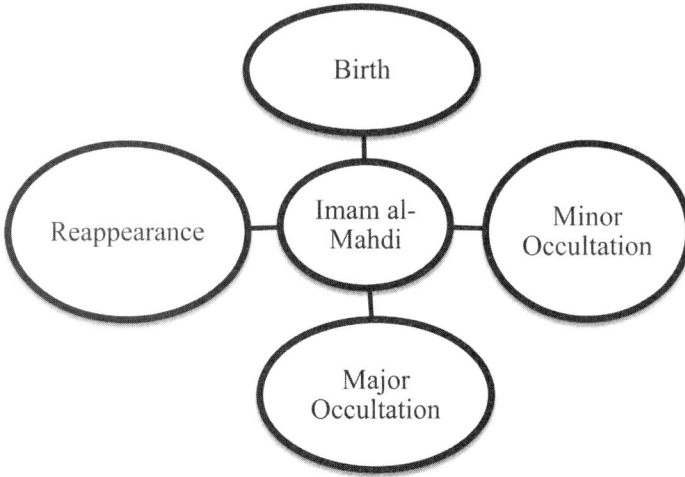

- *First Period*: AD 869 to AD 874
- *Second Period*: AD 874 to AD 941
- *Third Period*: AD 941 to reappearance of Imam
- *Fourth Period*: reappearance of Imam until his death

During the first period of five years since birth, Imam Mohammad al-Mahdi is introduced and recognized. The second period is the minor occultation that lasts sixty-seven years, a time in which the Imam communicated to the ummah through four pious deputies. In the service of Imam al-Mahdi, these deputies presented the problems of the Shi'as to the Imam, who in turn provided the answers to be conveyed back to the people:

- First Deputy: Abu Amr Usman Ibn Saeed Amri (AD 874–AD 880)
- Second Deputy: Abu Jafar Mohammad Ibn Usman Ibn Saeed Amri (AD 880–AD 917)
- Third Deputy: Abul Qasim Husain Ibn Ruh Nawbakhti (AD 917–AD 938)
- Fourth Deputy: Abul Hasan Ali Ibn Mohammad Seymouri (AD 938–AD 941)

Source: Abu Ja'far Muhammad b. al-Hasan b. Ali b. al-Hasan al-Tusi, *Ghaibat-e-Tusi*, p. 353 (first deputy); p. 362 (second deputy); p. 387 (third deputy); and p. 394 (fourth deputy). Dates are estimates from various sources.

The third period is the major occultation. Direct relations with the ummah began with the death of the fourth deputy and lasts until the Imam's reappearance. It is a time of struggle and endeavor for Shi'a scholars and Muslims to have a spiritual connection with the Imam. The fourth period begins with the Imam's reappearance from his major occultation and lasts until his death, the dates which are known only to Allah. During this time, the Imam reemerges to free the people from aggression and oppression and to rid the world of tyranny and injustice.

Over the centuries, the question of the Hidden Imam, Mohammad al-Mahdi, has been questioned, researched, and discussed. Skeptics take the view that there is no benefit in having an Imam that cannot be seen in order to address the ills of the society and needs of mankind. On the other hand, the true believers and faithful hold steadfastly and tenaciously to the premise that there are, in fact, numerous benefits derived during his major occultation. For example, Imam Mahdi is the link to the spiritual world that helps us escape from the pitfalls of materialism and complacency.

Birth of Imam al-Mahdi

Relative to the birth of Imam al-Mahdi, Shi'a and Sunni scholars are divided. While the Shi'a unequivocally state that he was the son of the eleventh Imam, Hassan al-Askari, some Sunni scholars agree with the Shi'a premise while other Sunni scholars refute it. Let us examine just some of the many Sunni scholars that agree Imam al-Mahdi is the son of Imam Hassan al-Askari:

+ "Abu al-Qasim Muhammad b. Hasan was born in the year 255 AH/873 CE in Samarra. His father's name was Hasan Khalis.

Among the titles (of this last Imam) are: Hujjat, Khalaf Salih (righteous offspring) and Muntazar (awaited one) … These hadith-reports confirm the existence of Imam Hasan 'Askari's son, who is in concealment and will appear later." (Inlagg 2013 [Muhammad b. Talha Shafi'i, *Matalib al-Su'al*, 1287 AH edition, p. 89])

+ "Section Twelve on the Life of Abu al-Qasim Muhammad, Hujjat, Khalaf Salih, the son of Abu Muhammad Hasan Khalis: He is the Twelfth Imam of Shi'a." (Inlagg 2013 [Ibn Sabbagh Maliki, *Fusul al-Muhimma*, 2nd ed., p. 273 and p. 286])

+ "His (Imam Hasan al-Askari) son's name is Muhammad, and his patronymic is Abu 'Abd Allah and Abu al-Qasim. He is the Proof of Allah's existence, the Master of the Age, the Qa'im, and the Muntazar. The Imamat has come to an end with him." (Inlagg 2013 [Yusuf b. Qazughli, *Tadhkirat Khawass al-Umma*, p. 363])

+ "Muhammad is the son of Hasan 'Askari. His mother was a slave girl by the name of Narjis or Sayqal or Sawsan. His patronymic is Abu al-Qasim. The Twelver Shi'ites know him as: Hujjat, Mahdi, Khalaf Salih, Qa'im, Muntazar, and Master of the Age." (Inlagg 2013 [Shablanji, *Nur al-Absar*, Cairo edition, p. 342])

+ "He has not left a son besides Abu al-Qasim, who is known as Muhammad and Hujjat. That boy was five years old when his father died." (Inlagg 2013 [Ibn Hajar, *al-Sawa'iq al-Muharriqa*, p. 206])

+ "Muhammad, who is also known as Mahdi, was five years old at the time of his father's death." (Inlagg 2013 [Muhammad Amin Baghdadi, *Saba'ik al-Dhahab*, p. 78])

+ "Abu al-Qasim Muhammad b. al-Hasan al-'Askari is the Twelfth Imam of the Imamiyya, that is the Twelver Shi'ites. The Shi'ites believe that is the one who is the awaited Qa'im and the Mahdi." (Inlagg 2013 [Ibn Khallikan, *Wafayat al-A'yan*, 1284 AH edition, Vol. 2., p. 24])

+ "Muhammad was the son of Hasan. His patronymic is Abu al-Qasim. The Imamiyya acknowledge that he is the Hujjat, the

Qa'im, and the Mahdi." (Inlagg 2013 [Mir Khwand, *Rawdat al-Safa*, Vol. 3, p. 143])

Furthermore, Sunni scholars (*Sahih Bukhari*, *Sahih Muslim*, *Al-Tirmidhi*, *Ibn Majah*, *Abu Dawud*, and *Al-Nasa'i*) authenticate the following:

- Imam al-Mahdi will return to fill the Earth with justice. (*Abu Dawud*, Vol. 4, Book 35, Hadith 4290)
- Imam al-Mahdi is from Prophet Mohammad's Ahl al-Bayt. (*Ibn Majah*, Vol. 5, Book 36, Hadith 4085)
- Imam al-Mahdi is from the children of Fatima, daughter of Prophet Mohammad. (*Ibn Majah*, Vol. 5, Book 36, Hadith 4086)
- Prophet Jesus will follow Imam al-Mahdi and pray behind him. (*Sahih Muslim*, Vol. 1, Book 1, Hadith 395)
- The antichrist, Dajjal, will be slain by Prophet Jesus. (*Ibn Majah*, Vol. 5, Book 36, Hadith 4077)

According to Sunni scholars, Prophet Jesus will kill the antichrist. However, according to Shia scholars, Imam al-Mahdi will kill the antichrist (Al-Qarashi 2006; Bilgrami 2005).

Al-Mahdi's Occultation

Sunni and Shi'a Muslims are awaiting a person referred to as Mohammad al-Mahdi. However, some Sunni scholars claim that the Mahdi is just a Muslim leader who will act as a caliph. On the other hand, Shi'a Muslims say that al-Mahdi disappeared at the age of five and went into hiding (occultation) to return in the future, the date known only by Allah. Following are the quotes of Sunni scholars regarding Imam Mohammad al-Mahdi:

- "Al-Mahdi is one of us, the members of the Household (Ahl al-Bayt)." (*Ibn Majah*, Vol. 5, Book 36, Hadith 4085; *Abu Dawud*,

Vol. 4, Book 35, Hadith 4284; *Al-Tirmidhi*, V4, Book 31, Hadith 2230)

+ "The Messenger of Allah said: 'Al-Mahdi is one of the children of Fatima (the Prophet's daughter).'" (*Ibn Majah*, Vol. 5, Book 36, Hadith 4086)

+ "We, the sons of Abdul-Muttalib, will be the leaders of the people of Paradise: myself (Prophet Mohammad), Hamzah, Ali, Ja'far, Hasan, Husain, and Mahdi." (*Ibn Majah*, Vol. 5, Book 36, Hadith 4087)

+ "It was narrated from Ali that the Prophet said: 'If there were only one day left of time, Allah would send a man from my family who would fill it with justice as it was filled with injustice.'" (*Abu Dawud*, Vol. 4, Book 35, Hadith 4283)

+ "It was narrated from Abdullah bin Ja'far Ar-Raqqi (he said): Abu Al-Malih Al-Hasan bin Umar narrated to us, from Ziyad bin Bayan, from Ali bin Nufail, from Sa'eed bin Al-Musayyab, from Umm Salama, who said: 'I heard the Messenger of Allah say: The Mahdi is of my offspring, one of the descendants of Fatimah.'" (*Abu Dawud*, Vol. 4, Book 35, Hadith 4284)

Regarding Imam al-Mahdi's occultation, the following Sunni scholars confirm it:

+ "Al-Mahdi is from my progeny. His name is similar to mine and his epithet is similar to mine. In his physique and character he looks like me. He will be in a state of occultation and there will be confusion (Hayra) in which people will wander about. Then he will come forth like a shooting star to fill the earth with justice and equity as it was filled before with injustice and inequity." (*Al-Tirmidhi*, Vol. 4, pp. 505–506)

+ "He is the 12th Imam and is known by the titles 'Abu Qasim', 'Al Hujjut' (The Proof), 'Al Qaim' (The Standing), 'Al Mahdi' (The Guide), 'Al-Muntazir' (The Awaited), and 'Sahib az Zaman' (Honor of our time) ... people are of the opinion he entered a cave in Sarman Rai, his followers still await his coming, this happened 265 Hijri some say 270 Hijri ..." (ShiaPen Newsletter, *Revealing the Truth*, www.shiapen.com [*Shawahid Nabuwat*, p. 198])

- "Allama in his book titled 'Mustahab al Yawaqiat Wa al Jawahir fi Aqaid' says, 'The condition for Qayyamat include the reappearance of Imam al-Mahdi, appearance of Dajjal, sudden appearance of many new diseases, sunset from the west, disappearance of Qur'an, appearance and victory of Gog and Magog.' After this he says, 'These events would occur ... and that is the time when Imam Mahdi reappearance is expected, who is the son of Imam Hasan al Askari, and was born on 15th Shaban, 255 Hijri and is still alive, and would end up meeting Isa-ibn-Maryam. At present, he is 706 years old.'" (ShiaPen Newsletter, *Revealing the Truth*, www.shiapen. com [*Al-Yawaqit Wal Jawahir*, 2nd ed., p. 127])

- "It is said that he was martyred by being poisoned, and apart from Abul Qasim Mohammad, had no other sons, who was at the tender age of five when his father passed away. But Allah provided him with knowledge, and he is known as the awaited savior, for he went into occultation and no one knows his whereabouts." (ShiaPen Newsletter, *Revealing the Truth*, www. shiapen.com [Ibn Hajar al-Haythami, *al-Sawa'iq al-Muhriqah*, p. 208])

- "According to Sheikh Iraqi, Imam al-Mahdi was born in 255 Hijri. According to Sheikh Ali al Khawas, during his times, which was 958 Hijri, Imam al-Mahdi's age would be 703 years. Ahmed Ramli also said that Imam al-Mahdi is real, as Imam Abdul Wahab Sharani has said." (ShiaPen Newsletter, *Revealing the Truth*, www.shiapen.com [Grand Mufti Diyar al-Hazarma Abdur Rehman bin Mohammed bin Husain bin Umar al-Mashoor Alvi, *Baghiyat ul Mustarshadeen*, p. 296])

- "At the time of his father's death, Imam Abu al Qasim Muhammad ibn Hasan al Askari was five years old ... vanished in a cave at Baghdad in 266 Hijri … who would reappear just before Judgment Day and before that he would go into two occultations, one the minor one and the other one would be the major one. During the minor occultation, which would start following his birth, there would be contact between him and his Shia, whereas the major occultation would start after the minor one and would continue till he reappears …" (ShiaPen Newsletter, *Revealing the Truth*, www.shiapen.com [Abdu al Abbas Ahmed ibn Yousuf Demashqi al Qirmani al Mutawafi, 1019 Hijri, *Tarikh Akhbar al-Daul Fi Asar al-Awal*, p. 118])

+ "Imam Mahdi al Muntazir al Hujjat son of Imam Hasan Askari was born in 255 Shabaan and was born five years before his father's death. Due to the fear of the Leaders his father kept his birth a secret. Imam Muhammad is the awaited Khalifa, the pious Imam of our time, his title is known as 'Mahdi.'" (ShiaPen Newsletter, *Revealing the Truth*, www.shiapen.com [Shaykh al-Shabrawi al-Shafiyee, *Kitab Itehaf Bejub al-Ashraaf*, p. 189])

+ "Imam al-Mahdi is Imam Hasan al Askari's son, who is alive and living. He is alive since his disappearance until now. This is just like Prophet Isa, Khizr and Ilyas, Imam al-Mahdi is likewise also alive." (ShiaPen Newsletter, *Revealing the Truth*, www. shiapen.com [Sheikh al Muhadduth Qadhi Abu Abdullah Mohammed bin Yousaf bin Mohammad Gangi Shafi, *Al Biyan fi Akhbar*, chapter 20; Al-Ganji al-Shafiyee (recorded by Imam of Ahle Sunnah Mustafa ibn Abdullah Chulpi), *Kifayaat al-Talib*, p. 308])

Reappearance of Imam al-Mahdi

The foregoing affirms the reemergence of Imam al-Mahdi and the necessity for an Imam throughout the ages. If there is no Imam, then mankind's link to Allah will lessen until disbelief triumphs over faith. Moreover, if there is no Imam, the purpose of worshipping Allah will diminish and eventually become pointless. As Muslims, we become immersed in the Imam al-Mahdi's creative energy that illuminates our hearts and minds by sustaining us within the sanctity of Islam and belief in Allah. Even though the Imam's physical presence is hidden, he will reappear to fulfill Allah's decree in all its manifestation. Likewise, followers of the Jewish and Christian religions also adhere to the concept of the awaited Messiah. Christians and Muslims believe that Jesus was the Messiah expected by the Jews, but the Jews reject this idea, alleging that Jesus was a false Messiah. However, the belief in the eventual coming of the Messiah (Mashiach or anointed one) is a basic fundamental part of traditional Judaism.

The metaphor of the reemergence of Imam al-Mahdi is like that of the sun. Just as the clouds hide the rays of the sun, its rays reappear and provide the energy that sustains life on earth. Similarly, the Imam will reappear from his major occultation, along with Prophet Jesus, to enlighten mankind and bring justice to the world. Imam Ja'far as-Sadiq put it in proper perspective:

> Sulayman, the narrator, asked Imam Ja'far as-Sadiq: "How does mankind benefit from an invisible and hidden representative?" Imam Ja'far said: "Just as they benefit from the sun behind the clouds." (*Bihar al-Anwar*, Vol. 52, Chapter 20, p. 92)

There is wisdom about the sun being hidden by the clouds, as only Allah knows what it is. However, we believe that the sun is there without actually seeing it at that time. Likewise, we also believe in the existence of Imam al-Mahdi without seeing him while he is in his major occultation. Just as there is hope that the rays of the sun will reemerge, so too is their hope that Imam al-Mahdi will reemerge. Even though the sun is hidden behind the clouds, it continues to bring benefit to mankind. Likewise, Imam al-Mahdi, the expected one, also brings benefit to mankind, as sincere believers do not give up hope but remain patient, awaiting his reappearance.

Optimism triumphs over pessimism as hope advances the Islamic ideal even in the presence of despair, injustice, poverty, genocide, immorality, and wars. Hence, the Imam in his major occultation is evident and apparent to the faithful who are hopeful and hold steadfast to his existence, purpose, and meaning of wilayat (guardianship). As Muslims, we should embrace the Straight Path and the certainty of Imam al-Mahdi's major occultation and be firm in our belief that his presence can be felt and seen within our hearts.

Opposing Views Relative to Occultation

Throughout history, the question of the major occultation of Imam al-Mahdi has been debated between Sunnis and Shi'as. The prevailing inquiry centers around whether he should be born at the time when he will rid the world of injustice and tyranny or be born centuries before that time. Sunnis would espouse the view that his minor occultation at the age of five was far too young to have prepared him to assume the role since he would not have had the intellectual development or religious and scientific knowledge.

Additionally, the Sunnis question that if al-Mahdi were in his major occultation, why hasn't he reappeared earlier to establish justice since he would have witnessed the political disasters, genocides, wars, and the many social upheavals that have afflicted the innocent? Moreover, non-Muslims question the validity of a single person having the ability to rid the world of injustice and tyranny whereas a nation that has the military capability cannot. For non-Muslims, doubt plays an important role in totally rejecting the concept of al-Mahdi, since for one to live for many centuries is unfathomable and unrealistic.

Even if medical research can result in scientifically being able to prolong one's life, can it justify the notion of one living for over a thousand years? Undeniably, scientific progress of today is far distant from the realization of this possibility, although the transformation of prolonging life is both scientific and logical. Hence, the prolongation of life is scientifically possible. However, as al-Mahdi's transformation via the major occultation precedes current scientific knowledge, the likelihood of being able to survive for over a thousand years is possible only by the grace of Allah.

The birth of Jesus and his return to accompany Imam al-Mahdi is another indication of the prolonging of one's life. Why do Sunnis accept the return of Jesus after his absence of over a thousand years and not accept the reappearance of Imam al-Mahdi from his major occultation? Or why should Sunnis believe that Noah lived among his people for 950 years and reject the reality of al-Mahdi living for over a thousand years?

Undeniably, the prolongation of life for Noah, Jesus, and Imam al-Mahdi runs counter to natural laws; however, Allah protected them and preserved their lives for a purpose. Furthermore, our Sunni brethren need to be reminded of chapter 18 of the Qur'an, *Al-Kahf* (The Cave), that describes how some youth wanted to escape from the worldly injustices and false rulers who transgressed and substituted lies for truth. While hiding in the cave, Allah made the youth sleep for 309 years. When Allah awakened them from their long sleep, they witnessed the collapse of transgression and the triumph of truth over falsehood. Isn't this a form of occultation?

If we can accept the verses of the Qur'an describing occultation and longevity of life, then why is it difficult for our Sunni brothers and sisters to come to the realization that the miracle of occultation for Imam al-Mahdi is just another miracle of Allah? Then the question arises as to why a minor occultation and then a major occultation? Why not just a single occultation? Simply, during al-Mahdi's minor occultation of about seventy years, it was necessary for his four deputies to be the mediators between him and the ummah (community) to address their concerns. Therefore, the ummah would be better prepared to accept the notion of ghayba (absence) in anticipation of the gradual return of the Imam. Thereafter, the Muslims themselves, without mediation from deputies, would feel the presence of al-Mahdi and believe in his second return (major occultation). Moreover, Muslims would adapt themselves to his absence, thereby enabling them to accept the major occultation and his reappearance.

Often, too much time and effort is spent on trying to determine when Imam al-Mahdi will reemerge and what his appearance will look like. These are unknowns to mankind, as only Allah knows these secrets. Furthermore, Imam al-Mahdi's role differs from the prophets who came with the message and the other infallible Imams who explained the details of the message. Moreover, the main role of Imam al-Mahdi is to change the world for the better, while the role of the other infallible Imams was to guard the Qur'an from distortion, bring about unity of the ummah, and strengthen Ahl al-Bayt. There is no need for him to discuss the details of the message but rather to bring about equity and justice to a world filled with tyranny and injustice.

Undoubtedly, Imam al-Mahdi is Allah's conclusive argument to make equity and justice prevail. Are we ready to support his cause, which is the cause of Allah? We are reminded that many of the Kufans who initially pledged and supported Imam Hussein reneged and directed their swords against him. Therefore, our responsibility is to prepare to be firm in our commitment and to be enlisted among his soldiers and leaders of the Straight Path. This enables us to pursue the path of Imam al-Mahdi by educating others about Islam and to face the numerous challenges that are directed against Islam. We can also prepare ourselves to be responsive to the true nature of Islam and carry out our Islamic responsibilities and obligations to the fullest extent possible.

Responsibilities of Muslims Prior to Return of Imam al-Mahdi

The return of Imam al-Mahdi from his major occultation is inevitable. As we await his return, we must conduct ourselves with the utmost sense of piety and righteousness. This necessitates a great deal of patience, preparation, and an attitude and behavior that are based on the Islamic personality:

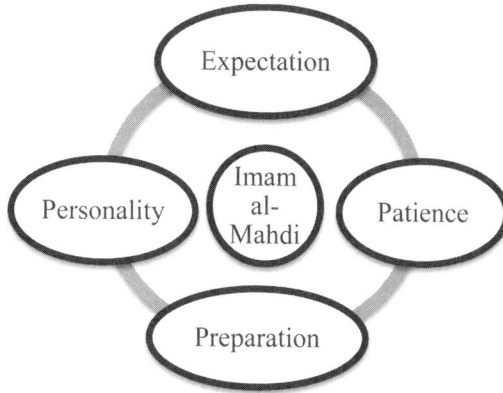

The essence of this expectation is our patience (sabr) that enables us to endure the trials and tribulations of life with all its hardships and adversities. It is patience that self-actualizes the unity within our self in order to bring about an Islamic personality that nurtures us to become better Muslims. Certainly, self-discovery, self-development, self-awareness, and self-confidence are essentials of patience that take a great deal of concentration and effort to acquire. Patience will help us be what we want to be because attainment is within reach if we persevere. But remember, patience is not passive; on the contrary, it is active. It is concentrated strength. Patience is preparation of the self toward the Straight Path.

Before the return of Imam al-Mahdi, we have a great deal of preparation that needs to be done. Once we have prepared ourselves to attain the Islamic personality that sets us on the Straight Path, we will be better equipped to overcome biases and prejudices based on tribalism, culture, race, color, creed, and other obstacles that separate people and erode the unity of humanity. Preparation also takes on a social obligation insofar as we strive to rid ourselves of injustice and tyranny. We cannot be complacent about the inhumane treatment of people throughout the world but must take an active part in abolishing and eliminating unjust systems of government. Justice must prevail in all aspects of human life whether cultural, social, political, government, legal, ethical, or economical. It is justice that is a major symbol of Imam al-Mahdi's global government, as Allah will fill the Earth with justice and eradicate injustice through him.

The foundation of justice is the inner self that seeks peace, harmony, and a sense of positive direction. In today's society, we seek instant gratification. However self-fulfillment through one's perspective is not instant. Becoming who we want to be is not instant. We cannot do everything at once, but we can do something at once! Controlling the Islamic self is not an easy task. It requires control of one's inner thoughts and actions. Becoming enlightened in Islam is to understand one's self-concept, control one's self-esteem, and attain self-fulfillment by way of patience. Control is achieved by way of order and harmony within the self.

Within our personality structure, we have individual selves. Each of these selves has a unique system. For example, the self has its own goals and priorities. Each has its own perceptions and motives. Each has its own style and development cycle. Each has its own limits of tolerance and emotional sensitivity. Dynamic and interactive, our sub-selves can communicate with each other to form a decision. When making decisions, the sub selves condition our true basic self. We are not born with a personality. Our personality is formed, shaped, and developed in the framework of our relationships with our family and environment. Personality is consistent with individuality, as we behave in a manner consistent within each of us. It is the consistency of our behavior that defines the kind of personality we are associated with.

We need to develop unity within ourselves by holding fast to the rope of Allah. The Islamic personality makes the believer cherish his human dignity and prestige and accept his responsibilities as a Muslim. The best example of the Islamic personality is that of Prophet Mohammad and his progeny. The justification of Islamic morality promises the continuance of life in the hereafter for the morally good individuals. Faith, righteous deeds, truth, and patience are the basic virtues of Islamic morality. We gain eternal happiness through moral virtues. We must cleanse our thoughts and our hearts in order to attain ultimate and final perfection, which leads us to the Straight Path. We must free ourselves from the spider's web of this frail world. We must walk the path of struggle against immoral tendencies.

All that we can do is to strive in the way of Allah. With firmness of purpose, determination, and patience, we can attain the mercy of Allah. The ideal Islamic personality is one where faith leads to good deeds and good deeds lead to faith. By helping others, we are in effect helping ourselves to become better Muslims. We sincerely concentrate on every aspect of life as we continue to understand the beauty and wisdom of Islam. We must continue to remember Allah and to win the satisfaction of the Creator.

Development of the Islamic personality takes a great deal of preparation. We must prepare ourselves against the ego, which is the belief that self-interest is the just and proper motive for all human conduct. It is the excessive preoccupation with one's own well-being and interests, usually accompanied by an inflated sense of self-importance. It is the tendency to evaluate everything in relation to one's own interests— that is, self-centeredness. This self-centeredness and self-absorption within oneself immensely diminishes the chances of ever reaching moral fulfillment and self-respect. Keeping occupied with thoughts and actions of materialism, greed, center of attention, and conceit, the person continues to fall deeper into a spiral pit he cannot escape. The obedience to the self further erodes the soul, as the person commits every act of transgression, deception, and sedition in order to achieve superiority or authority over others. In a nutshell, he begins to worship himself, thereby becoming totally impervious to spirituality and the common good.

A Muslim fulfills his needs by devoting himself to spirituality and not to vanity and conceit. Spirituality helps mold one's personality and sets the individual on the right track. With humility and self-sacrifice, one can recover his sense of worth and regain his spirituality, free of pride and complacency. Preparation to become better Muslims also includes self-forgiveness and self-criticism. The self-realization of forgiveness is when one is willing to forgive when he has the power to take revenge. Forgiveness is an acknowledgment of a person's pledge to not inflict harm on anyone and to make a concerted effort to remedy his inner self toward one of peace and harmony. Toward this end, forgiveness benefits both the one who harms as well as the one who is harmed.

Self-criticism is a necessary requirement for one to bring his thoughts and actions in harmony with righteousness. A righteous Muslim constantly evaluates his actions and seeks improvement in order to bring him closer to Allah. The Muslim becomes unified within his self by overcoming his inner weakness of sins and deviant behavior. Through self-criticism, one can seek and discover his spirituality. Self-criticism brings us closer to Allah, as it intensifies and heightens our piety. It enjoins what is right and forbids what is wrong. It is the Islamic way and the Straight Path! It is the purpose and goal of Imam al-Mahdi and the Imamat of Ahl al-Bayt!

Commentary

Numerous books, articles, and analyses on both sides of the equation, Sunni and Shi'a, have been written relative to each of their positions regarding who should have been the successor to Prophet Mohammad, the issue of *fadak*, infallibility, the authenticity of hadiths and the chain of narrations, the wording of *Hadith al-Thaqalayn* (two weighty things), the site location of the *Farewell Sermon* by Prophet Mohammad, the issue of the pen and paper, the birth of Imam Mohammad al-Mahdi, the prophet's companions, members of Prophet Mohammad's Ahl al-Bayt (house of Prophet Mohammad), and myriad other issues. All of these discussions have widened the gap between their respective schools of thought and have left the Muslims in utter confusion. As author of this book, I have conducted extensive research into these issues and have documented them. Undeniably, both sides will look for loopholes within the recorded hadiths to justify their points of view.

Let's review one of the issues, the pen and paper. Sunnis and Shi'as have analyzed the issue relative to Umar ibn Khattab denying Prophet Mohammad's request for pen and paper. The Sunnis believe Umar's statement that the Qur'an is sufficient for Muslims is justified, given the prophet's failing health condition at that time. In addition, the Sunnis further state that Umar was concerned about the unconsciousness of the prophet's health and his inability to have a statement written. But then there has been no discussion as to why Umar didn't come back the next day or the day after and honor the prophet's request for pen and paper. After all, Umar was his father-in-law.

The Shi'as would contend that verses from the Qur'an unequivocally state that Allah and Prophet Mohammad must be obeyed without question; therefore, the pen and paper should have been given to him. On this note, the reliable collection of hadiths by the six Sunni historians confirms that "whoever obeys Mohammad obeys Allah, and whoever disobeys the Prophet, disobeys Allah" (appendix 5). However, Imam Ali could have later provided the prophet with pen and paper. If Imam Ali had done so, then there would have been cries from the Muslim ummah that the statement was forged.

The bottom line on this issue is that no one knows what the prophet wanted to write in his statement. Could it have been that he wanted to write his will? The prophet has instructed us all to have a written will and not to wait until we are on our deathbed to write one. Hence, not knowing what the prophet wanted to write has generated a number of what-if scenarios. Moreover, Prophet Mohammad made his will known to tens of thousands of Muslims who witnessed his *Farewell Sermon* stating that his successor was Imam Ali. Even when Imam Ali was a child and the first male convert to Islam, Prophet Mohammad made him his executor and successor, which is confirmed by both Sunni and Shi'a hadiths.

According to *Sahih Bukhari* (Vol. 6, Book 65, Hadith 4481), Umar said: "Our best judge is Ali." Even three of the six reliable Sunni collectors of hadith, *Ibn Majah*, *Al-Tirmidhi*, and *Al-Nasa'i* recorded, "My Lord ordered me (Mohammad) that nobody can discharge my duty except myself or Ali" (appendix 5). Furthermore, five of the six reliable collectors of hadith, including *Sahih Bukhari* and *Sahih Muslim*, recorded that the prophet said, "You (Ali) are to me (Mohammad) as Aaron was to Moses, but there will be no Prophet after me" (appendix 5). Relative to this quote, Prophet Mohammad never made that statement about any of the other companions. Did not Prophet Aaron lead the community during the absence of Prophet Moses? Hence, Imam Ali would also lead the community during the absence or death of Prophet Mohammad.

Since both Sunnis and Shi'as accept the many virtues and leadership of Imam Ali, he would be the logical person to unify the Muslim community in partnership with Prophet Mohammad. Unity cannot come about relative to the other companions, as the wounds are too deep relative to how each looks at them, positively or negatively. Imam Ali supported the companions of Prophet Mohammad, only for the sake of unity. Imam Ali and the eleven Imams of his progeny that followed all preached unity of the ummah even when they were harassed and tormented, which led to their martyrdom. Can there be greater nobility than preaching unity in the midst of their oppression and persecution? Moreover, a review of the Sunni hadiths does not indicate any negative remarks regarding the twelve Imams of Ahl al-Bayt; rather they extol their virtues.

Today, we are in the twenty-first century. All of the companions of Prophet Mohammad have long since passed. It is not wise or healthy to continue to abase any of them in the mosques or media. If any of the prophet's companions have done wrong, then Allah will judge accordingly.

We are reminded by the courage of Caliph Umar ibn Abdul Aziz when he banned the negative speeches and slurs against Imam Ali in the mosques and in the community, only to have his life shortened at thirty-eight years of age. Imam Ali named three of his children, Abu Bakr, Umar, and Uthman, two of whom were martyred with their half brother, Imam Hussein, on the field of Karbala. The name Abu Bakr was not a common name at that time. Perhaps Imam Ali named his children after these companions so as to emphasize the importance of unity within the Muslim ummah. So let us follow the lifestyle and behavior of Imam Ali as we move forward to unify Sunni and Shi'a Muslims. The price we pay not to unify is already witnessed in the global arena, as non-Muslims are preying on this fragmentation to benefit their own whims, desires, and capitalistic notions. Let us escape the snake pit of this entrapment and begin a new dawn of brotherhood and solidarity.

Epilogue

When writing this book, the author viewed the concept of the Imamat with an open mind and intense concentration regarding its significance and meaning within the realm of Islam. In the course of connecting each piece of information with an adjacent piece, the understanding and manifestation of Imamat became evident and clear. Undoubtedly, one's interpretation of Qur'anic verses and hadiths (traditions) is gained not just by a piece of information or the specific view of one verse or tradition but also by how each fits within the notion of Islam. Hence, all of the pieces must fit. In addition, each of us, whether Sunni or Shi'a, comes to understand Islam with our own set of assumptions, which we have learned over the years. Undeniably, these assumptions are important to each of us. Unfortunately, how we come to understand what Prophet Mohammad has taught us has generated various interpretations that have put a barrier to unifying the Muslim ummah (community).

These roadblocks to unity have caused a great deal of animosity, hatred, and fear among those espousing different views. However, the only way we can realistically assess if a piece of information fits is to first find the common piece or pieces that are accepted by everyone, and then begin to build on that premise. We must arrive at this understanding with a mind free from presuppositions and preexisting ideas and views. Therefore, the author began with two pieces of information that are accepted by all Sunnis and Shi'as—Prophet Mohammad and Imam Ali ibn Abi Talib. Moreover, the author chose these two luminaries of Islam as the foundation of a paradigm that begins with everyone's acceptance. That being the case, we must accept the teachings and guidance of these two luminaries and those to whom they passed on the leadership (i.e., the infallible Imams).

There are no negative narrations concerning Ahl al-Bayt recorded in any of the six reliable Sunni collectors of hadiths. Rather, these hadiths give only positive descriptions, commentaries, and accounts of Ahl al-Bayt as to their virtues and moral ethics, such as nobility, truthfulness, piety, knowledge, wisdom, patience, leadership, personality, character, and the right of succession to lead the ummah.

Although it often appears that there is no common ground between Sunnis and Shi'as, usually there is. Even though uncompromising conflicts tend to be characterized by wide and deep-rooted interests and value differences between them, with concerted effort they can find areas of commonality. Each of us has similar fundamental needs, such as security, sense of identity, sense of belonging, and sense of value. Undeniably, we all value human life and family relationships. By coming together, we can find areas of commonality that lead to better relationships, effective interaction, and conflict transformation. As we explore our feelings, fears, and sense of hurt and hopelessness, we can come to the realization that we are very similar to others on both sides of the conflict.

As we begin to understand the needs of each other, our lives will be enriched and our children will be the heirs of our unity. Each of us has distinct, inherent qualities that make us who we are. Each piece of information is important and unifies with other pieces to contribute and enhance the beauty of the total picture.

In Islam, the key to unity is for Sunnis and Shi'as to respect and develop bonds of trust with each other. With trust, we can withstand anything and unite as one idea, one people, and one community.

Sunnis and Shi'as have debated the issue of the Imamat of the Twelve Infallible Imams for centuries. A great deal of confusion enters into the discussion because neither have fully understood the message of unity that Imam Ali ibn Abi Talib lived and died for, although they both revere him highly. The pursuit of this unity has resulted in the martyrdom of the Imams, as they stood steadfast in propagating it in order to protect the Straight Path and safeguard Islam.

A primary objective of each of the Twelve Infallible Imams of Ahl al-Bayt was to promote a change in the religious, social, economic, and political structure in order to unify the Islamic society. As such, they steadfastly espoused the premise that the life of Muslims must conform to the Islamic laws and principles established by Prophet Mohammad.

Just as Allah sent prophets and messengers to warn and guide mankind, so too did Allah appoint Imams as guardians to continue the guidance of Prophet Mohammad. That guidance was to instill in the minds of the Muslims the correct teachings of the Qur'an and hadiths. Hence, this guidance could not be given to just anyone but rather to those who are imbued with the knowledge, wisdom, obedience, authority, and infallibility to protect the Qur'an from distortion, corruption, and misinterpretation. The Qur'an and Ahl al-Bayt complement each other. As the Qur'an is a guide, so too are Prophet Mohammad and the Imamat guides.

As infallible personalities, the Imamat of Ahl al-Bayt are always in a state of ritual purity, which is why Allah endorsed their purification:

> Verily, Allah intendeth but to keep off from you (every kind of) uncleanness, O' ye the People of the House, and purify you (with) a thorough purification. (Qur'an 33:33)

In addition to this verse, there are numerous other verses in the Qur'an that make it abundantly clear that an understanding of the inner and implied meaning of the Qur'an is relegated to the purified few that Allah has chosen. Allah has provided them with the innate capability to interpret and disseminate their understanding of the Qur'an to the entire Muslim community. They are the ones who have the ability to come in contact with and fully understand the abundant source of knowledge and wisdom in the Qur'an:

> Whoever taketh as his guardian, Allah and His Apostle (Mohammad) and those who believe, verily, (he hath joined) Allah's battalion; they are those that shall (always) be triumphant. (Qur'an 5:56)

The term *triumphant* in this verse refers to the triumph of Islam as a way of life, its culture and civilization, and in the fulfillment of the Islamic ideals. The Twelfth Infallible Imam is in his major occultation, and he will return to earth with Prophet Jesus, at which time they will be in unison with each other as they *triumph* and address the ills of the societies. In the interim, another channel of religious teaching and training is available. These are the ulema, or religious teachers and scholars, who are not infallible but are schooled in the philosophy and jurisprudence of Prophet Mohammad and the Imamat of Ahl al-Bayt to impart knowledge to their followers.

We are going to have to revive a passion for the principle of unity among all schools of Islamic thought. Having the commitment to abide by Allah's commands is the avenue toward brotherhood and solidarity. We must be cognizant of the fact that our passion to reject each other over issues of politics, theology, and provinciality is not virtuous. It is an indication that we are too often controlled by our ego and not by Allah's commandments.

We need a passion for unity. Unity is not something we invent; it is Allah's gift. Let us exhaust every possibility and leave no stone unturned in the quest for unity. Let our efforts be the result of an earnest desire and willingness to succeed as we celebrate our differences as windows of opportunities. Let us uproot ignorance with knowledge as we learn to cooperate with one another. As Allah has already given us that passion for unity, we must move forward to fulfill his command. Our pledge to unity must begin within ourselves, within our families, within our communities, and with each other. As we engage in dialogue, let us seek to understand before we seek to be understood. In winning the unity, we must overcome our prejudice in order to rebel against the ignorance of intolerance and fanaticism.

As Muslims, we should embrace Imam Ali ibn Abi Talib as the rightful successor to Prophet Mohammad to *know* the Straight Path and embrace Prophet Mohammad and the Twelve Infallible Imams as the Imamat of Ahl al-Bayt to *follow* the Straight Path.

May Allah guide us to the Straight Path that leads to eternal bliss in the hereafter!

Appendix 1

Brief Timeline of Islamic Events

AD 570   - Birth of Mohammad

610   - Mohammad visited by Angel Gabriel in cave near Mecca

         - Angel Gabriel recites revelations of the Qur'an

         - Angel Gabriel informs Mohammad he is Allah's Seal of Prophets

622   - Prophet's hijra from Mecca to Medina

         - Foundation of ummah

         - Prophet establishes first Islamic community

         - Prophet establishes the first interfaith constitution (Charter of Medina)

624   - Battle of Badr, first victory for Muslims over Meccans

         - Direction of prayer is changed from Jerusalem to Mecca

         - Fast of Ramadan instituted

625   - Battle of Uhud where Muslims are defeated by Meccans outside Medina

627   - Battle of the Trench where Meccans and Jews fail to conquer Muslims in Medina

630   - Conquest of Mecca and rededication of the Ka'bah to monotheism

632   - Farewell Sermon of Prophet Mohammad at Ghadir Khumm

         - Prophet receives final revelation of Qur'an

         - Prophet declares Imam Ali ibn Abi Talib as his successor (mawla)

	- Death of Prophet Mohammad and Fatima as-Zahra
634	- Death of Caliph Abu Bakr (caliph from 632 to 634)
644	- Assassination of Caliph Umar (caliph from 634 to 644)
656	- Assassination of Caliph Uthman (caliph from 644 to 656)
632–661	- Period of the caliphate of Abu Bakr, Umar, Uthman, and Imam Ali
	- Collection of Qur'anic chapters and verses in written form by Imam Ali
	- Beginning of collection of hadiths (traditions)
	- Islamic Empire consists of Syria, Palestine, Mesopotamia, Egypt, North Africa, Persian, and Byzantine Empires
661	- Martyrdom of Caliph Imam Ali ibn Abi Talib (Caliph from 656 to 661)
661–750	- Umayyad Dynasty ruled from Damascus
670	- Martyrdom of Imam Hassan ibn Imam Ali
680	- Martyrdom of Imam Hussein and followers at Karbala (Iraq)
	- Imam Ali ibn Imam Hussein continues line of infallible Imams
682	- Death of Lady Zainab
711	- Muslims enter Spain, India, and most of the Iberian Peninsula
712	- Martyrdom of Imam Ali ibn Imam Hussein
732	- Muslims are defeated in France by Charles Martel
733	- Martyrdom of Imam Mohammad al-Baqir ibn Imam Ali
750–1258	- Abbasid Dynasty ruled from Baghdad
765	- Martyrdom of Imam Ja'far as-Sadiq ibn Imam Mohammad al-Baqir
799	- Martyrdom of Imam Musa al-Kazim ibn Imam Ja'far as-Sadiq
818	- Martyrdom of Imam Ali al-Rida ibn Imam Musa al-Kazim

835	- Martyrdom of Imam Mohammad al-Jawad ibn Imam Ali al-Rida
868	- Martyrdom of Imam Ali al-Hadi ibn Imam Mohammad al-Jawad
869	- Birth of Imam Mohammad al-Mahdi ibn Imam Hassan al-Askari
874	- Martyrdom of Imam Hassan al-Askari ibn Imam Ali al-Hadi
	- Minor occultation of Imam Mohammad al-Mahdi
941	- Major occultation of Imam Mohammad al-Mahdi
973–1171	- Fatimid Dynasty ruled from Cairo
1000	- Islam spreads through continent of Africa
1099	- Crusaders take Jerusalem
1120	- Islam spreads through continent of Asia
1171	- Fatimid Dynasty toppled in Egypt by Saladin al-Ayyubi
1187	- Saladin al-Ayyubi retakes Jerusalem
1258–1517	- Mamluk Sultanate ruled from Cairo
1299	- Earliest Ottoman state is formed in Anatolia, Turkey
1453	- Ottomans conquer Byzantine seat at Constantinople (renamed Istanbul)
1492	- End of Umayyad rule in Spain
	- Spain conquered by Christians
1517–1924	- Ottoman Empire ruled from Constantinople (Istanbul)
1870–1924	- Muslim immigrants from the Arab world voluntarily come to the United States, until the Asian Exclusion Act is passed in 1924
	- World War I ends with defeat and dissolution of Ottoman Empire
	- European colonization of Muslim regions in Africa and Asia
1888	- Muslims from Lebanon, Syria, and Jordan migrate to the United States
1893	- Muslims from India settle in the western region of the United States

1914–1922	- Arab Muslims arrive in the metropolitan area of Detroit, Michigan
1979	- Iranian Revolution establishes Islamic Republic of Iran
2014	- Muslim population in the United States estimated at 6–7 million with over 2,000 mosques

Sources: Data derived from the following: (1) *Islam Timeline*, One-Islam.org, United Wisdom of Allah, www.one-Islam.org, 2006; (2) *Islam Timeline*, Faithology, LLC, www.faithology.com, 2014; (3) *A Chronology of the Muslim Religion: Timeline of Islam*, Religious Facts, www.religiousfacts.com, 2014.

Appendix 2

Key Achievements of Ahl al-Bayt

Prophet Mohammad

Name: Mohammad ibn Abdullah, Abu al-Qasim
Title: Rasul Allah (Messenger of Allah)
Designation: Seal of all Prophets
Birth-Death: AD 570–AD 632
Birthplace: Mecca, Saudi Arabia
Place of Death and Burial: Died of natural causes in Medina, Saudi Arabia. Buried in Medina, Saudi Arabia.

Key Achievements:

- delivered the revelations of the Qur'an to the ummah
- related the hadiths (traditions) to the ummah
- became the seal of the prophets and final messenger
- completed the Night Journey of the Ascent (Isra' and Mi'raj)
- transferred power and leadership to the Imamat
- declared Imam Ali ibn Abi Talib as his successor
- founded a state and religion
- established the Islamic brotherhood
- ratified programs for solidarity and unity
- transcended the limitations of the human mind to bring about a code of ethics, virtues, justice, and tolerance
- built the Islamic civilization

- turned a weak society into a strong, disciplined society
- enforced equality for everyone, irrespective of gender, race, ethnicity, or religion
- ended racial segregation
- made freedom of religion and thought compulsory
- instituted social institutions and social reforms to replace old Arab social order
- liberated women
- initiated first genuine interfaith dialogue (Charter of Medina)
- proclaimed general amnesty to everyone after the conquest of Mecca, even to those who had persecuted and tortured him and his followers
- rendered mercy to his enemies

Fatima

Name: Fatima
Title: as-Zahra (Shining One)
Designation: Leader of all women in this world and in paradise
Birth: AD 605–AD 615 (Est.*)
Death: AD 632
Birthplace: Mecca, Saudi Arabia
Place of Death and Burial: Cause of death not verified. Buried in Jannat al-Baqi, Medina, Saudi Arabia (exact location of grave is unknown).

Key Achievements:

- mothered Imam Hassan and Imam Hussein as well as Lady Zainab and Umm Kulthum
- stood as lone defender of Prophet Mohammad's declaration at Ghadir Khumm
- admonished those who rejected Prophet Mohammad's appointment of Imam Ali as his successor, thereby awakening the community to the injustice
- received the title as-Zahra (Shining One) and al-Batul (Chaste and Pure One)
- considered to be the leader (sayyidah) of all women in this world and in paradise
- named after her is the Fatimid Dynasty
- claimed property rights of her father by challenging Abu Bakr's refusal to cede them, particularly Fadak and a share in the produce of Khaybar

*Sources of Fatima's date of birth conflict between AD 605 and AD 615. According to Al-Kafi (Shi'a), Fatima was born in AD 614.

Imam Ali ibn Abi Talib

Name: Ali ibn Abi Talib, Abu al-Hassan
Title: Amir al-Mu'minin (Commander of the Faithful); al-Murtaza (Approved)
Designation: First of the Twelve Infallible Imams and rightful successor to Prophet Mohammad
Birth-Death: AD 600–AD 661
Birthplace: Mecca, Saudi Arabia
Place of Death and Burial: Assassinated by Abd-al-Rahman ibn Muljam, a Kharijite, in Kufa, Iraq, who slashed him with a poisoned sword while he was in prayer. Buried at the Imam Ali Mosque in Najaf, Iraq.

Key Achievements:

- compiled the entire Qur'an and arranged it in order of revelation
- appointed as the first infallible Imam of the Imamat
- proclaimed by the prophet at Ghadir Khumm to be his successor (mawla)
- declared by Prophet Mohammad as the "Gate" to the City of Knowledge
- blessed by Allah in the Qur'an as a guardian of Islam, after he gave his ring to a poor beggar while prostrating in prayer
- became caliph of the Muslim ummah
- born inside the Ka'bah
- embraced Islam as a youngster and was first to accept its invitation
- accepted the prophet's offer, as a youngster, to be his brother, executor of his will, and successor, while the prophet's uncles and relatives stood silent in their refusal
- slept in Prophet Mohammad's bed, thereby risking his own life for the safety of the prophet
- volunteered to shield the prophet from the enemies and was ready to sacrifice his life to protect the prophet

- destroyed the idols at the Ka'bah, as a directive from Allah
- given the standard bearer (flag) by Prophet Mohammad to lead the Muslims to victory at the Battle of Khyber
- during the Battle of the Trench, displayed power and energy as he defeated Amru ibn Abd Wid, the champion of the enemy
- demonstrated his creative energy in the two-powered personality of polar opposites: attraction and repulsion when dealing with his followers and enemies
- authored the book, *Peak of Eloquence (Nahjul Balagha)*

Imam Hassan ibn Ali

Name: Hassan ibn Ali, Abu Mohammad
Title: al-Mujtaba (Chosen)
Designation: Second Infallible Imam
Birth-Death: AD 625–AD 670
Birthplace: Medina, Saudi Arabia
Place of Death and Burial: Poisoned by his wife, Ja'da, on the orders of the Caliph Muawiyah. Buried in Jannat al-Baqi, Medina, Saudi Arabia.

Key Achievements:

- supported peace for the sake of Islamic unity and harmony
- devoted to peacefully propagating Islam and the teachings of Prophet Mohammad and his father, Imam Ali ibn Abi Talib
- exposed the treachery and deception of Muawiyah's peace treaty by accepting it, only to save lives from the ravages of war and stop a civil war that could have destroyed Islam
- exhibited utmost level of piety by never letting the poor and the humble feel inferior to him, as he constantly met with them in complete humility
- carried out the duties of trusteeship (as testament of Allah's covenant between Prophet Mohammad and mankind) at the highest level of sincerity and modesty, winning the praise of numerous scholars in the centuries that followed
- exhausted all means for peace that withered away during the reign of Muawiyah (who later named Yazid, his son, his successor), which necessitated and justified the revolt of Imam Hussein

Imam Hussein ibn Ali

Name: Hussein ibn Ali, Abu-Abdallah
Title: Sayed al-Shuhada (Leader of the Martyrs)
Designation: Third Infallible Imam
Birth-Death: AD 626–AD 680
Birthplace: Medina, Saudi Arabia
Place of Death and Burial: Martyred at Battle of Karbala, Iraq. Buried in the Imam Hussein Shrine in Karbala, Iraq.

Key Achievements:

-   remained completely obedient to his brother, Imam Hassan, in all matters
-   took on the responsibility, following the martyrdom of his brother, Imam Hassan, of leading the Islamic society by preaching the genuine truth of Islam
-   refused to pledge allegiance under the tyranny of Yazid, the Umayyad caliph
-   revolted and resisted against the tyranny and oppression of Yazid that led to the tragedy at Karbala
-   sacrificed his life and the life of his followers at Karbala to restore the sanctity of Islam
-   distinguished in all qualities and ethics possessing the human perfection within his personality
-   demonstrated to the world how to attain victory while being oppressed
-   instilled in the minds of Muslims and non-Muslims that the message of Karbala is intrinsic and fundamental within the ten days of Ashura
-   symbolized the essence of heroism, redemption, and sacrifice for the sake of justice and equality
-   manifested the highest principles of humanity by restoring life to human consciousness

- restored the people to the Straight Path of Islam by giving them back their dignity and self-respect
- redefined the meaning of devotion by persevering with steadfastness in times of overwhelming hardship and suffering
- fought against injustice, tyranny, and oppression by exposing hypocrisy and corruption

Lady Zainab bint Imam Ali

Name: Lady Zainab bint Ali, Abu-Abdallah
Title: Siddiqah (Truthful One) or Sabirah (Patient One)
Designation: Savior of Islam
Birth-Death: AD 627–AD 682
Birthplace: Medina, Saudi Arabia
Place of Death and Burial: Died of natural causes. Claims of where she is buried range from Medina to Damascus to Egypt. However, the most popular belief is that she was buried in Damascus.

Key Achievements:

- counseled her brother, Imam Hussein, during the tragedy at Karbala
- played a major role in spreading the account of the tragedy at Karbala
- continued to recount the tragedy of Karbala for the remainder of her life
- rebuked the people of Kufa with her eloquence by exposing their false faith in Islam
- exposed and disgraced Ibn Ziyad in Kufa with her rebuttal to his speech
- offered to be killed if Ibn Ziyad went with his plan to kill her nephew, Imam Ali al-Sajjad
- admonished Yazid by referring to his false elation as victorious in the encounter at Karbala
- reproached Yazid for taking the harem of Prophet Mohammad's household as captives
- protected and supported Imam Ali al-Sajjad
- aroused the people in Kufa and Damascus who were deceived by the tyranny of Ibn Ziyad and Yazid
- convinced a whole new generation of Muslims to the way of Ahl al-Bayt

- captured her audience with eloquent communication and touched them emotionally
- educated, encouraged, and counseled the Muslim community to be more vigilant and actionable with their Islamic obligations
- inspired trust and demonstrated leadership as she created an environment where her followers took pride in being Muslims
- restored the ummah to the morals, ethics, and ideals of Islam

Imam Ali ibn al-Hussein

Name: Ali ibn al-Hussein, Abu Mohammad
Title: Zainul-Abedin (Adornment of the Worshippers), Imam al-Sajjad (Prostrating Imam)
Designation: Fourth Infallible Imam
Birth-Death: AD 659–AD 712
Birthplace: Medina, Saudi Arabia
Place of Death and Burial: Poisoned on the order of Caliph al-Walid I in Medina, Saudi Arabia. Buried in Jannat al-Baqi, Medina, Saudi Arabia.

Key Achievements:

- safeguarded the culture of Ashura and the tragedy of Karbala with his supplications and fervent sermons
- sowed the seeds of awareness and awakened the dormant conscience of the Muslim community
- revealed the crimes of the enemies of Ahl al-Bayt
- presented the true image of the despotic Umayyad rulers to the people
- publicized the merits and virtues of Ahl al-Bayt
- possessed oceans of knowledge and traditions that jurists have reported within the religious sciences
- recorded on his authority are sermons, prayers, merits of the Qur'an, accounts of the laws of what is permitted and what is forbidden, and the raids (*maghazi*) and battles (*ayyam*) during the time of the prophet
- became an authority on prophetic traditions and shari'ah
- authored the *Sahifa al-Sadjadiyya*, commonly referred to as the Psalms of the household of Mohammad
- reawakened the Muslim community by preaching the true Islam and guiding them to the Straight Path

Imam Mohammad ibn Ali

Name: Mohammad ibn Ali, Abu Ja'far
Title: al-Baqir al-Ulum (Splitting Open the Knowledge)
Designation: Fifth Infallible Imam
Birth-Death: AD 676–AD 733
Birthplace: Medina, Saudi Arabia
Place of Death and Burial: According to some Shi'a scholars, he was poisoned by Ibrahim ibn Walid ibn 'Abdallah in Medina, Saudi Arabia. Buried in Jannat al-Baqi, Medina, Saudi Arabia.

Key Achievements:

- recounted reports of the beginnings of history (*mubtada'*) and of the prophets
- related stories of the prophet's campaigns (maghazi)
- relied on by Muslims who followed his practices relative to the prophet (*sunan*) and the rites of the pilgrimage
- documented commentaries of the Qur'an were written on his authority
- reported traditions by both the Shi'a (*khassa*) and the non-Shi'a (*amma*) were based on his authority
- credited with shaping the Shi'a approach to hadith
- debated with the exponents of individual reasoning (*ahl al-ara'*), as they learned a great deal of theology ('*ilm al-kalam*) from him
- initiated the first Islamic coin to be minted with the inscription of "La Ilaha Illallah" on one side and "Mohammad Rasul Allah" on the other side
- convinced the Caliph Umar ibn Abdul Aziz to hand back to Ahl al-Bayt the land of Fadak that was wrongly taken from Fatima, daughter of Prophet Mohammad
- derived income from the land of Fadak and opened up schools in Medina to educate thousands of students about Islam and the Qur'an

- achieved vast knowledge of jurisprudence, sciences, theology, philosophy, and history that brightened the Islamic civilization
- brought to light the hidden origins of some sciences
- educated over 25,000 students who learned jurisprudence (*fiqh*), theology, and science from him
- directed his students, under his guidance, to compile over four hundred books on hadith
- split open knowledge in order to scrutinize and examine its depths

Imam Ja'far ibn Mohammad

Name: Ja'far ibn Mohammad, Abu Abdallah
Title: al-Sadiq (Trustworthy)
Designation: Sixth Infallible Imam
Birth-Death: AD 702–AD 765
Birthplace: Medina, Saudi Arabia
Place of Death and Burial: Poisoned by the order of Caliph al-Mansur in Medina, Saudi Arabia. Buried in Jannat al-Baqi, Medina, Saudi Arabia.

Key Achievements:

- initiated and promoted the school of jurisprudence (fiqh)
- expanded the First Grand Islamic University in which he taught over four thousand students in the fields of jurisprudence, tafsir, and hadith, including Abu Hanifa and Malik ibn Anas who were the Imams of two of the four Sunni schools of thought
- made many contributions to understanding the concept of energy and its relationship to philosophy and science
- exhibited perfection in medicine, theology, philosophy, mathematics, chemistry, and other aspects of science
- recognized as the Father of the Renaissance, at least in the field of astronomy
- discovered hydrogen in water
- championed the theory that as the light reflected by different objects comes to us, only a part of the rays enter our eyes
- espoused the theory of matter and anti-matter
- adopted and proved the theory that stars in the universe are billions of times brighter than the sun, now called quasars
- advocated the theory of perpetual motion by stating that everything in the universe, including inanimate objects, is always in motion, although we may not see it
- rejected Aristotle's Theory of Four Elements (earth, water, air, and fire) as the only four elements by stating that air is not an

element but contains many elements, and likewise each metal in
the Earth is also an element

- advanced his theory that the Earth rotates on its own axis
- recognized the importance of electromagnetic energy on the
  human system
- educated and trained Abu Musa Jabir ibn Hayyan al Azdi, also
  known as Geber, the Father of Chemistry, yet Imam Ja'far was
  the teacher and Geber the student

Imam Musa ibn Ja'far

Name: Musa ibn Ja'far, Abu al-Hassan I
Title: al-Kazim (One Who Controls His Anger)
Designation: Seventh Infallible Imam
Birth-Death: AD 746–AD 799
Birthplace: Medina, Saudi Arabia
Place of Death and Burial: Imprisoned and poisoned on the order of Caliph Harun al-Rashid in Baghdad, Iraq. Buried in the Kazimayn Shrine in Baghdad, Iraq.

Key Achievements:

- authored a number of books, the most famous being the *Musnad of Imam Moosa-e-Kazim*
- regarded as the most learned and highest authority in the science of Islamic jurisprudence and tradition during his Imamat
- surrounded by religious scholars and narrators who recorded his religious edicts, sayings, and morals
- considered famous for his outstanding qualities, virtues, wisdom, and morals relative to his scientific talents, acts of worship, reverential fear, self-discipline, self-denial, forgiveness, generosity, and helping the distressed
- helped people solve their problems, set the slaves free, and paid the debts of the indebted
- advanced the Institute of Ahl al-Bayt whereby the intellectual centers were blooming and millions of non-Muslims were accepting Islam
- cared for the poor and indebted by providing them with food, clothing, and money, without letting them know that he was their benefactor
- enlightened his followers on the dynamics of monotheism and the powers of reason and intellect in order to combat the

philosophical ideas and atheist tendencies infiltrating the minds of the society

- restrained his anger (*al-Kazim*) with extreme endurance and patience, in the face of severe persecution, imprisonment, adversities, and torture but always forgave those who inflicted such harm on him

Imam Ali ibn Musa

Name: Ali ibn Musa, Abu al-Hassan II
Title: al-Rida (Contented)
Designation: Eighth Infallible Imam
Birth-Death: AD 765–AD 818
Birthplace: Medina, Saudi Arabia
Place of Death and Burial: Poisoned by the order of Caliph al-Ma'mun in Mashhad, Iran. Buried in Imam Reza Shrine, Mashhad, Iran.

Key Achievements:

- successfully pursued a simultaneous, twofold strategy of peace and revolution to counteract the evil acts of Caliph al-Ma'mun by accepting to be his heir apparent
- undertook the position of peace in accepting to be the heir apparent, similar to Imam Hassan's acceptance of peace in order to safeguard Islam and Ahl al-Bayt
- embarked on the position of revolution that Imam Hussein pursued not only to follow martyrdom but to embrace it as well
- created an opposition within the regime of Caliph al-Ma'mun on an ideological, political, and popular level
- preserved the general order of the society and safety and freedom of movement for Ahl al-Bayt and its followers by accepting to be the heir apparent
- met with the foremost writers and intellectual thinkers promoting the views of Ahl al-Bayt
- protected Islam from being distorted, falsified, and misinterpreted, and protected the followers of the principle of nass from ignorance, deviation, and liquidation
- disclosed the ambiguity that was exploited in the slogan *al-rida min aal* Mohammad in order to reawaken the consciousness of the society with regard to the principle of nass and the Imamat
- played the role of an active leader, as his precise and universal

plan enabled him not only to counter the problems he faced but also to carry out his duties of supreme leadership in the ummah

- safeguarded Islam against the distorted meanings of certain Qur'anic verses
- defended Islam against narration of forged and corrupted hadiths (traditions) ascribed to Prophet Mohammad
- expanded and attracted a larger number of Muslims to the circle of Ahl al-Bayt
- continued the majalis (meetings) depicting the Karbala tragedy and the martyrdom of Imam Hussein and his companions
- authored books, *Al-Risala al-Dahabiyya fil Tibb* (*Golden Dissertation in Medicine*) and *Sahifat al-Reza* that deals with fiqh (jurisprudence)

Imam Mohammad ibn Ali

Name: Mohammad ibn Ali, Abu Ja'far
Title: al-Taqi (Pious), al-Jawad (Most Generous)
Designation: Ninth Infallible Imam
Birth-Death: AD 811–AD 835
Birthplace: Medina, Saudi Arabia
Place of Death and Burial: Poisoned by his wife, al-Ma'mun's daughter, on the order of Caliph Mu'tasim in Baghdad, Iraq. Buried in the Kazimayn Shrine in Baghdad, Iraq.

Key Achievements:

- enriched the scholarly school of Ahl al-Bayt
- exemplified two points: dependence on text and narration of Prophet Mohammad and an accurate understanding and deduction of both the Qur'an and the prophet's hadiths (traditions)
- promoted intellectual knowledge and science by developing, enriching, and expanding Islamic thought and shari'ah within the circles of Ahl al-Bayt and their students
- taught and instructed his students and scholars by urging them to write, classify, record, and publish as well as to sustain what comes from the Holy Imams of Ahl al-Bayt
- appointed deputies and commanded them to spread out in different parts of the Muslim world to convey Islam's divine laws
- encouraged scholarly debates and discussions in different kinds of sciences, and defended and fixed the pillars of Islam in the fields of monotheism, jurisprudence, interpretation, and narrations
- defended Islam and countered perverse ideas and deviated philosophies and ideologies that existed
- repaired ideological deviations, such as exaggeration and incarnations, and explained and clarified the diverse fields of Islam

- dispatched letters to his companions, followers, and representatives to expose the ideological and political situation of the Abbasid regime
- weakened the Waqifia movement that had been formed on the death of Imam Musa Kazim and which had been a cause of serious trouble to Imam Ali al-Rida

Imam Ali ibn Mohammad

Name: Ali ibn Mohammad, Abu al-Hassan III
Title: al-Naqi (Holy), al-Hadi (Guide)
Designation: Tenth Infallible Imam
Birth-Death: AD 827–AD 868
Birthplace: Surayya, a village near Medina, Saudi Arabia
Place of Death and Burial: Poisoned on the order of Caliph Al-Mu'tazz
in Samarra, Iraq. Buried in the Al-Askari Mosque in Samarra, Iraq.

Key Achievements:

- endowed with the knowledge of the languages of the Persians,
  Slavs, Indians, and Nabataeans in addition to foreknowing
  unexpected storms and accurately predicting other events
- invalidated the theological misconceptions regarding Islam by
  contributing to the books of argumentation that were compiled
  by Shi'a scholars to further refute misguided beliefs about Islam,
  such as the impossibility of the Muslim ummah to describe
  Allah's essence
- rejected the claim that he was the Creator, preached by heretics
  such as Ibn Hasakah who claimed to be a prophet abolishing
  prayer, fasting, zakat, and haj
- spread the sublime principles and commandments of Islam
- attended meetings in order to refute the deviated trends by
  explaining every religious issue quietly, clearly, and with reason
  and logic
- received letters from all over the Muslim world and accepted the
  religious revenues to be spent according to religious instructions
  for the welfare of the Muslim community
- confronted the extremists by exposing their deviation and
  declaring them on the wrong path
- dedicated to teaching and even paid for student's supplies if they
  needed it

- utilized the Prophet's mosque in Medina as a place to teach people about knowledge, principles, and morals that could be derived from Islam
- explained the Islamic laws of jurisprudence to the Muslim community, as he was dedicated to upholding shari'ah law with regards to its verdicts, teachings, and principles

Imam Hassan ibn Ali

Name: Hassan ibn Ali, Abu Mohammad
Title: al-Askari (Soldier)
Designation: Eleventh Infallible Imam
Birth-Death: AD 846–AD 874
Birthplace: Medina, Saudi Arabia
Place of Death and Burial: Poisoned on the order of Caliph Al-Mu'tamid in Samarra, Iraq. Buried in Al-Askari Mosque in Samarra, Iraq.

Key Achievements:

-   imprisoned for most of his short life of twenty-eight years but still able to teach and compile commentaries on the Qur'an
-   represented the front of opposition to the Abbasid rule by criticizing the rulers for appropriating the wealth unlawfully and using followers of Islam as slaves
-   stood up against the deviate and oppressive Abbasid rule and spared no effort in achieving truth and justice among people
-   appointed agents in Muslim countries and entrusted them to receive the legal dues and spend them on the poor and the deprived, to reconcile between people and the general welfare
-   curtailed the flood of atheism and disbelief that ensued from the philosophers of that time
-   undertook the fatal issues of the Islamic ummah and defended the rights of Muslims
-   personified the essence of patience (sabr), as the virtue and symbolism of sabr became associated with his name
-   exhibited such high morals that even some of his enemies and opponents turned to be his loyal supporters
-   refrained from communicating or cooperating with the kings who took the wealth of Allah as theirs and the people as their slaves

- sided with the poor and the deprived who were victims of the kings who robbed the wealth of the ummah and left the state in economical imbalance
- appointed his son, Imam Mohammad al-Mahdi, as his successor

Imam Mohammad ibn al-Hassan

Name: Mohammad ibn al-Hassan, Abu al-Qasim
Title: al-Mahdi (Guided One), Hidden Imam, al-Hujjah (Proof)
Designation: Twelfth Infallible Imam (Final Infallible Imam)
Birth-Death: AD 869–Present
Birthplace: Samarra, Iraq
Place of Death and Burial: Still living. He will descend in the future with
the Messiah, Jesus, to defeat al-Dajjal, the antichrist.

Key Achievements:

- presided over the funeral of his father, Imam Hassan al-Askari, when he was five years old, at which time he became the Twelfth and Final Infallible Imam
- appointed four deputies in his minor occultation (874), lasting about seven decades, to represent him in the Muslim societies
- declared the beginning of his major occultation (941) during which time he is not in contact with his followers
- reemerges by the will of Allah in the future, along with Jesus in order to fulfill their mission of bringing peace and justice to the world
- returns when all types of ideologies are tested and have failed, at which time people will come to understand that they do not have any more solutions and must accept the solution of Imam al-Mahdi
- upon his return, will be joined by 313 of the most virtuous and faithful supporters that possess supreme knowledge and wisdom, to help him govern the world

Appendix 3

Twelve Infallible Imams
Shi'a Sources of Hadiths

Following is a list of some of the major Shi'a collections of hadiths (traditions) compiled by renowned Shi'a scholars authenticating the Twelve Infallible Imams of Ahl al-Bayt:

Al-Kafi (*Al-Kafi fi 'ilm al-din*) (*The Sufficient in the Knowledge of Religion*)
Author: Thiqat al-Islam al-Shaykh Abu Ja'far Muhammad b. Ya'qub b. Ishaq al-Kulayni (d. AH 329/AD 940); eight volumes containing 16,099 traditions with their authorities and sources, related to both Usul and Furu.

Man la Yahduruhu al-Faqih (*For him not in the Presence of Jurisprudent*)
Author: al-Shaykh Abu Ja'far Muhammad b. 'Ali b. Husayn b. Babawayh al-Qummi (al-Shaykh al-Saduq) (d. AH 381/AD 991); four volumes containing 666 chapters, 5,998 traditions.

Tahdhib al-Ahkam (*Rectification of the Statutes*)
Author: Shaykh al-Ta'ifah, Abu Ja'far Muhammad b. Hasan al-Tusi (d. AH 460/AD 1067); ten volumes containing 1,359 hadiths, 393 sections.

Al-Istibsar (*al-Istibsar fi ma ukhtulif fihi min al-akhbar*) (*Reflection upon the Disputed Traditions*)
Author: al-Shaykh Abu Ja'far Muhammad b. Hasan al-Tusi (d. AH 460/AD 1067); four volumes containing 5,511 hadiths.

Bihar al-Anwar (*Oceans of Lights*)
Author: Muhammad Baqir b. Muhammad Taqi al-Majlisi (d. AH 1110/ AD 1698); 110 volumes.

Wasa'il al-Shi'ah ila Tahsil Masa'il al-Shari'ah
Author: al-Shaykh Muhammad b. Hasan al-Hurr al-'Amili (d. AH 1104/AD 1693); twenty-nine volumes containing 35,868 hadiths.

Mustadrak al-Wasa'il wa Mustanbat al-Masa'il
Author: al-Hajj Mirza Husayn al-Nuri al-Tabarsi (d. AH 1320/AD 1902); eighteen volumes containing 23,000 traditions.

Appendix 4

Twelve Infallible Imams
Sunni Sources (Selected Hadiths)

Following are some of the hadiths (traditions) narrated by renowned Sunni scholars who confirm that the succession of the caliphate is only from the Twelve Infallible Imams of Ahl al-Bayt:

1. Ḥafiẓ Abū 'Abd Allāh al-Bukhārī, in his *Ṣaḥīḥ*, relates via Jābir b. Samara from the Apostle of Allah who stated: There will be **twelve chiefs (Amīrs)** [after me]. Then he said something that I could not hear. My father said: the Apostle of Allah said: All of them are from the **Quraysh.**
Al-Bukhārī, *Ṣaḥīḥ*: *Kitāb al-Aḥkām*, chapter 51; Ibn Kathīr, *Al-Bidāya wa al-Nihāya*, I, 153, Maktaba al-Ma'ārif; Aḥmad b. Ḥanbal, *Musnad*, V, 90, 93, 95, Dār al-Fikr; Bayhaqqī, *Dalā'il al-Nabuwwa*, VI, 569, Dār al-Kutub al-'Ilmiyya; Ṭabarānī, *Mu'jam al-Kabīr*, II, 277, Printed in Iraq.

2. Muslim, in his *Ṣaḥīḥ*, relates via Jābir b. Samara from the Apostle of Allah who stated: Islam will remain mighty and glorified as long as **twelve caliphs** come [to rule], all of whom from the **Quraysh.**
Muslim, *Ṣaḥīḥ*: *Kitāb al-Amāra*, chapter I, *ḥadīth* 7; Aḥmad b. Ḥanbal, *Musnad*, V, 90, 100, 106; Muttaqī al-Hindī, *Kanz al-'Ummāl*, XII, 32, Mu'assisa al-Risāla; Ibn Ḥajar 'Asqalānī, *Fatḥ al-Bārī*, XIII, 211; Dār al-Ma'rifa; Muḥammad 'Umarī Tabrīzī, *Mishkāt al-Masābīḥ*, *ḥadīth* 5974, Al-Maktab al-Islāmī.

3. Tirmidhī, in his *Sunan*, quotes the Apostle of Allah as stating: There will be **twelve Amīrs** after me, all of whom from the **Quraysh**.
TIrmidhī, *Sunan: Kitāb-i Fitan*, chapter 46, *ḥadīth*, 1; *Mu'jam al-Kabīr*, II, 214; Āamad b. Ḥanbal, *Musnad*, V, 99; *Kanz al-'Ummāl*, XII, 24; Muḥammad Nāṣir al-Dīn al-Bānī, *Silsilatu al-Aḥādīth al-Ṣaḥīḥa*, Al-Maktab al-Islāmī, No. 1075.

4. Ḥāfiẓ b. Abū Dāwūd Sajistānī has quoted Jābir b. Samara in his *Sunan* as saying: I heard the Apostle of Allah say: This Religion will ever remain upright as long as there will be among you **twelve Caliphs**, all of whom to be accepted by the *Umma*. [Jābir b. Samara goes on to say:] Then I heard the Prophet say something that I did not comprehend. I asked my father what the Prophet said, and my father replied: [he said:] All of them are from the **Quraysh**.
Ibn Dāwūd, *Sunan*, Kitāb al-Mahdī, *ḥadīth* 1; Al-Siyūṭī, *Tārīkh al-Khulafā*, 18, Dār al-Qalam; *Dalā'il al-Nabuwwa*, VI, 520; *Fatḥ al-Bārī*, XIII, 212.

5. Ahmad b. Ḥanbal in his *Musnad* has related via Jābir b. Samara from the Apostle of Allah who stated: There will be **twelve Caliphs** for this *Umma*.
Aḥmad b. Ḥanbal, *Musnad*, V, 106; *Kanz al-'Ummāl*, XII, 33.

6. Ḥākim-i Nīshābūrī in his *Mustadrak* quotes Awn b. Abū Jaḥīfa as relating from his father that the Apostle of Allah stated: My *Umma* will ever remain righteous as long as there will come [to rule] **twelve Caliphs**, all of whom from the **Quraysh**.
Ḥākim-i Nīshābūrī, *Al-Mustadrak 'alā Ṣaḥīḥīn*, III, 618, Dār al-Kitāb.

7. Al-Siyūṭī relates via Jābir b. Samara from the Apostle of Allah who stated: This affair (*amr*) will ever remain glorified, and **twelve Caliphs** who are all from the **Quraysh** will defend it against those who are hostile to it.
Al-Siyūṭī, *Tārīkh al-Khulafā*, 10, Raḍī Publication.

8. Khaṭīb al-Baghdādī relates via Jābir b. Samara from the Apostle of Allah who stated: There will be after me **twelve Amīrs**, all of whom from the **Quraysh**.

Khaṭīb al-Baghdādī, *Tārīkh-i Baghdād*, XIV, 353 & VI, 263, Dār al-Kutub al-ʿIlmiyya; Aḥmad b. Ḥanbal, *Musnad*, V, 92; Muḥammad Bukhārī Jaʿfī, *Al-Tārīkh al-Kabīr*, I, 446, Dār al-Fikr.

9. Ṭabarānī relates via Jābir b. Samara from the Apostle of Allah who stated: This religion will remain powerful and invincible as long as **twelve caliphs** come [to rule], all of whom from the **Quraysh**.

Muʿjam al-Kabīr, II, 195, Dār-i Iḥyā al-Turāth; Aḥmad b. Ḥanbal, *Musnad*, V, 99; *Kanz al-ʿUmmāl*, XII, 32; Muslim, *Ṣaḥīḥ*, chapter one, *ḥadīth* 9, Kitāb al-Amāra.

10. Abū Naʿīm relates via Jābir b. Samara from the Apostle of Allah who stated: There will be **twelve Amīrs** after me, all of whom from the **Quraysh**.

Abū Naʿīm, *Ḥilya al-Awliyā*, IV, 333, Dār al-Kutub al-ʿIlmiya; *Muʿjam al-Kabīr*, II, 216, Printed in Iraq; *Kanz al-ʿUmmāl*, XII, 33.

11. The author of *Al-Tāj* relates via Jābir from the Apostle of Allah who stated: Islam will remain powerful as long as **twelve caliphs** come [to rule], all of whom from the **Quraysh**.

Manṣūr ʿAlī Nāṣif, *Al-Tāj al-Jāmiʿ li al-Uṣūl fī Aḥādīth al-Rasūl*, III, 39, printed in Istanbul; Muslim, *Ṣaḥīḥ*, Kitāb al-Imāra, chapter 1, *ḥadīth* 7; Aḥmad b. Ḥanbal, *Musnad*, 5, 90; *Fatḥ al-Bārī*, XIII, 212.

12. Bayhaqqī relates via Jābir from the Apostle of Allah who stated: This Religion will ever remain upright as long as there will be among you **twelve Caliphs**, all of whom to be accepted by the Umma.

Dalāʾil al-Nabuwwa, VI, 520; *Fatḥ al-Bārī*, XIII, 212.

13. Muttaqī Hindī relates via Anas from the Apostle of Allah who stated: This Religion will ever remain upright as long as there will be

among you **twelve Caliphs** from the **Quraysh**; when they perish, the earth and its inhabitants will be thrown into disorder.
Kanz al-'Ummāl, XII, 34.

14. Also in *Muntakhab-i Kanz al-'Ummāl*, it is related via Ibn Masūd from the Apostle of Allah who stated: There will be **twelve guardians** to this *Umma*; those who abandon them will inflict no loss on them.
Muntakhab-i Kanz al-'Ummāl, marginal notes to *Musnad* of Aāmad b. Ḥanbal, V, 312, Dār al-Fikr.

15. Ḥanafī al-Qandūzī relates via Jābir b. Samara from the Apostle of Allah who stated: I am the chief (*sayyid*) of the Prophets and **Ali** is the chief of the *Waṣīs* (successors; trustees); indeed my trustees after me will be **twelve**, of whom the first is **Ali** and the last will be **Mahdī**, the Qā'im.
Ḥanafī al-Qandūzī, *Yanābī' al-Mawidda*, II, 534, Raḍī Publication.

16. Siyūṭī relates from Aḥmad, Bazzāz, quoting Ibn Mas'ūd as saying: The Prophet was asked about the number of Caliphs who were going to rule this *Umma*. His Holiness stated: They are **twelve**; [the same as] the number of the chieftains
to the children of Israel.
Tārīkh al-Khulafā, 10.

17. My *Umma* will ever remain in righteous condition as long as there will come [to rule] **twelve Caliphs**.
Al-Mustadrak 'alā al-Ṣaḥīḥīn, III, 618; Haythamī, *Majma' al-Zawā'id wa Manba' al-Farā'id*, V, 190, Qudsī Edition. *Kanz al-'Ummāl*, ḥadīth 33849; *Fatḥ al-Bārī*, XIII, 211; *Tārīkh al-Kabīr*, VIII, 411; Zubaydī, *Itḥāf al-Sādat al-Muttaqīn*, VII, 489, Dār al-Fikr; *Mu'jam al-Kabīr*, II, 216, 236.

18. This affair [i.e., religious condition] will ever remain glorified as long as there will come [to rule] **twelve Caliphs**, all from among the **Quraysh**.
Al-Bidāya wa al-Nihāya, I, 153; *Tārīkh al-Khulafā*, 10.

19. Abū Dāwūd quotes the Prophet in another tradition as saying: Even if there remains only one day on earth, Allah will elongate that day until He will raise up a man from among **my progeny, whose name will be my name** and whose father's name will be my father's name, and will fill the earth with justice and equity as it is filled with injustice and tyranny. Abū Dāwūd, *Sunan*, IV, *Kitāb al-Mahdī*; *Muʿjam al-Kabīr*, X, 166; *Kanz al-ʿUmmāl*, *ḥadīth* 38676; *Al-Ḥāwī al-Fatāwā*, II, 215; Aḥmad Ḥanbal, *Musnad*, V, 86; Siyūṭī, *Durr al-Manthūr*, VI, 58, Islāmiya Edition; Ibn Māja, *Sunan*, II, *Kitāb al-Fitan*, chapter 34.

20. In his *Sunan*, Ibn Māja has also related numerous traditions from the Apostle of Allah on this issue; such as the following: When you see him, swear allegiance to him, even if you [will have to] crawl toward him on snow. Verily, he is **Mahdī, the Caliph of Allah**.
Ibn Māja, *Sunan*, II, *Kitāb al-Fitan*, chapter 34.

21. In his *Sunan*, Tirmidhī relates from the Apostle of Allah: The world will not come to pass until **a man from my Ahl al-Bayt, whose name will be my name**, will come to rule over Arabs.
Al-Tirmidhī, *Sunan*, *Kitāb al-Fitan*, Chapter 52; Aḥmad b. Ḥanbal, *Musnad*, I, 377, 430; Abū Naʿīm, *Ḥilaytu al-Awliyā*, V, 75; *Kanz al-ʿUmmāl*, *ḥadīth* 38655.

22. **Ali** has related from the Apostle of Allah who stated: **Mahdī** is of us; the Religion will end up to him as it has been set up by us.
ʿAjlūnī, *Kashf al-Khulafā wa Muzīl al-Ilbās*, II, 380, Muʾassisa al-Risāla.

23. Imam Aḥmad Ḥanbal relates via Abī Saʿīd al-Khudrī from the Apostle of Allah who stated: I leave behind for you two heavy things (*Thaghalayn*), one of which is superior to the other; the Book of Allah, stretched from heaven down to earth; and **my offspring, [that is] my Ahl al-Bayt**; and they will never separate from each other until they come to [join] me at the Fountain [of Kawthar].

Aḥmad b. Ḥanbal, *Musnad*, III, 14 & IV, 371; *Maj‘ al-Zawā’id*, IX, 257; *Ithāf al-Sāda al-Muttaqīn*, X, 502, 506; *Tahdhīb Tārīkh-i Damishq*, V, 439; Yaḥyā Shajarī, *Kitāb al-Amālī*, I, 143, 149, 154, ‘Ālam al-Kutub.

24. In his *Sunan*, Dārimī relates via Zayd b. Arqam from the Apostle of Allah who stated: I leave behind for you two heavy things; the first is the Book of Allah, in which there is guidance and light, so adhere to the Book of Allah and take hold of it. After that, he urged and encouraged to turn to it. Then he said three times: **And my Ahl Al-Bayt; I remind you to fear Allah with regard to my Ahl al-Bayt.**
Al-Dārimī, *Sunan*, II, 432, Dār al-Fikr; Bayhaqqī, *Al-Sunan al-Kubrā*, II, 148 & VII, 30 & X, 114, Dār al-Ma‘rifa; Ibn Khuzayma, *Ṣaḥīḥ*, No. 2357, Al-Maktab al-Islāmī.

25. Likewise, Ḥākim al-Nīshābūrī relates via Zayd b. Arqam from the Apostle of Allah who stated: I leave behind for you two heavy things; the Book of Allah and **my Ahl Al-Bayt**; and they will never separate from each other until they come to [join] me at the Fountain [of Kawthar].
Al-Mstadrak alā al-Ṣaḥīḥīn, III, 148 asserting the soundness of the *ḥadīth*, Aḥmad b. Ḥanbal, *Musnad*, III, 17; Al-Ṭabarānī, *Mu‘jam al-Ṣaghīr*, I, 131, I, 131, Dār al-Fikr; Al-Ṭaḥāwī, *Mushkil al-Āthār*, IV, 368, 369, Dār al-Niẓām, asserting the soundness of the *ḥadīth*, *Mu‘jam al-Kabīr*, V, 190, 205 “Iraq Edition.”

26. In his *Fayḍ al-Ghadīr*, Munāwī relates via Zayd b. Thābit from the Apostle of Allah who stated: I leave behind two successors (*khalīfatayn*) for you, the Book of Allah, stretched down between heaven and earth; and my offspring, [that is] **my Ahl al-Bayt**; and they will never separate [from each other] until they come to [join] me at the Fountain [of Kawthar].
Munāwī, *Fayḍ al-Qadīr*, II, 14, Dār al-Fikr; asserting the soundness of the *ḥadīth*; Aḥmad b. Ḥanbal, *Musnad*, V, 182, 189; *Maj‘ al-Zawā’id*, IX, 162; *Durr al-Manthūr*, II, 60.

27. In his *Sunan*, Tirmidhī relates via Zayd b. Arqam from the Apostle of Allah who stated. I leave behind for you the things that if you hold fast unto, you will never go astray, one of which is superior to the other; the Book of Allah, stretched from heaven down to earth; and my offspring, [that is] **my Ahl al-Bayt**; and they will never separate from each other until they come to [join] me at the Fountain [of Kawthar]. So, see how you take them as a substitute for me.

Al-Tirmidhī, *Sunan*, V, 329, "Salfiya Edition"; *Kanz al-'Ummāl*, I, 173; *Durr al-Manṣūr*, II, 60; Qāḍī 'Ayāḍ, *Al-Shifā bi Ta'rīf-i Ḥuqūq al-Muṣṭafā*, II, 105, "Fārābī Edition"; 'Umarī Tabrīzī, *Mishkāt al-Maṣābīḥ*, *ḥadīth* 6144, Al-Maktab al-Islāmī; *Itḥāf al-Sāda al-Muttaqīn*, X, 507.

28. In his *Ṣaḥīḥ*, Muslim b. Ḥajjāj Nīshābūrī relates via Zayd b. Arqam from the Apostle of Allah who stated: The Apostle of Allah delivered a sermon to us in Al-Ghadīr al-Khumm; after praising and glorifying Allah, he stated: Now then. O People! Truly, I am a man about to meet my Lord's envoy [Angel of Death] to which I would respond. And I leave behind for you two heavy things; the first is the Book of Allah, in which there is guidance and light, so adhere to the Book of Allah and take hold of it. After that, he urged and encouraged to turn to it. Then he said, **And my Ahl Al-Bayt; I remind you to fear Allah with regard to my Ahl al-Bayt, I remind you to fear Allah with regard to my Ahl al-Bayt, I remind you to fear Allah with regard to my Ahl al-Bayt.**

Muslim, *Ṣaḥīḥ*, *ḥadīth* 36, *Kitāb-i Faḍā'il al-Ṣaḥāba*; *Kanz al-'Ummāl*, *ḥadīth* 37620; Bayhaqqī, *Al-Sunan al-Ṣaqīr*, II, 212, Dār al-Kutub al-'Ilmiya; *Mu'jam al-Kabīr*, V, 183.

29. Anas b. Mālik relates from the Apostle of Allah who stated: Truly, my Ahl al-Bayt and I are comparable to the Noah's Ark, those who embark it will be rescued, and those who fail to will be drowned.

Durr al-Manṣūr, III, 334; *Tārīkh-i Baghdād*, 12, 91; *Al-Mustadrik 'alā al-Ṣaḥīḥīn*, II, 343, asserting on the soundness of the *ḥadīth*.

30. Abū Dhar relates from the Apostle of Allah: Truly, **my Ahl al-Bayt** among you is comparable to the Noah's Ark, those who embark it will be rescued, and those who fail to will be perished.
Muʿjam al-Kabīr, III, 45; *Kanz al-ʿUmmāl*, XII, 98.

31. Zayd b. Arqam relates from the Apostle of Allah who stated: Whoever I am his master; **Ali** is his master, too.
Tirmidhī, *Sunan*, V, 297; Aḥmad b. Ḥanbal, *Musnad*, I, 84, 118, 119; *Muʿjam al-Kabīr*, III, 199, Iraq Edition; *Al-Mustadrik ʿalā al-Ṣaḥīḥīn*, III, 110; *Ḥilya al-Awliyā*, IV, 23.

32. Tirmidhī relates via ʿUmrān b. Ḥusayn from the Apostle of Allah who stated: Truly, **Ali** is of me and I am of him, and he is the master (*Walī*) of all the faithful after me.
Tirmidhī, *Sunan*, V, 296; Ibn Mājja, *Sunan*, *ḥadīth* 119; Aḥmad b. Ḥanbal, *Musnad*, IV, 164, 165; *Muʿjam al-Kabīr*, IV, 19, 20, Iraq Edition; *Kanz al-ʿUmmāl*, XIII, 142.

33. Saʿd b. Abī Waqqāṣ says: I heard the Prophet saying to **Ali**: Are you not satisfied with being unto me what Hārun was unto Mūsā, except that there would be no prophet after me?
Al-Bukhārī, *Ṣaḥīḥ*, *Kitābu Faḍāʾil Ṣaḥāba*, Chapter on Virtues of Ali; Tirmidhī, *Sunan*, V, 302; Ibn ʿAsākir, *Tārīkhu Madīnati Damishq*, XVII, 347, Dār al-Fikr, Damascus; *Tārīkh al-Khulafā*, 168.

34. Burayda relates from the Apostle of Allah: **Ali b. Abī Ṭālib** is the master of whomever I am his master; and **Ali b. Abī Ṭālib** is the master of all faithful men and women, and he will be your master after me.
Tārīkhu Madīnati Damishq, XVII, 348.

35. Zayd b. Arqam relates from the Apostle of Allah: Let whoever is pleased to live like me and die like me and inhabit Eden's Paradise which my Lord - the Almighty and Glorious - has promised me and has planted

its trees by His Hands take **Ali b. Abī Ṭālib** as his master, since he would never lead you away from guidance, and would never lead you astray.
Majmaʿ al-Zawāʾid, IX, 137.

36. Barāʾ b. ʿĀdhib relates from the Apostle of Allah: **Ali** to me is like my head to my body.
Tārīkh-i Baghdād, VII, 12; *Kanz al-ʿUmmāl*, XI, 603, *ḥadīth* 32914.

37. Anas b. Mālik relates from the Apostle of Allah who stated: Who is the master of Arabs? They replied, You! O Rasūl Allah. Then he said: I am the master of the children of Adam and **Ali** is the master of Arabs.
Majmaʿ al-Zawāʾid, IX, 152.

38. Abū Maryam Thaqafī says: I heard the Apostle of Allah saying to **Ali**: O **Ali**! Blessed is he who loves you and approves you; and woe on him who hates you and disapproves you.
Ibid, 179.

39. Umm Salama relates from the Apostle of Allah: The hypocrites do not like **Ali**, and the faithful do not hate him.
Tirmidhī, *Sunan*, V, 298; *Majmaʿ al-Zawāʾid*, IX, 181.

40. Abī Saʿīd al-Khudrī says: Verily, I get to know the hypocrites through their hatred of **Ali b. Abī Ṭālib**.
Tārīkh al-Khulafā, 170; Tirmidhī, *Sunan*, V, 298.

41. Abū Rāfiʿ says: The Apostle of Allah said concerning **Ali**: Whoever loves him does indeed love me, and whoever loves me does indeed loves Allah; and whoever hates him does indeed hate me and whoever hates me does indeed hate Allah, the Almighty and Glorified.
Majmaʿ al-Zawāʾid, IX, 177; *Tārīkh al-Khulafā*, 173.

42. Zayd b. Arqam relates from the Apostle of Allah: The first one who turned Muslim was **Ali**.

Tirmidhī, *Sunan*, V, 306.

43. Ibn 'Abbās relates from the Apostle of Allah: The First one who performed *ṣalāt* (ritual prayer) was **Ali**.
Ibid, V, 305.

44. Umm Salama relates from the Apostle of Allah who said: **Ali** is with the Truth and the Truth is with **Ali**; they will not separate until they come to me at the Fountain of Kawthar on the Day of Resurrection.
Tārīkh-i Baghdād, XIV, 321; *Majma' al-Zawā'id*, VII, 235; *Kanz al-'Ummāl*, XI, 603.

45. Likewise, Umm Salama says: I heard from the Apostle of Allah who stated: **Ali** is with the Qur'an and the Qur'an is with **Ali**; they will not separate until they come by the Fountain of Kawthar.
Ṭabarānī, *Mu'jam al-Awsat*, V, 455; *Kanz al-'Ummāl*, *ḥadīth* 32912; *Majma' al-Zawā'id*, IX, 183.

46. Abū Sakhīla relates from the Apostle of Allah: **Ali** was the first man who acknowledged his faith in me and will be the first one who will shake hands with me on the Day of Resurrection; and he is the most veracious; and he is the distinguisher, who distinguishes between the true and the false.
Tārīkhu Madīnati Damishq, XVII, 306, 307.

47. Ibn Mas'ūd relates from the Apostle of Allah who stated: Looking at **Ali** is worship.
Tārīkh al-Khulafā, 172; *Majma' al-Zawā'id*, IX, 157.

48. Jābir says: The Apostle of Allah said to **Ali**: The one who persecutes you has [indeed] persecuted me; and the one who persecutes me has [indeed] persecuted Allah.

Tārīkhu Madīnati Damishq, XVII, 352; *Tārīkh al-Khulafā*, 173; *Al-Mustadrih 'alā al-Ṣaḥīḥīn*, III, 122, asserting the soundness of the *ḥadīth*; *Al-Tārīkh al-Kabīr*, VI, 307; *Dalā'il al-Nabuwwa*, V, 395.

49. Umm Salama relates from the Apostle of Allah who stated: The one who curses **Ali** has indeed cursed me.
Majma' al-Zawā'id, IX, 175; *Tārīkh al-Khulafā*, 173.

50. Abū Rāfi' says: I had an audience with the Apostle of Allah. His holiness took my hand and said:O Abū Rāfi'! After me there will come a folk who will murder **Ali**. Allah, the Exalted, has deemed it rightful to fight against them; those who are unable to fight with their hands, then fight with their tongues; and then if unable to fight with their tongues, fight with their heart; there is no way beyond that.
Ibid, 182.

51. Abī Sa'īd al-Khudrī says: The Apostle of Allah said to **Ali**: You will make war over the esoteric interpretation (*ta'wīl*) of the Qur'an, as I made war over its Revelation.
Tārīkh al-Khulafā, 173.

52. Ibn Mas'ūd relates from the Apostle of Allah who said: **Al-Ḥasan and al-Ḥusayn are the masters of the Youth of Paradise.**
Kanz al-'Ummāl, XII, 112; Tirmidhī, *Sunan*, V, 321; *Mu'jam al-Kabīr*, XII, 35; *Majma' al-Zawā'id*, IX, 286.

53. Anas relates from the Apostle of Allah: Verily, **al-Ḥasan and al-Ḥusayn** are my two fragrant flowers of this world.
Tirmidhī, *Sunan*, V, 322; *Kanz al-'Ummāl*, XII, 113.

54. Ya'lā b. Marra relates from the Apostle of Allah: **Al-Ḥusayn is of me and I am of Al-Ḥusayn.**
Mu'jam al-Kabīr, XII, 32, Dār Iḥyā al-Turāth; Tirmidhī, *Sunan*, V, 324.

55. Abū Hurayra relates from the Apostle of Allah: Whoever loves them has loved me and whoever hates them has indeed hated me.
Majmaʿ al-Zawāʾid, IX, 286.

56. Saʿd b. Abī Waqqāṣ says: When the *Āyah* of *Mubāhila* (Al-Qurʾan, 3:61) was revealed, the Apostle of Allah prayed **Ali, Fāṭima, Al-Ḥasan and al-Ḥusayn**, and said: O Allah! These are **my Ahl al-Bayt**.
Tirmidhī, *Sunan*, V, 302, asserting the soundness of the *ḥadīth*.

57. Umm Salama says: The *Āyah* of *Taṭhīr* (Indeed Allah desires to repel all impurity from you, O People of the Household…) (Al-Qurʾan, 33:33) was revealed in my house. When this *Āyah* was revealed, the Apostle of Allah sent for **Ali, Fāṭima, Al-Ḥasan and al-Ḥusayn**, and then said: These are **my Ahl al-Bayt**.
Al-Mustadrik ʿalā al-Ṣaḥīḥīn, III, 146.

58. Salama b. Akwaʿ relates from the Apostle of Allah: The stars are made as safeguards for the inhabitants of the heaven, and **my Ahl al-Bayt** are indeed safeguards for my *Umma*.
Majmaʿ al-Zawāʾid, IX, 277; *Muʿjam al-Kabīr*, XII, 22, Dār Iḥyāʾ al-Turāth; *Kanz al-ʿUmmāl*, XII, 101.

59. Zayd b. Thābit relates from the Apostle of Allah: **My Ahl al-Bayt** are safeguards for the inhabitants of the earth; when they go away, the inhabitants of the earth will go away, too.
Fayḍ al-Qadīr, III, 15.

60. Ibn ʿAbbās relates from the Apostle of Allah: The stars are safeguards for the inhabitants of the heaven from dispersing, and **my Ahl al-Bayt** are safeguards for my *Umma* from disuniting; so, if any tribes from the Arab dispute about them, they will disunite and turn into the cabal of the Satan.
Al-Mustadrik ʿalā al-Ṣaḥīḥīn, III, asserting the soundness of the *ḥadīth*; *Kanz al-ʿUmmāl*, XII, 102.

61. **Ali** relates from the Apostle of Allah: O **Ali**! Indeed, Islam is naked; its garment is fear of Allah (*taqwā*) … and the basis of Islam is love of me and love of **my Ahl al-Bayt.**
Kanz al-'Ummāl, XII, 105.

62. Abī Sa'īd al-Khudrī relates from the Apostle of Allah: I swear by the One in Whose Hand lies my life that no one will bear a grudge against us, the **Ahl al-Bayt**, unless Allah will get him into Fire.
Al-Mustadrik 'alā al-Ṣaḥīḥīn, III, 150, asserting the soundness of the *ḥadīth*; See also Ibn 'Abbās' tradition in: Ibid, III, 149, asserting the soundness of the *ḥadīth*; *Kanz al-'Ummāl*, XII, 42.

63. Anas relates from the Apostle of Allah: We are the **Ahl a-Bayt**; no one is comparable with us.
Kanz al-'Ummāl, XII, 104.

64. Abū Na'īm relates from Ibn 'Abbās quoting the Apostle of Allah as saying: Let whoever likes to live like me and die like me and inhabit Eden's Paradise which my Lord cultivated take **Ali** as his master after me, and let him obey whoever he places in charge over him, and let him follow the example of **my Ahl al-Bayt** after me, for they are **my progeny**: they are created of my own mold and blessed with my own comprehension and knowledge. Woe unto those from among my *Umma* who deny their excellence and separate me from them! May Allah never permit them to enjoy my intercession.
Ḥilyat al-Awliyā, I, 86; *Kanz al-'Ummāl*, XII, 106.

65. Abū Hurayra says: **The Prophet looked at Ali, Fāṭima, Ḥasan and Ḥusayn and said: I am at war with those who are at war with you at peace with those who are at peace with you.**
Al-Mustadrik 'alā al-Ṣaḥīḥīn, III, 149, asserting the soundness of the *ḥadīth*, Aḥmad b. Ḥanbal, *Musnad*, II, 422; *Mu'jam al-Kabīr*, III, 31; *Tahdhīb-i Tārīkh-i Damishq al-Kabīr li Ibn 'Asākir*, IV, 139; *Tārīkh-i Baghdād*, VII, 137; *Durr al-Manṣūr*, V, 199.

Source: Data derived from *The Twelve Imams in the Sunni Sources: Fiqh ul-Hadith*, by Gulam Husayn Zaynali. Translator: Ahmad Rezwani; Editor: Mahdi Baqi. Qum, Iran: Dar ul-Hadith Scientific Cultural Institute, 2010.

Appendix 5

Selected Hadiths on Ahl al-Bayt
Six Books (*Kutub al-Sittah*) of
Major Sunni Sources (Including
Musnad Ahmad ibn Hanbal)

Hadith	Sunni Source of Hadith S (Sahih/Authentic); H (Hasan/Good); D (Dha'eef/Weak)
Blessings on Mohammad and his Household. (Qur'an 33:33; 33:56; 42:23)	*Sahih Bukhari*, V4, Book 60, Hadith 3370 (S) *Sahih Muslim*, V1, Book 4, Hadith 907 (S) *Ibn Majah*, V2, Book 5, Hadith 904 (S) *Abu Dawud*, V1, Book 2, Hadith 976 (S) *Al-Tirmidhi*, V1, Book 3, Hadith 483 (S) *Al-Nasa'i*, V2, Book 13, Hadith 1286 (S) *Ahmad ibn Hanbal*, V4, pp. 241, 243–244
Whoever obeys me (Mohammad) obeys Allah; and whoever disobeys me, disobeys Allah. (Qur'an 4:80; 72:23)	*Sahih Bukhari*, V5, Book 64, Hadith 3951 (S) *Sahih Muslim*, V2, Book 7, Hadith 2010 (S) *Ibn Majah*, V1, Book 1, Hadith 3 (S) *Abu-Dawud*, V1, Book 2, Hadith 1099 (S) *Al-Tirmidhi*, V3, Book 21, Hadith 1672 (S) *Al-Nasa'i*, V5, Book 39, Hadith 4198 (S)

Thaqalayn (Qur'an and Ahl al-Bayt).	Sahih Bukhari, al Ta'rikh al Kabir, V3, p. 96 Sahih Muslim, V6, Book 44, Hadith 6225 (S) Abu Dawud, Tadhkirat Khawass al-Ummah, 322 Al-Tirmidhi, V6, Book 46, Hadiths 3786, 3788 (S) Al-Nasa'i, Al-Khasais, p. 96, Hadith 79 Ahmad ibn Hanbal, V5, pp. 182, 189, 350, 366, 419
Twelve Caliphs are all from Quraysh.	Sahih Bukhari, V9, Book 93, Hadiths 7222–7223(S) Sahih Muslim, V5, Book 33, Hadith 4705 (S) Abu Dawud, V4, Book 35, Hadith 4280 (S) Al-Tirmidhi, V4, Book 31, Hadith 2223 (S) Ahmad ibn Hanbal, V5, p. 106
Cloak (Kisa) of Ahl al-Bayt.	Sahih Bukhari, Tafsir al-Kabir, V1, Part 2, p. 69 Sahih Muslim, V6, Book 44, Hadith 6261 (S) Al-Tirmidhi, V5, Book 44, Hadith 3205 (S) Al-Nasa'i, Al-Khasais, pp. 4, 8 Ahmad ibn Hanbal, V6, pp. 292, 298, 323
O Lord! These are my (Mohammad) family members (Ali, Fatima, Hassan, and Hussein).	Sahih Muslim, V6, Book 44, Hadith 6220 (S) Ibn Majah, Sunan, V1, p. 52 Al-Tirmidhi, V6, Book 46, Hadith 3724 (S) Ahmad ibn Hanbal, V1, p. 185
Prophet said: Who makes her (Fatima) angry makes me angry.	Sahih Bukhari, V5, Book 62, Hadith 3714 (S) Ibn Majah, Sunan, V1, p. 644 Al-Tirmidhi, Vol. 6, Book 46, Hadith 3867 (S) Ahmad ibn Hanbal, V5, p. 26

Umar denied Prophet's request for a pen and writing paper.	Sahih Bukhari, V1, Book 3, Hadith 114 (S) Sahih Muslim, V4, Book 25, Hadith 4234 (S)
You (Ali) are to me (Mohammad) as Aaron was to Moses, but there will be no Prophet after me.	Sahih Bukhari, V5, Book 64, Hadith 4416 (S) Sahih Muslim, V6, Book 44, Hadith 6218 (S) Ibn Majah, V1, Book 1, Hadith 121 (S) Al-Tirmidhi, V6, Book 46, Hadith 3730 (S) Al-Nasa'i, Al-Khasais, pp. 15–16 Ahmad ibn Hanbal, V1, p. 174
I (Mohammad) am the City of Knowledge (House of Wisdom) and Ali is its gate.	Al-Tirmidhi, V6, Book 46, Hadith 3723* (D)
Ali as Mawla after Prophet Mohammad.	Ibn Majah, V1, Book 1, Hadith 121 (S) Al-Tirmidhi, V6, Book 46, Hadith 3713 (S) Al-Nasa'i, Al-Khasais, pp. 4, 21–26, 40 Ahmad ibn Hanbal, V1, Hadith 641 (S)
Loving Ali is the sign of belief, and hating Ali is the sign of hypocrisy.	Sahih Muslim, V1, Book 1, Ch. 33, Hadith 235 (S) Ibn Majah, V1, Book 1, Hadith 114 (S) Al-Tirmidhi, V6, Book 46, Hadith 3718 (H) Al-Nasa'i, V6, Book 47, Hadith 5021 (S) Ahmad ibn Hanbal, V1, pp. 84, 95, 128
My Lord ordered me (Mohammad) that nobody can discharge my duty except myself or Ali.	Ibn Majah, V1, Book 1, Hadith 119 (H) Al-Tirmidhi, V6, Book 46, Hadith 3719 (H) Al-Nasa'i, Al-Khasais, p. 20

Karam Allahu Wajhah (May Allah bless his face) (Imam Ali).	Al-Nasai'i, V6, Book 51, Hadith 5614 (S) Ahmad ibn Hanbal, V3, Hadiths 1775, 1874
Umar said: You (Ali) have become my leader (mawla) and the leader of every faithful Muslim.	Ahmad ibn Hanbal, V4, p. 281, 368, 370
Umar said: Our best judge is Ali.	Sahih Bukhari, V6, Book 65, Hadith 4481 (S)
Imam al-Mahdi is from Prophet Mohammad's Ahl al-Bayt.	Ibn Majah, V5, Book 36, Hadith 4085 (H) Abu Dawud, V4, Book 35, Hadith 4284 (H) Al-Tirmidhi, V4, Book 31, Hadith 2230 (H)
Occultation of Imam al-Mahdi.	Al-Tirmidhi, V4, pp. 505–506; Al-Darimi, V4, p. 151

*Other Sunni references include:
Al Hakim, *Mustadrak*, iii, 126, 127
Al Khatib, *Tarikh Baghdad*, ii, 348, 377; vii, 172; xi, 48, 49
Al Muhibb al Tabari, *al Riyad al Nadirah*, ii, 193
Al Muttaqi, *Kanz al Ummal*, vi, 152, 156, 401
Ibn Hajar, *al Sawa'iq al Muhriqah*, 73
Al Manawi, *Kunuz al Haqaiq*, 43, and *Fayd al Qadir*, iii, 46
Al Haythami, *Majma al Zawa'id*, ix, 114
Ibn al Athir, *Usd al Ghabah*, iv, 22, and *Tahdhib al Tahdhib* (Hyderabad, 1325), vi, 152

Source: Data derived primarily from Darussalam Global Leader in Islamic Books, Riyadh, Saudi Arabia.

Appendix 6

Prophet Mohammad's *Farewell Sermon* at Ghadir Khumm
March 10, AD 632 (18th Dhu-l-Hijja, AH 10)

All Praise is due to Allah Who is Exalted in His Unity, Near in His Uniqueness, Sublime in His Authority, and Magnanimous in His Dominance. He knows everything; He subdues all creation through His might and evidence. He is Praised always and forever, Glorified and has no end. He begins and He repeats, and to Him every matter is referred.

Allah is the Creator of everything; He dominates with His power the earth and the heavens. Holy, He is, and Praised, the Lord of the angels and of the spirits. His favors overwhelm whatever He creates, and He is the Mighty over whatever He initiates. He observes all eyes while no eye can observe Him. He is Generous, Clement, and Patient. His mercy encompasses everything, and so is His giving. He never rushes His revenge, nor does He hasten the retribution they deserve. He comprehends what the breast conceals and what the conscience hides. No inner thought can be concealed from Him, nor does He confuse one with another. He encompasses everything, dominates everything, and subdues everything. Nothing is like Him. He initiates the creation from nothing; He is everlasting, living, sustaining in the truth; there is no god but He, the Omnipotent, the Wise One.

He is greater than can be conceived by visions, while He conceives all visions, the Eternal, the Knowing. None can describe Him by seeing Him, nor can anyone find out how He is, be it by his intellect or by a spoken word except through what leads to Him, the Sublime, the Mighty that He is.

I testify that He is Allah, the One Who has filled time with His Holiness, the One Whose Light overwhelms eternity, Who effects His will without consulting anyone; there is no partner with Him in His decisions, nor is He assisted in running His affairs. He shaped what He made without following a preexisting model, and He created whatever He created without receiving help from anyone, nor did doing so exhaust Him nor frustrated His designs. He created, and so it was, and He initiated, and it became visible. So He is Allah, the One and Only God, the One Who does whatever He does extremely well. He is the Just One Who never oppresses, the most Holy to Whom all affairs are referred.

I further testify that He is Allah before Whom everything is humbled, to Whose Greatness everything is humiliated, and to Whose Dignity everything submits. He is the King of every domain and the One Who places planets in their orbits. He controls the movements of the sun and of the moon; each circles till a certain time. He makes the night follow the day and the day follow the night, seeking it incessantly. He splits the spine of every stubborn tyrant and annihilates every mighty devil.

Never has there been any opponent opposing Him nor a peer assisting Him. He is Independent; He never begets nor is He begotten, and none can ever be His equal. He is One God, the Glorified Lord. His will is done; His word is the law. He knows, so He takes account. He causes death and gives life. He makes some poor and others rich. He causes some to smile and others to cry. He brings some nearer to Him while distancing others from Him. He withholds and He gives. The domain belongs to Him and so is all the Praise. In His hand is all goodness, and He can do anything at all.

He lets the night cover the day and the day cover the night; there is no god but He, the Sublime, the oft-Forgiving One. He responds to the supplication; He gives generously; He computes the breath; He is the Lord of the jinns and of mankind, the One Whom nothing confuses, nor is He annoyed by those who cry for His help, nor is He fed-up by those who persist. He safeguards the righteous against sinning, and He enables the winners to win. He is the Master of the faithful, the Lord of the Worlds Who deserves the appreciation of all those whom He created and is praised no matter what.

I praise Him and always thank Him for the ease He brings me and for the constriction, in hardship and in prosperity, and I believe in Him, in His angels, in His Books and messengers. I listen to His Command and I obey, and I initiate the doing of whatever pleases Him, and I submit to His decree hoping to acquire obedience to Him and fear of His penalty, for He is Allah against Whose designs nobody should feel secure, nor should anyone ever fear His "oppression."

I testify, even against my own soul, that I am His servant, and I bear witness that He is my Lord. I convey what He reveals to me, being cautious lest I should not do it, so a catastrophe from Him would befall upon me, one which none can keep away, no matter how great His design may be and how sincere His friendship. There is no god but He, for He has informed me that if I do not convey what He has just revealed to me in honor of 'Ali in truth, I will not have conveyed His Message at all, and He, the Praised and the Exalted One, has guaranteed for me to protect me from the (evil) people, and He is Allah, the One Who suffices, the Sublime. He has just revealed to me the following (verse):

"In The Name of Allah, the Most Gracious, the Most Merciful."

"(O' Our Apostle Mohammad!) Deliver thou what hath been sent down unto thee from thy Lord; and if thou dost it not, then (it will be as if) thou hast not delivered His message (at all); and surely will Allah protect thee from (the mischief) of men; verily, Allah guideth not an infidel people." (Qur'an 5:67)

O people! I have not committed any shortcoming in conveying what Allah Almighty revealed to me, and I am now going to explain to you the reason behind the revelation of this verse: Three times did Gabriel command me on behalf of the Peace, my Lord, Who is the source of all peace, to thus make a stand in order to inform everyone, black and white, that: 'Ali ibn Abu Talib is my Brother, Wasi, and successor over my Ummah and the Imam after me, the one whose status to me is like that of Aaron to Moses except there will be no prophet after me, and he is your master next only to Allah and to His Messenger, and Allah has already revealed to me the same in one of the fixed verses of His Book saying, *"Verily, your guardian is (none else but) Allah and His Apostle (Mohammad) and those who believe, those who establish prayer and pay the poor-rate, while they be (even) bowing down (in prayer)."* (Qur'an, 5:55) and Ali ibn Abu Talib, the one who keeps up prayers, who pays zakat even as he bows down, seeking to please Allah, the Sublime, the Almighty, on each and every occasion.

I asked Gabriel to plead to the Peace to excuse me from having to convey such a message to you, O' people, due to my knowledge that the pious are few while the hypocrites are many, and due to those who will blame me, and due to the trickery of those who ridicule Islam and whom Allah described in His Book as saying with their tongues contrarily to what their hearts conceal, thinking lightly of it, while it is with Allah magnanimous, and due to the abundance of their harm to me, so much so that they called me "ears" and claimed that I am so because of being so much in his ('Ali's) company, always welcoming him, loving him and being so much pleased with him till Allah, the Exalted and the Sublime One, revealed in this regard the verse saying: *"Among them are those who hurt the Apostle (Mohammad) and say they (that) 'he is (all)-ear' (uthun; i.e. he always listens to 'Ali). Say: One who listens (to 'Ali) is good for you; he believeth in Allah and hath faith in the believers and a mercy unto those of you who believe, and those who hurt the Apostle of Allah (Mohammad) for them is a grievous chastisement."* (Qur'an, 9:61)

Had I wished to name those who have called me so, I would have called them by their names, and I would have pointed them out. I would have singled them out and called them by what they really are, but I, by Allah, am fully aware of their affairs. Yet despite all of that, Allah insisted that I should convey what He has just revealed to me in honor of Ali. Then the Prophet recited the following verse:

"(O' Our Apostle Mohammad!) Deliver thou what hath been sent down unto thee from thy Lord (with regard to 'Ali); and if thou dost it not, then (it will be as if) thou hast not delivered His message (at all); and surely will Allah

protect thee from (the mischief) of men; verily, Allah guideth not an infidel people." (Qur'an, 5:67)

O people! Comprehend (the implications of) what I have just said, and again do comprehend it, and be (further) informed that Allah has installed him ('Ali) as your Master and Imam, obligating the Muhajirun and the Ansar and those who follow them in goodness to obey him, and so must everyone who lives in the desert or in the city, who is a non-Arab or an Arab, who is a free man or a slave, who is young or old, white or black, and so should everyone who believes in His Unity. His decree shall be carried out. His ('Ali's) word is binding; his command is obligating; cursed is whoever opposes him, blessed with mercy is whoever follows him and believes in him, for Allah has already forgiven him and forgiven whoever listens to him and obeys him.

O people! This is the last stand I make in such a situation; so listen and obey and submit to the Command of Allah, your Lord, for Allah, the Exalted and the Sublime One, is your Master and Lord, then next to Him is His Messenger and Prophet who is now addressing you, then after me 'Ali is your Master and Imam according to the Command of Allah, your Lord, then the Imams from among my progeny, his offspring, till the Day you meet Allah and His Messenger.

Nothing is permissible except what is deemed so by Allah, His Messenger, and they (the Imams), and nothing is prohibitive except what is deemed so by Allah and His Messenger and they (the Imams). Allah, the Exalted and the Sublime One, has made me acquainted with what is permissible and what is prohibitive, and I have conveyed to you what my Lord has taught me of His Book, of what it decrees as permissible or as prohibitive.

O people! Prefer him ('Ali) to all others! There is no knowledge except that Allah has divulged it to me, and all the knowledge I have learned I have divulged to Imam al-Muttaqin (leader of the righteous), and there is no knowledge (that I know) except that I divulged it to 'Ali, and he is al-Imam al-Mubin (the evident Imam) whom Allah mentions in Surat Ya-Sin: *"… and everything have We confined (recorded) into a Manifesting Imam (Guide)."* (Qur'an, 36:12)

O people! Do not abandon him, nor should you flee away from him, nor should you be too arrogant to accept his authority, for he is the one who guides to righteousness and who acts according to it. He defeats falsehood and prohibits others from acting according to it, accepting no blame from anyone while seeking to please Allah. He is the first to believe in Allah and in His Messenger; none preceded him as such. And he is the one who offered his life as a sacrifice for the Messenger of Allah and who was in the company of the Messenger of Allah while no other man was. He is the first of all people to offer prayers and the first to worship Allah with me. I ordered him, on behalf of Allah, to sleep in my bed, and he did, offering his life as a sacrifice for my sake.

O people! Prefer him (over all others), for Allah has preferred him, and accept him, for Allah has appointed him (as your leader).

O people! He is an Imam appointed by Allah, and Allah shall never accept the repentance of anyone who denies his authority, nor shall He forgive him; this is a must decree from Allah never to do so to anyone who opposes him, and that He shall torment him with a most painful torment for all time to come, for eternity; so, beware lest you should oppose him and thus enter the fire the fuel of which is the people and the stones prepared for the unbelievers.

O people! By Allah! All past prophets and messengers conveyed the glad tiding of my advent, and I, by Allah, am the seal of the prophets and of the messengers and the argument against all beings in the heavens and on earth. Anyone who doubts this commits apostasy similar to that of the early jahiliyya, and anyone who doubts anything of what I have just said doubts everything which has been revealed to me, and anyone who doubts any of the Imams doubts all of them, and anyone who doubts us shall be lodged in the fire.

O people! Allah, the most Exalted and the Almighty, has bestowed this virtue upon me out of His kindness towards 'Ali and as a boon to 'Ali and there is no god but He; to Him all praise belongs in all times, for eternity, and in all circumstances.

O people! Prefer 'Ali (over all others), for he is the very best of all people after me, be they males or females, so long as Allah sends down

His sustenance, so long as there are beings. Cursed and again cursed, condemned and again condemned, is anyone who does not accept this statement of mine and who does not agree to it. Gabriel himself has informed me of the same on behalf of Allah Almighty Who he said (in Gabriel's words): "Anyone who antagonizes 'Ali and refuses to accept his wilayat shall incur My curse upon him and My wrath." *"… Let every soul (carefully) look well to what it hath sent on for the morrow (the Day of Reckoning); and fear ye (the wrath of) Allah; verily Allah is All-Aware of whatsoever ye do."* (Qur'an, 59:18) *"And take ye not your oaths a means of deceit between you, lest slippeth a foot after it hath been firmly fixed…."* (Qur'an, 16:94) *"…Allah is All-Aware of what ye do."* (Qur'an, 58:13)

O people! He ('Ali) is janb-Allah mentioned in the Book of Allah, the Sublime One: The Almighty, forewarning his ('Ali's) adversaries, says, *"Lest a soul should say: 'Oh! Alas, Woe unto me! for what I failed (in my duty) unto Allah, and certainly was I of those who mocked."* (Qur'an, 39:56)

O people! Study the Qur'an and comprehend its verses, look into its fixed verses and do not follow what is similar thereof, for by Allah, none shall explain to you what it forbids you from doing, nor clarify its exegesis, other than the one whose hand I am taking and whom I am lifting to me, the one whose arm I am taking and whom I am lifting, so that I may enable you to understand that: Whoever among you takes me as his master, this, Ali is his master, and he is 'Ali ibn Abu Talib, my Brother and wasi, and his appointment as your wali is from Allah, the Sublime, the Exalted One, a commandment which He revealed to me.

O people! 'Ali and the good ones from among my offspring from his loins are the Lesser Weight, while the Qur'an is the Greater One: each one of them informs you of and agrees with the other. They shall never part till they meet me at the Pool (of Kawthar). They are the Trustees of Allah over His creation, the rulers on His earth.

Indeed now I have performed my duty and conveyed the Message. Indeed you have heard what I have said and explained. Indeed Allah, the Exalted One and the Sublime, has said, and so have I on behalf of Allah, the Exalted One and the Sublime, that there is no Ameerul-Mo'mineen

(Commander of the Faithful) save this Brother of mine; no authority over a believer is permissible after me except to him.

[Then the Prophet patted 'Ali's arm, lifting him up. Since the time when the Messenger of Allah ascended the pulpit, Ameerul-Mo'mineen was one pulpit step below where the Messenger of Allah had seated himself on his pulpit, while 'Ali was on his (Prophet's) right side, one pulpit step lower, now they both appeared to the gathering to be on the same level; the Prophet lifted him up. The Prophet then raised his hands to the heavens in supplication while 'Ali's leg was touching the knee of the Messenger of Allah. The Prophet continued his sermon thus:]

O people! This is 'Ali, my Brother, Wasi, the one who comprehends my knowledge, and my successor over my Ummah, over everyone who believes in me. He is the one entrusted with explaining the Book of Allah, the Most Exalted One, the Sublime, and the one who invites people to His path. He (Ali) is the one who does whatever pleases Him, fighting His enemies, befriending His friends who obey Him, prohibiting disobedience to Him. He is the successor of the Messenger of Allah and Ameerul- Mo'mineen, the man assigned by Allah to guide others, killer of the renegades and of those who believe in equals to Allah, those who violate the Commandments of Allah. Allah says, *Changeth not the word with Me, nor am I (in the least) unjust unto (any of) the servants.* (Qur'an, 50.29) and by Your Command, O Lord, do I (submit and) say, O Allah! Befriend whoever befriends him (Ali) and be the enemy of whoever antagonizes him; support whoever supports him and abandon whoever abandons him; curse whoever disavows him, and let Your Wrath descend on whoever usurps his right.

O Lord! You revealed a verse in honor of 'Ali, Your wali, in its explanation and to effect Your own appointment of him this very day did You say, *"… This day have I perfected for you, your religion, and have completed My favor on you, and chosen for you Islam (to be) the Religion …"* (Qur'an, 5.3); *"And whosoever seeketh any religion other than Islam (total resignation unto Allah), never shall it be accepted from him, and in the next world he shall be among the losers."* (Qur'an, 3:85)

Lord! I implore You to testify that I have conveyed (Your Message).

O people! Allah, the Exalted and the Sublime, has perfected your religion through his ('Ali's) Imamat; so, whoever rejects him as his Imam or rejects those of my offspring from his loins who assume the same status (as lmams) till the Day of Judgment when they shall all be displayed before Allah, the Exalted and the Sublime, these are the ones whose (good) deeds shall be nil and void in the life of this world and in the hereafter, and in the fire shall they be lodged forever, "... *torment shall not be lightened for them nor shall they have respite.*" (Qur'an, 2:162)

O people! Here is 'Ali, the one who has supported me more than anyone else among you, the one who most deserves my gratitude, the one who is closest of all of you to me and the one who is the very dearest to me. Both Allah, the Exalted and the Sublime, and I are pleased with him, and no verse of the Holy Qur'an expressing Allah's Pleasure except that he is implied therein, nor has any verse of praise been revealed in the Qur'an except that he is implied therein, nor has the Lord testified to Paradise in the (Qur'anic) Chapter starting with "*Surely did come over man to pass an occasion of time when he was nothing, mentioned of?*" (Qur'an, 76:1) nor was this Chapter revealed except in his praise.

O people! He is the one who supports the religion of Allah, who argues on behalf of the Messenger of Allah. He is the pious, the pure, and the guide, the one rightly guided. Your Prophet is the best of all prophets, and your wasi is the best of all wasis, and his offspring are the best of wasis.

O people! Each prophet's progeny is from his own loins whereas mine is from the loins of Ameerul-Mo'mineen 'Ali.

O people! Iblis caused Adam to be dismissed from the garden through envy; so, do not envy him lest your deeds should be voided and lest your feet should slip away, for Adam was sent down to earth after having committed only one sin, and he was among the elite of Allah's creation. How, then, will be your case, and you being who you are, and among you are enemies of Allah?

Indeed, none hates 'Ali except a wretch, and none accepts 'Ali's wilayat except a pious person. None believes in him except a sincere mu'min, and in honor of, Ali was the Chapter of 'Asr (Ch. 103) revealed, I swear to it by Allah: *"In the Name of Allah, the Beneficent, the Merciful. By the time! Verily man is in loss!"* (Qur'an, 103:1–2), except 'Ali who believed and was pleased with the truth and with perseverance.

O people! I have sought Allah to be my Witness and have conveyed my Message to you, and the Messenger is obligated only to clearly convey (his Message).

O people! *"... Fear ye Allah as ye should: and (see that) ye die not but as Muslims."* (Qur'an, 3:102) O people! *"... Believe in what We have sent down confirming what is (already) with you, ere We change their faces (features) and turn them towards their backs, or as We cursed the people of Sabath ..."* (Qur'an, 4:47) By Allah! He did not imply anyone in this verse except a certain band of my sahaba whom I know by name and by lineage, and I have been ordered (by my Lord) to pardon them; so, let each person deal with 'Ali according to what he finds in his heart of love or of hatred.

O people! The nur from Allah, the Exalted One and the Sublime, flows through me then through 'Ali ibn Abu Talib then in the progeny that descends from him till al-Qa'im al-Mahdi, who shall effect the justice of Allah, and who will take back any right belonging to us because Allah, the Exalted and the Sublime, made us Hujjat over those who take us lightly, the stubborn ones, those who act contrarily to our word, who are treacherous, who are sinners, who are oppressors, who are usurpers, from the entire world.

O people! I warn you that I am the Messenger of Allah; messengers before me have already passed away; so, should I die or should I be killed, are you going to turn upon your heels? And whoever turns upon his heels shall not harm Allah in the least, and Allah shall reward those who are grateful, those who persevere. 'Ali is surely the one described with perseverance and gratitude, then after him are my offspring from his loins.

O people! Do not think that you are doing me a favor by your accepting Islam. Nay! Do not think that you are doing Allah such a favor lest He should void your deeds, lest His wrath should descend upon you, lest He should try you with a flame of fire and brass; surely your Lord is ever watchful.

O people! There shall be Imams after me who shall invite people to the fire, and they shall not be helped on the Day of Judgment.

O people! Allah and I are both clear of them.

O people! They and their supporters and followers shall be in the lowest rung of the fire; miserable, indeed, is the resort of the arrogant ones. Indeed, these are the folks of the sahifa; so, let each one of you look into his sahifa!

O people! I am calling for it to be an Imamat and a succession confined to my offspring till the Day of Judgment, and I have conveyed only what I have been commanded (by my Lord) to convey to drive the argument home against everyone present or absent and on everyone who has witnessed or who has not, who is already born or he who is yet to be born; therefore, let those present here convey it to those who are absent, and let the father convey it to his son, and so on till the Day of Judgment.

And they shall make the Imamat after me a property, a usurpation; may Allah curse the usurpers who usurp, and it is then that you, O jinns and mankind, will get the full attention of the One Who shall cause a flame of fire and brass to be hurled upon you, and you shall not achieve any victory!

O people! Allah, the Exalted and the Sublime, is not to let you be whatever you want to be except so that He may distinguish the bad ones from among you from the good, and Allah is not to make you acquainted with the unknown.

O people! There shall be no town that falsifies except that Allah shall annihilate it on account of its falsehood before the Day of Judgment, and He shall give al-Imam al-Mahdi authority over it, and surely Allah's promise is true.

O people! Most of the early generations before you have strayed, and by Allah, He surely annihilated the early generations, and He shall annihilate the later ones. Allah Almighty has said, "What! Destroyed We not the former people? Then did We make the later people follow them, thus We deal with the guilty ones. Woe on the Day unto the beliers." (Qur'an, 77: 16–19)

299

O people! Allah has ordered me to do and not to do, and I have ordered 'Ali to do and not to do, so he learned what should be done and what should not; therefore, you should listen to his orders so that you may be safe, and you should obey him so that you may be rightly guided. Do not do what he forbids you from doing so that you may acquire wisdom. Agree with him, and do not let your paths be different from his.

O people! I am al-Sirat al-Mustaqeem (the Straight Path) of Allah whom He commanded you to follow, and it is after me 'Ali then my offspring from his loins, the Imams of Guidance: they guide to the truth and act accordingly.

Then the Prophet recited the entire text of Surat al-Fatiha and commented by saying: It is in my honor that this (Sura) was revealed, including them (the Imams) specifically; they are the friends of Allah for whom there shall be no fear, nor shall they grieve; truly the Party of Allah are the winners. Indeed, it is their enemies who are the impudent ones, the deviators, the brethren of Satan; they inspire each other with embellished speech out of their haughtiness.

Indeed, their (Imams) friends are the ones whom Allah, the Exalted One, the Great, mentions in His Book saying, *"Thou shall find not a people who believe in Allah and in the hereafter befriending those who oppose Allah and His Apostle, be they even their own fathers, or their sons, or their own brothers, or their kinsmen, they are those Allah hath inscribed faith in their hearts and hath strengthened them …"* (Qur'an, 58:22) Indeed, their (Imams) friends are the mu'mins (believers) whom Allah, the Exalted One, the Sublime, describes as: *"Those who believe and mix not their faith with iniquity, those are they for whom is security, and they are (the ones) guided aright."* (Qur'an, 6:82)

Indeed, their friends are those who believed and never doubted. Indeed, their friends are the ones who shall enter Paradise in peace and security; the angels shall receive them with welcome saying, "Peace be upon you! Enter it and reside in it forever!"

Indeed, their friends shall be rewarded with Paradise where they shall be sustained without having to account for anything.

Indeed, their enemies are the ones who shall be hurled into the fire.

Indeed, their enemies are the ones who shall hear the exhalation of hell as it increases in intensity, and they shall see it sigh.

Indeed, their enemies are the ones thus described by Allah: "... *Everytime a (new) people entereth (it) it shall curse its sister ...*" (Qur'an, 7:38)

Indeed, their enemies are the ones whom Allah, the Exalted One and the Sublime, describes thus: "*As it would burst with rage; whenever a group is flung into it, its keepers shall ask them; 'Came not there unto you a warner?' They shall say: 'Yea! Indeed a warner did come unto us, but we belied (him)' and said we: 'Allah hath sent not down aught, ye are in naught but a vast delusion!' And they shall say: 'Had we but hearkened (unto them) or pondered (over what they said), we would not have been amidst the fellows in the flaming fire. So shall they confess their sins, but far will be (from mercy) the fellows in blazing fire.'*" (Qur'an, 67:8–11)

Indeed, their friends are the ones who fear their Lord in the unseen; forgiveness shall be theirs and a great reward.

O people! What a difference it is between the fire and the great reward!

O people! Our enemy is the one whom Allah censures and curses, whereas our friend is everyone praised and loved by Allah.

O people! I am the Warner (nathir) and 'Ali is the one who brings glad tidings (bashir).

O people! I am the one who warns (munthir) while 'Ali is the guide (hadi).

O people! I am a Prophet (nabi) and 'Ali is the successor (wasi).

O people! I am a Messenger (rasul) and 'Ali is the Imam and the Wasi after me, and so are the Imams after him from among his offspring. Indeed, I am their father, and they shall descend from his loins.

Indeed, the seal of the Imams from among us is al-Qa'im al-Mahdi. He, indeed, is the one who shall come out so that the creed may prevail. He, indeed, is the one who shall seek revenge against the oppressor. He, indeed, is the one who conquers the forts and demolishes them. He, indeed, is the one who subdues every tribe from among the people of polytheism and the one to guide it.

He is the one who shall seek redress for all friends of Allah. He is the one who supports the religion of Allah. He ever derives (his knowledge) from a very deep ocean. He shall identify each man of distinction by his distinction and every man of ignorance by his ignorance. He shall be the choicest of Allah's beings and the chosen one. He is the heir of all (branches of) knowledge, the one who encompasses every perception. He conveys on behalf of his Lord, the Exalted and the Sublime, who points out His miracles. He is the wise, the one endowed with wisdom, the one upon whom (divine) authority is vested.

Glad tidings of him have been conveyed by past generations, yet he is the one who shall remain as a Hujja, and there shall be no Hujja after him, or any right except with him, or any nur (light) except with him. None, indeed, shall subdue him, nor shall he ever be vanquished. He is the friend of Allah on His earth, the judge over His creatures, and the custodian of what is evident and what is hidden of His.

O people! I have explained (everything) for you and enabled you to comprehend it, and this 'Ali shall after me explain everything to you.

At the conclusion of my khutba, I shall call upon you to shake hands with me to swear your allegiance to him and to recognize his authority, and then to shake hands with him after you have shaken hands with me.

I had, indeed, sworn allegiance to Allah, and 'Ali had sworn allegiance to me, and I on behalf of Allah, the Exalted One and the Sublime, I require you to swear the oath of allegiance to him: *"Verily those who swear their fealty unto thee do but swear fealty unto Allah; the hand of Allah is above their hands; so whosoever violateth his oath, doth violate it only to the hurt of his (own) self; and whosoever fulfilleth what he hath convenanted with Allah, soon will Allah grant him a great recompense."* (Qur'an, 48:10)

O people! The pilgrimage (haj) and the 'umra are among Allah's rituals; *"Verily, 'Safa' and 'Marwa' are among the signs of Allah; whoever therefore maketh a pilgrimage to the House or performeth 'Umra'. Therefore it shall be no blame on him to go round them both …"* (Qur'an, 2:158)

O people! Perform your pilgrimage to the House, for no members of a family went there except that they became wealthy, and receive glad tidings! None failed to do so except that their lineage was cut-off and were impoverished.

O people! No believer stands at the standing place [at 'Arafa] except that Allah forgives his past sins till then; so, once his pilgrimage is over, he resumes his deeds.

O people! Pilgrims are assisted, and their expenses shall be replenished, and Allah never suffers the rewards of the doers of good to be lost.

O people! Perform your pilgrimage to the House by perfecting your religion and by delving into fiqh, and do not leave the sacred places except after having repented and abandoned (the doing of anything prohibited).

O people! Uphold prayers and pay the zakat as Allah, the Exalted One and the Sublime, commanded you; so, if time lapses and you were short of doing so or you forgot, 'Ali is your wali and he will explain for you.

He is the one whom Allah, the Exalted and the Sublime, appointed for you after me as the custodian of His creation. He is from me and I am from him, and he and those who will succeed him from my progeny shall inform you of anything you ask them about, and they shall clarify whatever you do not know.

Halal and haram things are more than I can count for you now or explain, for a commandment to enjoin what is permissible and a prohibition from what is not permissible are both on the same level, so I was ordered (by my Lord) to take your oath of allegiance and to make a covenant with you to accept what I brought you from Allah, the Exalted One and the Sublime, with regards to 'Ali Ameerul-Mo'mineen and to the wasis after him who are from me and from him, a standing Imamat whose seal is al-Mahdi till the Day he meets Allah Who decrees and Who judges.

O people! I never refrained from informing you of everything permissible or prohibitive; so, do remember this and safeguard it and advise each other to do likewise; do not alter it; do not substitute it with something else.

I am now repeating what I have already said: Uphold the prayers and pay the zakat and enjoin righteousness and forbid abomination.

The peak of enjoining righteousness is to resort to my speech and to convey it to whoever did not attend it and to order him on my behalf to accept it and to (likewise) order him not to violate it, for it is an order from Allah, the Exalted and the Sublime, and there is no knowledge of enjoining righteousness nor prohibiting abomination except that it is with a ma'soom Imam.

O people! The Qur'an informs you that the Imams after him are his ('Ali's) descendants, and I have already informed you that they are from me and from him, for Allah says in His Book, *"And he made it a word (doctrine) to continue in his progeny that they may return (unto Allah)."* (Qur'an, 43:28) while I have said: "You shall not stray as long as you uphold both of them (simultaneously)."

O people! (Uphold) piety, (uphold) piety, and be forewarned of the Hour as Allah, the Exalted and the Sublime, has said, *"O' ye people! Fear ye your Lord! Verily, the quake of the Hour (of Doom) is a thing tremendous!"* (Qur'an, 22:1)

Remember death, resurrection, the judgment, the scales, and the account before the Lord of the Worlds, and (remember) the rewards and the penalty. So whoever does a good deed shall be rewarded for it, and whoever commits a sin shall have no place in the Gardens.

O people! You are more numerous than (it is practical) to shake hands with me all at the same time, and Allah, the Exalted and the Sublime, commanded me to require you to confirm what authority I have vested upon 'Ali Ameerul-Mo'mineen and to whoever succeeds him of the Imams from me and from him, since I have just informed you that my offspring are from his loins.

You, therefore, should say in one voice: "We hear, and we obey; we accept and we are bound by what you have conveyed to us from our Lord and yours with regard to our Imam 'Ali Ameerul-Mo'mineen, and to the Imams, your sons from his loins. We swear the oath of allegiance to you in this regard with our hearts, with our souls, with our tongues, with our hands. According to it shall we live, and according to it shall we die, and according to it shall we be resurrected. We shall not alter anything or substitute anything with another, nor shall we doubt nor deny nor suspect, nor shall we violate our covenant nor abrogate the pledge. You admonished us on behalf of Allah with regard to 'Ali Ameerul-Mo'mineen, and to the Imams whom you mentioned to be from your offspring from among his descendants after him: al-Hasan and al-Husain and to whoever is appointed (as such) by Allah after them. The covenant and the pledge are taken from us, from our hearts, from our souls, from our tongues, from our conscience, from our hands. Whoever does so by his handshake, it shall be so, or otherwise testified to it by his tongue, and we do not seek any substitute for it, nor shall Allah see our souls deviating there from. We shall convey the same on your behalf to anyone near and far of our offspring and families, and we implore Allah to testify to it, and surely Allah suffices as the Witness and you, too, shall testify for us."

O people! What are you going to say? Allah knows every sound and the innermost of every soul; *"Whosoever getteth guided aright, verily he getteth guided aright for his ownself; and he who goeth astray, verily he goeth astray against his ownself ..."* (Qur'an, 17:15)

O people! Swear the oath of allegiance to Allah, and swear it to me, and swear it to 'Ali Ameerul-Mo'mineen, and to al-Hasan and al-Husain and to the Imams from their offspring in the life of this world and in the hereafter, a word that shall always remain so. Allah shall annihilate anyone guilty of treachery and be merciful upon everyone who remains true to his word: *"... whosoever violateth his oath, doth violate it only to the hurt of his (own) self; and whosoever fulfilleth what he hath covenanted with Allah, soon will Allah grant him a great recompense."* (Qur'an, 48:10)

O people! Repeat what I have just told you to, and greet 'Ali with the title of authority of "Ameerul-Mo'mineen" and say: *"... We have heard and obeyed (and we implore) Thy forgiveness, O' Our Lord! And unto Thee is our march."* (Qur'an, 2:285) and you should say: *"... All praise be (only) to Allah who guided us to this and we would not have been guided had not Allah guided us ..."* (Qur'an, 7:43)

O people! The merits of 'Ali ibn Abu Talib with Allah, the Exalted and the Sublime, the merits which are revealed in the Qur'an, are more numerous than I can recount in one speech; so, whoever informs you of them and defines them for you, you should believe him.

O people! Whoever obeys Allah and His Messenger and 'Ali and the Imams to whom I have already referred shall attain a great victory. O people! Those foremost from among you who swear allegiance to him and who pledge to obey him and who greet him with the greeting of being the Commander of the Faithful are the ones who shall win the Gardens of Felicity.

O people! Say what brings you the Pleasure of Allah, for if you and all the people of the earth disbelieve, it will not harm Allah in the least.

O Lord! Forgive the believers through what I have conveyed, and let Your Wrath descend upon those who renege, the apostates, and all Praise is due to Allah, the Lord of the Worlds.

References: *Farewell Sermon* at Ghadir Khumm:

1.   Jalaal ad-Deen al-Sayyuti, Kitab Al-Itqaan, Vol. 1, p. 31.
2.   al-Majlisi, Bihar al-Anwar, Vol. 21, pp. 360–90, Vol. 37, pp. 111–235, and Vol. 41, p. 228.
3.   Al-Bidaaya wal Nihaaya, Vol. 5, p. 208.
4.   Badee' al-Ma'aani, p. 75.
5.   Tareekh Baghdad, Vol. 1, p. 411 and Vol. 8, p. 290.
6.   Tareekh Dimashq, Vol. 5, p. 210.
7.   Ibn al-Jawziyya, Tadh'kirat al-Khawaas, pp. 18–20.
8.   Ibn al-Sa'ud's Tafseer, Vol. 8, p. 292.
9.   Al-Tibari, Tafseer al-Qur'an, Vol. 3, p. 428 and Vol. 6, p. 46.
10.   al-Fakhr al-Razi, Al-Tafseer al-Kabeer, Vol. 3, p. 636.
11.   Al-Tamhid fi Usool al-Deen, p. 171.
12.   Tayseer al-Wusul, Vol. 1, p. 122.
13.   Ghiyaath ad-Din ibn Hammaam, Tareekh Habib al-Siyar, Vol. 1, p. 144.
14.   al-Maqrizi, Khutat, p. 223.

15. al-Sayyuti, Al-Durr al-Manthur, Vol. 2, pp. 259, 298.

16. Thakhaa'ir al-'Uqba, p. 68.

17. Ruh al-Ma'aani, Vol. 2, p. 348.

18. Mohibb al-Tabal-; Al Riyadh al-radhirah, Vol. 2, p.169.

19. Al-Siraaj al-Munir, Vol. 4, p. 364.

20. al-Hakim, Al-Seera al-Halabiyya, Vol. 3, p. 302.

21. Shar'h al-Mawaahib, Vol. 7, p. 13.

22. Ibn Hajar al-' Asqalaani, Al-Sawaa'iq al-Muhriqa, p. 26.

23. Ibn al-Badriq, Al-'Umda, p. 52.

24. Badr ad-Deen, 'Umdat al-Qari fi Shar'h al-Bukhari, Vol. 8, p. 584.

25. al-Ghadeer, Vol. 2, p. 57.

26. Sharafud-Deen al-Musawi, AI-Fusul al-Muhimma, pp. 25–27.

27. Fadha 'il al-Sahaaba, p. 272.

28. Faydh al-Ghadeer, Vol. 6, p. 218.

29. Kashf al-Ghumma, p. 94.

30. Kifaayat al- Taalib, pp. 17, 28.

31. al-Muttaqi al-Hindi, Kanz al-'Ummaal, Vol. 6, p. 397.

32. Imam Ibn Hanbal, Musnad, Vol. 4, p. 281.

33. Mishkaat al-Masabeeh, p. 272.

34. Mushkil al-aathaar, Vol. 3, p. 196.

35. Mataalib al-Su'ul, p. 16.

36. Muftah al-Najaat, p. 216.

37. al-Shahristaani, AI-Milal wal Nihal, V 01. 1, p. 220.

38. al-Khawarizmi, Manaaqib, pp. 80, 94.

39. Ibn al-Maghaazli, Manaaqib, p. 232.

40. al-Qastalani, Al-Mawaahib, Vol. 2, p. 13.

41. al-Samhudi, Wafaa' al-Wafaa', Vol. 2, p. 173.

42. al-Qanduzi, Yanabi al-Mawadda, p. 120.

Source: Darul Islam Center, Inc. (Duas.org), March 1999.

Appendix 7

Sunni Collectors of Hadiths (Living at the Time of the Emirs and Caliphs)

Collectors of Hadiths

Caliph (Birth-Death Year AD)	Sahih Bukhari (810–870)	Sahih Muslim (818–875)	Abu Dawud (817–888)	Ibn Majah (824–886)	Al Tirmidhi (824–892)	Nasa'i (829–915)
Umayyad Emirs:						
Abd Ar-Rahman II (822–852)	X	X	X	X	X	X
Muhammad I (852–886)	X	X	X	X	X	X
Al-Mundhir (886–888)			X	X	X	X
Abdallah ibn Muhammad (888–912)					X	X
Abd-ar-Rahman III (912–929)						X
Abbasid Caliphs:						
Al-Ma'mun (813–833)	X	X	X	X	X	X
Al-Mu'tasim (833–842)	X	X	X	X	X	X
Al-Wathiq (842–847)	X	X	X	X	X	X
Al-Mutawakkil (847–861)	X	X	X	X	X	X

Caliph (Birth-Death Year AD)	Sahih Bukhari (810–870)	Sahih Muslim (818–875)	Abu Dawud (817–888)	Ibn Majah (824–886)	Al Tirmidhi (824–892)	Nasa'i (829–915)
Al-Muntasir (861–862)	X	X	X	X	X	X
Al-Musta'in (862–866)	X	X	X	X	X	X
Al-Mu'tazz (866–869)	X	X	X	X	X	X
Al-Muhtadi (869–870)	X	X	X	X	X	X
Al-Mu'tamid (870–892)	X	X	X	X	X	X
Al-Mu'tadid (892–902)						X
Al-Muktafi (902–908)						X
Al-Muqtadir (908–932)						X
Fatimid Caliphs:						
Al-Mahdi Billah (909–934)						X
Imams of Ahl al-Bayt:						
Mohammad al-Jawad (811–835)	X	X	X	X	X	X
Ali al-Hadi (827–868)	X	X	X	X	X	X
Hassan al-Askari (846–874)	X	X	X	X	X	X
Mohammad al-Mahdi (869–Present)	X	X	X	X	X	X
Shi'a Hadiths (Al Kafi):						
Al-Kulayni (864–940)	X	X	X	X	X	X

X signifies Sunni collector of hadiths living at the time of the Emirs and caliphs.

Source: Analysis by Tallal Alie Turfe on data derived from Wikipedia.

Appendix 8

Sunni Prerequisites to Becoming a Caliph

Based on the following seven Sunni prerequisites to becoming a caliph, undeniably and unequivocally, Imam Ali ibn Abi Talib was the only one who not only self-actualized in each prerequisite but also overwhelmingly was superior to anyone else in this regard.

1, 2, and 3: Muslim, Male, Tribe of Quraysh

+ Imam Ali ibn Abi Talib is from the clan of Banu Hashim in the Quraysh tribe and the first male (after Prophet Mohammad) to accept Islam.

4: Knowledgeable in Islam, Able to Make Independent Decisions

+ Prophet Mohammad said: "I am the City of Knowledge and Ali is its Gate." (*Al-Tirmidhi*, V6, Book 46, Hadith 3723)
+ Prophet Mohammad said: "The most knowledgeable person in my nation after me is Ali." (Imam Reza Network [*Manaqib al-Imam Ali ibn Abi Talib*, ibn al-Maghazeli al-Shafi'i])
+ Abu Bakr said: "May Allah never put me in a situation where I can not have access to Abul Hasan (Imam Ali) to solve a problem"; Umar ibn Khattab used to beg Allah to preserve him from a perplexing case which the father of al-Hasan (Imam Ali) was not present to decide. "Umar ibn Khattab said: "If there were not

Ali, Umar would have been ruined." (Ahlul-Bayt Islamic Library [*Fadha'il al-Sahaba*, Ahmad ibn Hanbal, V2, p. 647, Hadith 1100; *Al-Isti'ab*, Ibn Abd al-Barr, V3, p. 39; *Manaqib*, al-Khawarizmi, p. 48; *Al-Tabaqat*, Ibn Sa'd, V2, p. 338; *Al-Riaydh al-Nadhirah*, Muhibbuddin al-Tabari, V2, p. 194; and *Tarikh al-Khulafaa*, Jalaluddin al-Suyuti, p. 171])

5: Just, Moral, and Trustworthy

+ Umar ibn Khattab said: "Ali is the best in judgment among us ..." (Rizvi 2008 [*Musnad Ahmad ibn Hanbal*])
+ Ibn Abbas heard Umar ibn Khattab saying, "The best judge among us is Ali." (*Sahih Bukhari*, V6, Book 65, Hadith 4481)
+ Prophet Mohammad said: "Ali is the wisest and superior to all of you. He is the best judge among all." (Tahmasebi 2013 [*Ahmad ibn Hanbal*; *Manaqib*, al-Khawarizmi; *Sunan*, Abu Bakr al-Bayhaqi])
+ It was narrated from Zirr: Ali said: "The Unlettered Prophet made a covenant with me, that none but a believer would love me, and none but a hypocrite would hate me." (*Al-Nasai*, V6, Book 47, Hadith 5021)
+ It was narrated that Hubshi bin Junadah said: "I heard the Messenger of Allah say: 'Ali is part of me and I am part of him, and no one will represent me except Ali.'" (*Ibn Majah*, V1, Book 1, Hadith 119)
+ The Holy Prophet said, "May Allah bless Ali. O Lord! Render the truth always with Ali so that wherever he is the truth is with him too." (*Al-Tirmidhi*, V6, Book 46, Hadith 3714)

6: Physically Able, Spiritually Brave, and Protects the Ummah Against Its Enemies

+ Umar ibn al-Khattab said: "Congratulations, congratulations to you, O 'Ali; you have become my leader (mawla) and the leader of every faithful Muslim." (*Ahmad ibn Hanbal*, V4, pp. 281, 368, 370)

- Battle of Khandaq (The Trench): The horse-riders of Quraysh dreamt of a quick victory asking for a challenger and declared a hand-to-hand fighting. Among the Muslims, the first man who responded was Ali who defeated the giant warrior Amru ibn Abd Wid. Seeing Amru killed, the enemies found no benefit in continuing the fighting and thus were defeated. (Hilli 2007 (*Kashf al-Ghummah*, V1, p. 197)) Allah revealed the following verse in honor of Imam Ali: "And Allah turned back those who disbelieve in their rage, they achieved not any advantage; and Allah did suffice for the believers in fighting; for Allah is All-Strong, the Almighty." (Qur'an 33:25). (*Kashf al-Ghummah*, V1, p. 206)

- Battle of Badr: Prophet Mohammad said, "There is no man more valorous than Ali and there is no sword sharper than Dhu'l-Fiqar." (Hilli 2007 [*Tarikh Dimashq*, V1, p. 158, Hadith 197]) Ali was the first person to fight the atheists of Quraysh who outnumbered the Muslims, and he defeated Walid ibn 'Utbah, a man of courage and valor. (Hilli 2007 [*Kashf al-Ghummah*, V1, p. 183]) Then Imam Ali defeated Al-'As ibn Sa'id ibn al-'As, a man of courage and horror. (*Bihar al-Anwar*, V19, p. 338) Imam Ali was in the front line of the battle defeating the atheists of Quraysh. Imam Ali killed seventy of the Quraysh leaders. (*Kitab al-Irshad*, Sheikh Mufid, V1, Part 2, Chapter 18, p. 62)

- Battle of Uhud: After the Muslims broke their promises to Prophet Mohammad by escaping from the battle scene, having taken shelter on the mountain, Imam Ali protected and defended the Prophet and was prepared to sacrifice himself from every side the enemies attacked him. Imam Ali remained to repel the enemies. (*Kitab al-Irshad*, Sheikh Mufid, V1, Part 2, Chapter 22, p. 73) Those who escaped from the scene, though seeing the Prophet was being attacked, remained on the mountain, except fourteen of them who returned. (*Kitab al-Irshad*, Sheikh Mufid,

V1, Part 2, Chapter 22, p. 74) In this battle, Gabriel brought the deed of honor for Imam Ali: "There is no man more valorous than Ali and there is no sword sharper than Dhu'l-Fiqar." (*Kitab al-Irshad*, Sheikh Mufid, V1, Part 2, Chapter 22, p. 78) During this battle, Imam Ali killed many of the enemy's soldiers. The Muslims' final victory and their returning to the Messenger of Allah was due to Imam Ali's steadfastness and courage in the battlefield. (*Kitab al-Irshad*, Sheikh Mufid, V1, Part 2, Chapter 23, p. 81)

+ Battle of Khaybar: It was Imam Ali who achieved victory for Islam. After the Prophet gave the banner of Islam to Abu Bakr and thereafter to Umar ibn al-Khattab, both were facing defeat so they returned back. Seeing the defeat of the two, the Prophet gave the banner of Islam to Imam Ali who, unlike the others, never abandoned the battlefield by defeating the enemy with his successive attacks. (Hilli 2007 [*Al-Isabah*, V2, pp. 508–509]).

+ "The Messenger of Allah said on the Day of Khaybar: 'I shall give this flag to a man who loves Allah and His Messenger and Allah and His Messenger love him, and Allah will grant him victory at his hands.' Umar bin al-Khattab said: 'I never desired leadership except on that day.' He said, 'I came before him in the hope that I might be called to it, but the Messenger called Ali bin Abi Talib. He gave it to him and said: march, and do not turn around until Allah grants you victory.'" (*Sahih Muslim*, V6, Book 44, Hadiths 6222–6224)

+ Battle of Hunayn: Imam Ali was defending with his unsheathed sword in front of the Prophet. Imam Ali killed forty of the enemy troops. (*Kitab al-Irshad*, Sheikh Mufid, V1, Part 2, Chapter 16, p. 129)

+ Imam Ali was ready to sacrifice his life by putting on the Prophet's clothes and lying in his bed at the night the enemies came to kill him. The Prophet had left Mecca for Medina for his safety. Because Imam Ali was ready to risk his life to save the Prophet on the night of Hijra from Mecca to Medina, the following verse was revealed: "And among men there is one who selleth his self (soul) seeking the pleasure of Allah; and verily, Allah is affectionate unto His (faithful)) servants." (Qur'an 2:207)

7: Political, Military, and Administrative Experience

- UN Secretariat, the Committee of Human Rights in New York, under the chairmanship of the Secretary General of the United Nations, Kofi Annan, issued in AD 2002 this historic resolution: "The Caliph Ali Bin Abi Talib is considered the fairest governor who appeared during human history (after the Prophet Mohammad)." For this reason, the World Organization for Human Rights called the rulers of the world to follow the example of his sound and humanitarian method in ruling that revealed the spirit of social justice and peace. The United Nations has advised Arab countries to take Imam Ali bin Abi Talib as an example in establishing a regime based on justice and democracy and encouraging knowledge. (Jaffery 2012)
- The United Nations Development Programme (UNDP) in its 2002 Arab Human Development Report, distributed around the world, listed six sayings of Imam Ali about ideal governance. They include consultation between the ruler and the ruled, speaking out against corruption and other wrong doings, ensuring justice to all, and achieving domestic development (Arab Human Development Report 2002):

> (1) He who has appointed himself an Imam (ruler) of the people must begin by teaching himself before teaching others. His teaching of others must be first by setting an example rather than with his words, for he who begins by teaching and educating himself is more worthy of respect than he who teaches and educates others.

(2) Your concern with developing the land should be greater than your concern for collecting taxes, for the latter can only be obtained by developing; whereas he who seeks revenue without development destroys the country and the people.

(3) Seek the company of the learned and the wise in search of solving the problems of your country and the righteousness of your people.

(4) No good can come out in keeping silent to the government or in speaking out of ignorance.

(5) The righteous are men of virtue, whose logic is straightforward, whose dress is unostentatious, whose path is modest, whose actions are many and who are undeterred by difficulties.

(6) Choose the best among your people to administer justice among them. Choose someone who does not easily give up, who is unruffled by enmities, someone who will not persist in wrong doings, who will not hesitate to pursue right once he knows it, someone whose heart knows no greed, who will not be satisfied with a minimum of explanation without seeking the maximum of understanding, who will be the most steadfast when doubt is cast, who will be the least impatient in correcting the opponent, the most patient in pursuing the truth, the most stern in meting out judgment, someone who is unaffected by flattery and not swayed by temptation and these are but few.

+ Prophet Mohammad said to Imam Ali: "You are to me as Aaron was to Moses, but there will be no prophet after me." (*Sahih*

Bukhari, V5, Book 64, Hadith 4416; *Sahih Muslim*, V6, Book 44, Hadith 6218; *Ibn Majah*, V1, Book 1, Hadith 121; *Al-Tirmidhi*, V6, Book 46, Hadith 3730; *Al-Nasa'i*, Al-Khasais, pp. 15–16; *Ahmad ibn Hanbal*, V1, p. 174)

- With the exception of the Battle of Tabouk, Imam Ali took part in all military battles and expeditions fought for Islam. The reason he didn't participate in the Battle of Tabouk is because Prophet Mohammad ordered him to remain and protect Medina from external and internal forces. In addition to being the standard bearer in the battles, Imam Ali also commanded his soldiers into enemy territory. Furthermore, Imam Ali was the commander of the Muslim army in the Battle of Khaybar. His military skills and bravery earned him the title of *Asadullah* (Lion of Allah) bestowed upon him by Prophet Mohammad.

- Abu Bakr sought Imam Ali's counsel on whether to wage war against the Romans. Imam Ali said, "If you embark on this work, you will succeed." Abu Bakr happily responded, "May you receive good tidings," and thereafter he ordered the expedition under the leadership of Khalid bin Sa'id. (Shirazi 2008 [*Tarikh al-Ya'qubi*, V2, pp. 132–133])

- Umar ibn al-Khattab consulted with Imam Ali on how to spend Persia's immense wealth. Imam Ali said, "Once every year, distribute the riches among all people and leave none remaining in the treasury." (Shirazi 2008 [*Al-Mawirdi, Al-Ahkam al-Sultaniyyah*, p. 199])

- Imam Ali's governors were advised to deal fairly, impartially and justly with all, individually and collectively, without any discrimination. Ministerial positions were not distributed on the basis of wealth, relationship, tribalism, or influence in society but on the basis of merit. When accepted as advisors, they would speak the bitter truth unreservedly and without fear of the status of government officials. Therefore, through this type of counselors, Imam Ali bin Abi Talib sought to keep his men of authority in check.

Under the government of Imam Ali, there was a distribution of work and duties among various branches of Administration, and there was cooperation and coordination among government departments. Rules were laid down for controlling the civil servants and fighting corruption and oppression among officers of the State. In commercial activities, profiteering, hoarding and black marketing were prohibited. Importance was attached to equitable distribution of wealth, upbringing of orphans and maintenance of handicapped. Role of the army was defined and qualification of those entitled to join and those not entitled to join were specified. Rights of rulers over the ruled and rights of ruled over the rulers were pronounced.

Imam Ali bin Abi Talib's governors were guided to forget and forgive the shortcomings of their subjects. They were not to hurry over punishments. They were to refrain from being pleased and proud over their power to punish. They were advised not to get angry or lose temper over the mistakes and failures of their subjects. They were to be patient and sympathetic towards them. (Al-Ghamdy 2004)

Glossary

AD	Anno Domini (in the year of our Lord)
Adhan	Call to prayer
Adl	Justice
AH	After Hijrah
Ahl al-Bayt	House of the Family of Prophet Mohammad
Ahl al-Kisa	Family of the Cloak of Prophet Mohammad
Akhi	Brother
Al-Azeem	The Lofty and Great
Al-Fatiha	Opening chapter of the Qur'an
Al-Furqan	The Criterion
Al-Hakeem	The Wise and Learned
Al-Imam al-Asr	The Imam of the Period
Al-Kareem	The Generous and Bountiful
Al-Kitab	The Book
Al-Mahdi	The Guided One
Al-Majeed	The Glorious and Noble
Al-Qa'im	The One to Arise

Al-Rida Min Aal Mohammad	The Chosen from the Family of Prophet Mohammad
Al-Sahifa al-Sajjadiyyah al-Kamilah	The Psalms of Islam
Amir al-Mu'mineen	Commander of the Faithful
An-Nass al-Jali	Explicit designation
An-Nass al-Khafi	Implicit designation
Ansar	Supporters
AS	Alayhi Salam—upon him be peace
Asadullah	Lion of Allah
Ash Hadu Anna Mohammadan Rasulullah	I bear witness that Mohammad is Allah's Messenger
Ashura	Tenth Day of the month of Muharram
Bagiyyat Allah	Remnant of Allah
Baitul Maal	Islamic Treasury
Baqir	Split open or expounder of knowledge
BC	Before Christ
Buraq	Steed
Caliph	Successor, ruler
CE	Common Era, Current Era, or Christian Era
Dha'eef	Weak
Dajjal	Antichrist
Du'a	Supplication
Fiqh	Islamic jurisprudence
Fir-awn	Pharaoh Ramses II
Furqan	Criterion
Furu' al-Din	Secondary principles of practices
Ghayba	Occultation
Ghaybat-ul-Kubra	Major occultation
Ghaybat-us-Sughra	Minor occultation
Habib Allah	Allah's beloved friend

Hadi	Guide
Hadith	Tradition, narration
Hadith Qudsi	Sacred Hadith
Hadiyya	Gift
Haj	Major pilgrimage
Halal	Lawful
Haram	Unlawful
Hasan	Good
Hidaya	Guidance
Hijra	Migration
Ibadah	Worship
Iblis	Satan
Ihdina	Guide
Ihdina-Sirat-al-Mustaqim	Guide us to the Straight Path
Ijma'	Consensus
Ilham	Inspiration
Imam	Leader
Imam al-Muntazar	The Awaited Imam
Imamat	Twelve Infallible Imams of Ahl al-Bayt
Iman	Faith
Injil	Gospel
Iqamah	Call to prayer
Islam	Submission to the will of Allah
'Ismah	Infallibility
Isnad	Chain
Isra'	Night Journey of Prophet Mohammad
'Itrah	Ahl al-Bayt (House of the Family of Prophet Mohammad)
Jahil Murakkab	Closed-minded ignorance
Jihad	Struggle
Jinn	Unseen beings of fire
Ka'bah	Sacred house in Mecca
Kalim Allah	He to whom Allah has talked
Karam Allahu Wajhah	May Allah bless his face

Kawthar	Fountain in paradise
Khalifah	Vicegerent or steward
Khalil	Good friend
Kitab	Book
La Ilahi Illallah	There is no Allah but Allah
Lutf	Grace of Allah
Ma'sum	Sinless
Madhhab	School of thought
Mahdi	Guide
Majalis	Meetings
Majlis-Ash-Shura	Consultative Council
Marja'a	Islamic jurist
Masjid	Mosque
Matn	Text
Mawdoo'	Fabricated
Mawla	Master
Mi'raj	Ascension of Prophet Mohammad
Mu'min	Believer
Muazzin	One who summons people to prayer
Mujtahid	Authority in Islamic law
Musannaf	Collection of hadiths
Musnad	Chain of transmitters of hadiths (traditions)
Nabi	Prophet
Nafs	Self
Nahj al-Balagha	Peak of eloquence
Nass	Designation for appointment
Ni'mah	Blessing
Nur	Light
PBUH	Peace be upon him
Qayyamat	Day of Judgment
Qiblah	Direction of prayer
RA	Rathi Allahu Anhu (may Allah be pleased with him)

Rahma	Mercy
Raj'a	Return
Rakats	Units of prayer
Rasul	Messenger
Sabr	Patience
Safi Allah	Allah's sincere friend
Sahaba	Companions
Sahib al-Zaman	Master of the age
Sahih	Authentic
Salawat	Blessings
SAWS (SAW & SAAS)	Sallallahu Alahi Wa Sallam (may Allah honor him and grant him peace)
Shari'ah	Divine law of Islam
Shaykh	Spiritual master, cleric
Shi'a	Followers of Ahl al-Bayt
Shura	Consultation
Sirat-al-Mustaqim	Straight Path
Sunnah	Path or way of Prophet Mohammad
Sunni	Denomination of Islam
Sura	Chapter of the Qur'an
SWT	Subhanahu Wa Ta'ala (Glorious is He, and He is exalted)
Ta'wil	Interpretation
Tafsir	Commentary, explanation
Taqleed	Follow or imitate a Mujtahid
Tawhid	Oneness of Allah
Thaqalayn	Two things
Thikr	Reminder
Torah	Book of Moses
Ulema	Religious leaders
Ulu 'l-amr	Those entrusted with directing Muslims
Ummah	Community
'Umra	Lesser pilgrimage
Usul-al-Din	Fundamental principles of belief

Wali	Guardian
Wasiyyi	Successor
Wila'-e Imamat	Spiritual guidance
Wila'-e Muhabbat	Love, devotion
Wila'-e Tasarruf	Universal nature
Wila'-e Zi'amat	Sociopolitical guidance
Wilayat	Guardianship
Wilayat-ul-Faqih	Guardianship-based political system
Yoreedo	Intends
Zabur	Psalms of Prophet David
Zakat	Tax, alms

References

A Brief History of the Fourteen Infallibles. 1984. World Organization of Islamic Services (WOFIS).

A Chronology of the Muslim Religion: Timeline of Islam. Religious Facts. www.religiousfacts.com, 2014.

Administrator. May 2010. *Fatima Al-Zahra (as), the Lady of Light.* The World Forum for Proximity of Islamic Schools of Thought.

Ahlul Bayt Digital Islamic Library Project Team. "Fact Sheets About Islam and Shi'ism." *A Shi'ite Encyclopedia.* http://al-islam.org/nutshell/.

Ahlul-Bayt Islamic Library. www.alseraj.net/maktaba/kotob/english/.../Tokyo/Spa/.../index1.html.

Akbari, Javed. *Appointment of Imam Ali (a.s.) as Successor by the Prophet (pbuh).* http://imamalmahdi.com/main/eng/news.php?extend.725.

Algar, Hamid. *Religion and State in Iran, 1785–1906; The Role of the Ulema in the Qajar Period.* Berkeley: University of California Press, 1969.

Al-Ghamdy, Gharm Allah. *e Process of Choosing the Leader (Caliph) of the Muslims: The Muslim Khilafa.* April 25, 2004.

Al-Halabi, Nur al-Din. *Al-Sirah al-Halabiyah wa al-Athar al-Muhammadiyah,* Cairo: al-Matbaah al-Amirah, Vol. 3, p. 207 (1875).

Al-Hamawi, Yaqut. *Kitab Mau'jam-al-Buldan.* Vol. 14, p. 238 (1228).

Al-Haythami, Ahmad ibn Hajar. *Al-Sawa'iq al-Muhriqah (Loud/Frightening Lightning),* Maktabat al-Ma'arif (1965).

Al-Hilali, Sulaym ibn Qays. *Kitab e Sulaym Qays Al-Hilali.* Yasin Publications, 2014.

Al-Hilli. *Al-Bab al-Hadi 'Ashar*. Edited by Mahdi Muhaqqiq. Iran: McGill University Institute of Islamic Studies, 1986.

Ali, Abdullah Yusuf. *The Holy Qur'an: Text, Translation and Commentary*. Washington, DC: The Islamic Center, 1978.

Ali, S.V. Mir Ahmed. *The Holy Qur'an*. Elmhurst, New York: Tahrike Tarsile Qur'an, Inc., 1995.

Al-Khazraji, Khalid; Muhammad Ghoneim & M.S.M. Saifullah. "On the Nature of Hadith Collections of Imam al-Bukhari & Muslim." *Islamic Awareness*, August 24, 2005.

Al-Mawardi, Abu al-Hasan. *The Ordinances of Government*, Translated by Wafaa H. Wahba. Reading: Garnet Publishing, 1996.

Al-Mufid, Shaykh. *Kitab al-Irshad: The Book of Guidance into the Lives of the Twelve Imams*. Translated by I. K. A. Howard, University of Edinburgh. Qum, Iran: Ansariyan Publications, 2nd ed., 2004.

Al-Musawi, Hashim. *The Shia: Their Origins and Beliefs*. Translated by Dr. Hamid S. Atiyyah. Beirut: Al-Ghadeer Center for Islamic Studies, 1996.

Al Naysaburi, al-Hakim. *al-Mustadrak 'ala al-Sahihayn*. Haydarabad, Vol. 3., 1915–1923.

Al-Qarashi, Baqir Sharif. *The Life of Imam al-Mahdi Peace Be Upon Him*. Qum: Ansarian Publications, 2006.

Al-Qarashi, Baqir Sharif. *The Life of Imam Husain ('a)* Translated by Sayyid Athar Husain S. H. Rizvi. Qum, Iran: Ansariyan Publications, 1st ed., 2007.

Al-Qarashi, Baqir Sharif. *The Life of Imam Ali Bin Musa Al-Rida*. CreateSpace Independent Publishing Platform, 2014.

Al-Qazwini, Imam Muhammad bin Yazeed ibn Majah. *Sunan Ibn Majah*. Translated by Nasriddin al-Khattab. Riyadh: Darussalam, 2007.

Al-Qurashi, Baqir Sharif. *The Life of Imam Musa bin Ja'far al-Kazim*. Translated by Jasim al-Rasheed. Qum, Iran: Ansariyan Publications, 2005.

Al-Qurashi, Baqir Sharif. *The Life of Muhammad The Greatest Liberator The Holiest Prophet*. Translated by Abdullah al-Shahin. Qum, Iran: Ansariyan Publications, 2007.

Al Saduq, Al-Shaykh (Abu Ja'far Muhammad ibn 'Ali ibn Babawaih al-Qummi). *Al-Aamali (Majalis)*. Vancouver, Canada: World Federation website. 2012.

Al-Sajjad, Imam Ali Ibnul-Husayn Zaynul-Aa'bideen. *Al-Sahifah Al-Sajjadiyyah Al-Kamilah (The Psalms of Islam)*. Translated by William C. Chittick. 4th ed. Qum, Iran: Ansariyan Publications, 2006.

Alsamail, Ali. Imam Al-Jawad (AS): *The Manifestation of Magnanimity*. London: Ahlulbayt Islamic Mission, 2012.

Al-Samawi, Dr. Muhammad Tijani. *The Shi'a' Are (the real) Ahl al-Sunnah*. Translated by Yasin T. al-Jibouri. Bloomfield, New Jersey, 1995.

Al-Suyuti, Jalal al-Din. *Tarikh al-Khulafa'*. Beirut: Dar al-Ma'rifah, 1996.

Al-Suyuti, Jalal ad-Din. *Ad-Durr al-Manthur fi-t-Tafsir al-Ma'thur (I-VII)*. Gebunden, 2000.

Al-Tabari, Mohibbudin. *Riyadh Al Nadira*.

Al-Tirmidhi, Hafiz Abu Elsa. *Jami' al-Tirmidhi*. Translation by Abu Khaliyl. Dar-us-Salam: 6 vols, 2007.

Al-Yasin, Shaykh Radi. *Sulh al-Hasan (The Peace Treaty of al-Hasan)*. Translated by Jasim al-Rasheed. Qum: Ansariyan Publications, 1998.

An Analysis of the Characteristics of Imam Hussein. World Service of Islamic Republic of Iran Broadcasting website. 2000.

Anjum, Ovamir. *Politics, Law, and Community in Islamic Thought: The Taymiyyan Moment*. New York: Cambridge University Press, 2012.

Ansariyan, Allama Hussein. *Ahl Al-Bayt: The Celestial Beings on the Earth*. Translated by Dr. Ali Akbar Aghili Ashtiani. Qum: Ansariyan Publications, 2007.

Bahrani, Hashim ibn Sulayman. *Ghayat al-Maram*. Beirut: Muassasat al-Tarikh al-Arabi, 2001.

Bennison, Amira K. *The Great Caliphs: The Golden Age of the Abbasid Empire*. Yale University Press, 2009. New Haven, Connecticut.

Bilgrami, Sayed Tahir. *Essence of Life, A Translation of Ain al-Hayat by Allama Mohammad Baqir Majlisi*, Qum: Ansarian Publications, 2005.

Bokhari, Farhan. *Hazrat Ali's Legacy*. The News International. Jag Group of Newspapers: Pakistan. August 11, 2012.

Brown, Daniel W. *Rethinking Tradition in Modern Islamic Thought (Cambridge Middle East Studies)*, Cambridge University Press, 1999. Cambridge, England.

Choueiri, Youssef M. *A Companion to the History of the Middle East*. Chapter 4: "The Ulama: Status and Function" by Zouhair Ghazzal. Wiley-Blackwell, 2005. Malden, Massachusets.

Collection of Imam Shafi'i Poetry. Beirut: Dar al-Kitab al-Arabi, 1993.

Corbin, Henry. *History of Islamic Philosophy*. London: Kegan Paul International, 1993.

Crone, Patricia and Martin Hinds. *God's Caliph: Religious Authority in the First Centuries of Islam*. Cambridge: Cambridge University Press, 1986.

Darul Islam Center, Inc. (Duas.org). *Prophet Mohammad's Farewell Sermon at Ghadir Khumm*. March 1999.

Darussalam Global Leader in Islamic Books, Publishers and Distributors, Riaydh, Saudi Arabia.

Dindang, Dr. Norlain bint Muhammad. *The Sunnah and the Science of Hadith*. ("*Glossary of Islamic Terms* by Aisha Bewley"). Riyadh, Saudi Arabia. July 27, 2004.

Donner, Fred. *Muhammad and the Believers: At the Origins of Islam*. Cambridge: The Belknap Press of Harvard University Press, 2010.

Duderija, Adis. *Development of Secterianism in Islam: Second Part*. July 2005.

Elhadj, Elie. *The Islamic Shield: Arab Resistance to Democratic and Religious Reforms*. Brown Walker Press, 2007. Boca Raton, Florida.

Ferrari, G.R.F. *Plato: The Republic*. Translated by Tom Griffith. Cambridge University Press, 2000. Cambridge, England.

Gilchrist, John. *Muhammad and the Religion of Islam*. Publisher: Jesus to the Muslims, 1986.

Glad, Betty. "Why Tyrants Go Too Far: Malignant Narcissism and Absolute Power." *Political Psychology*, Vol. 23, No. 1 (March 2002): 1–37.

Hanne, Eric J. *Putting the Caliph in His Place: Power, Authority, and the Late Abbasid Caliphate.* Fairleigh Dickinson, 2007. Madison, New Jersey.

Haq, S. Moninul. *Ibn Sa'd's, Kitab al-Tabaqat al-Kabir (The Major Classes).* Islamic Book Service, Kitab Bhavan, India, 2009.

H.I. Abbas Ayleya. *Imam Hasan Al-Askari AS.* Video (1:04:10), Zainab TV, Zainab Center. January 9, 2014.

Hilli, Jamal al-Din ibn Yusuf Allamah. *Certainty Uncovered (Kashf al-Yaqin Virtues of Imam Ali).* Translated by Dr. Ali Akbar Aghili Ashtiani. 1st ed. Qum: Ansariyan Publications, 2007.

Horney, Karen. *Neurosis and Human Growth: The Struggle Toward Self-Realization.* New York: W. W. Norton & Company, 1991.

Hussain, Irshad. *Al Taqrib: A Journal of Islamic Unity.* Chapter on "Shaykh Muhammad Jawad Mughniyyah: A Jurisprudent." Tehran: The World Forum for Poximity of Islamic Schools of Thought, No. 4. Winter 2009.

Ibn Abi Talib, Imam Ali. *Nahjul Balagha (Peak of Eloquence): Sermons and Letters of Imam Ali Ibn Abi Talib.* 12th ed. Islamic Seminary Publications, 1999.

Ibn Kathir, Ismail Ibn Umar. *Al-Bidayah wa-l Nihayah (The Beginning and the End): Tarikh ibn Kathir (Ibn Kathir's History).* Dar ibn Hazm. Vols. 1–5, 2009.

Ibn Sa'd, Muhammad. *The Men of Madina II.* Translated by Aisha Bewley. London: Ta-Ha Publishers, 2000.

Ibn Sa'd, Muhammad. *Kitab al-Tabaqat al-Kabir.* New Delhi: Kitab Bhavan Publishers, 2009.

Ibn Shahrashub, Muhammad ibn Ali. *Manaqib Ali Abi Talib.* Qum: Allamah Publications, 1959.

Imam Reza Network. www.imamreza.net.

Inlagg. *The Truth and Nothing But the Truth!* March 26, 2013. Wakeup313. blogspot.com.

Insanul Ayun fi Seerah al Halbeeya. Chapter: "The Death of the Prophet." Vol. 3, pp. 487–488.

Islam Timeline. Faithology, LLC. www.faithology.com, 2014.

Islam Timeline. One-Islam.org, United Wisdom of Allah. www.one-Islam.org, 2006.

Jafari, Syed Muhammad Askari. *A Biographical Profile of Imam Ali,* 2009. www.alseraj.net.

Jaffer, Mohammed Yusuf. *Thaqalain—Part 9.* Quran and Hadith Regarding Ahlel Bait. April 17, 1998.

Jaffery, Sarah. *United Nations on Imam Ali ibn Abi Talib.* Ahlul-Bayt Student Association. November 16, 2012.

Jones, Alfred. *The Psychology of Tyrants,* posted by Alfred Jones, October 28, 2011, Historic Mysteries website.

Kandemir, M. Yasar. *Abu Huraira,* Diyanet Isleri Ansiklopedisi, X, Istanbul, 1994.

Khan, Dr. Muhammad Muhsin. *Sahih Bukhari.* Islamic University, Al-Medina Al-Munauwara. Vols. 1–9, 1994.

Khawarizmi, Ahmad. Abu'l-Muwayyid Muwafiq bin Ahmad Khawarizmi. *Manaqib.* Ansariyan Publications, Qum, Iran

Koelliker, Lee A. *The Minha: Ma'mun's Inquisition for Supremacy.* Lincoln College of Technology, USA. History Research, Vol. 1, No. 1 (December 2011): 35–46.

LagosShia. *Ali And His Shia Shall Be The Saved Party.* Nairaland Forum, Oluwaseun Osewa.

Lalani, Arizna R. *Early Shi'i Thought: The Teachings of Imam Muhammad Al-Baqir.* London, 2000. London, England.

Lari, Sayyid Mujtaba Musavi. *Imamate and Leadership: Lessons on Islamic Doctrine (Book Four)* Translated by Hamid Algar. 1st ed. Tehran: Foundation of Islamic Cultural Propagation in the World, 1996.

Lights and Disease. The Minister, 11:10 (1984): 5–7.

MacDonald, Duncan B. *Development of Muslim Theology, Jurisprudence and Constitutional Theory.* London: Routledge, 1903: 77–78.

Machiavelli, Niccolo. *The Prince.* New York: Bantam, 1966.

Majlisi, Mohammad Baqir. *Bihar al-Anwar (Ocean of Lights).* Beirut: Dar Ihya al-Turath al Arabi Publications, 1983.

Majlisi, Mohammad Baqir. *Hayat Al Qulub,* Qum: Ansariyan Publications, Vol. 3, Chapter 2, Part 33, 2003: 443–444.

Majlisi, Mohammad Baqir. *Hayat Al Qulub*, Qum: Ansariyan Publications, Vol. 2, Chapter 10, 2012: 293.

Mathews, Nathaniel. *The Createdness or Uncreatedness of the Quran.* December 19, 2012. www.azaniansea.com.

Mavani, Hamid. *Religious Authority and Political Thought in Twelver Shi'ism: From Ali to Post-Khomeini.* Routledge Publishers, 2013. London, England.

Meri, Josef W. *Medieval Islamic Civilization: An Encyclopedia.* Routledge, 2005. London, England.

Mirza, Kaukab Ali. *The Great Muslim Scientist and Philosopher Imam Jafar ibn Mohammed As-Sadiq.* Translated by Kaukab Ali Mirza. 2nd ed. Ontario: Willowdale Publishers, 1997.

Mugniyyah, Shaykh Muhammad Jawad. *Ahl al-Bayt (Shi'a 12 Imams) and Infallibility.* March 15, 2010. Free-Minds.org.

Muslim, Imam Abul-Husain. *Sahih Muslim (7 Vol. Set).* Translated by Nasiruddin al-Khattab. Dar-us-Salam Publications, Inc., 2007.

Mutahhari, Ayatollah Murtaza. *Wilayat the Station of the Master.* Tehran: World Organization for Islamic Services, 1982.

Mutahhari, Ayatollah Murtada. *Man and Universe.* (Chapter 32). 1st ed. Pakistan: Islamic Seminary Publications, 1990.

Mutahhari, Murtada. *Polarization around the Character of 'Ali Ibn Abi Talib.* 1st ed. Tehran, Iran: WOFIS, World Organization for Islamic Services, 1981.

Nasr, Vali. *The Shia Revival: How Conflicts Within Islam Will Shape the Future.* W.W. Norton & Company, Inc., 2006. New York, New York.

NationMaster.com. *Encyclopedia: Hadith of Fatimah, Fadak an Abu Bakr.*

Nawas, John A. "A Reexamination of Three Current Explanations for al-Ma'mun's Introduction of the Mihna." *International Journal of Middle East Studies* 26:4 (November 1994): 615.

Patton, Walter Melville. *Ahmed ibn Hanbal and the Mihna: A Biography of the Imam Including an Account of the Mohammedan Inquisition Called the Mihna, 218–234 A.H.* E. J. Brill, 1897. Leiden, The Netherlands.

Razwy, Sayed Ali Asgher. *A Restatement of the History of Islam and Muslims*. The World Federation "Of Khoja Shia Ithna-Asheri Muslim." 2nd ed. 2001.

Reis, Dr. David. *Shi'ite Identity Formation: Martyrdom Through Collective Memory*. University of Oregon, Winter 2013. Eugene, Oregon.

Revert Muslims Association. *To Know the Shia*. www.revertmuslims.com.

Rizvi, Hujjatul Islam Wal Muslimeen al-Haj Sayyid Muhammad Rizvi. *Islamic Correspondence Course: Advanced Book Two*. 1st ed. Dar Es Salaam, Tanzania: Bilal Muslim Mission of Tanzania, 2008.

Rizvi, Sayyid Sa'eed Akhtar. *Imamate: Vicegerency of the Prophet*. CreateSpace Independent Publishing Platform, 2014.

Rizvi, Syed Abbas. *Shattered: The Sectarian Divide and Start of the Feminist Revolution in Islam*. AuthorHouse, 2008.

Roland, Jon. *Principles of Tyranny*. Constitution Society, 2000.

Sarwar, Muhammad. *Kitab Al-Kafi*. Compiled by Thiqatu al-Islam, Abu Ja'far Muhammad ibn Ya'qub al-Kulayni. 1st e-book ed. The Islamic Seminary, Inc., 2013.

Shah, Ali Asghar. *Life of Ali bin Abu Talib, r.a, The Lion of Allah and Darling of Holy Prophet saws*. May 2009. Aliasgharshah23's,Blog.

Shahin, Badr. *Lady Zaynab (Peace Be Upon Her)*. Qum: Ansaryian Publications, 2002.

Shakir, Ahmad and Hamza Ahmad al-Zayn. *Al-Musnad Ahmad bin Hanbal*. 20 vols. Cairo: Dar-al-Hadith, 1995.

Shaltoot, Mahmood. *Verdict by His Excellency Shaikh al-Akbar Mahmood Shaltoot, Head of the al-Azhar University, on Permissibility of Following 'al-Shia al-Imamiyyah' School of Thought*. July 6, 1959.

Sharaf al-Din. Abd al-Husayn. *Al-Fusul al-Muhimmah fi Talif al-Ummah*, Rabitat al-Thaqafah wa-al-Alaqat al-Islamiyah, Idarat al-Tarjamah wa-al-Nashr, 1996.

Shariati, Dr. Ali. *From Where Shall We Begin & The Machine in the Captivity of Machinism*. Free Islamic Literature, 1980. Houston, Texas.

Shaykh al-Saduq (Ibn Babawayh al-Qummi). *Kitab al-Tawhid: The Book of Divine Unity*. Translated by Ali Adam. AMI Press, Al-Mahdi Institute: Birmingham, United Kingdom, 2013.

ShiaPen Newsletter, *Revealing the Truth*, chapters 3 and 6. www.shiapen.com.

Shirazi, Abd al-Karim Bi-Azar. "Imam Ali and the Caliphs: Their Relationship and Interaction." *Al-Taqrib: A Quarterly Journal of Islamic Unity*. Vol. 2, No. 3. Translated by D. D. Sodagar. The World Forum for Proximity of Islamic Schools of Thought, Tehran, Iran. Winter 2008.

Siddiqui, Abdul Hamid. *Sahih Muslim: English Translation*. Lahore: Sh. Muhammad Ashraf, Vols. 1–4, 1973–1975.

Siddiqui, Muhammed Zubayr. *Hadith Literatures: Its Origin, Development & Special Features*. Islamic Book Trust, 2006. Selangor, Malaysia.

Simpson, Peter. *The Politics of Aristotle*. University of North Carolina Press, 1997. Chapel Hill, North Carolina.

Superiority of Ali Ibne Abi Talib (a.s.) Over All Others. Verbatim text of the Video. http://www.abubakr.org/tenproofs.php.

Surur, Muhammad Jamal al-Din. *Al-Asr al-Abbasi al-Awwal*. [The First Abbasid Era]. Dar al-Fikr al-Arabi. 2001.

Syed, Hamid. *The Companions of Our Beloved Prophet Muhammad*. Iqra Islamic Publications. www.iqra.net.

Syed, Ibraham B. *52 Weak Ahadith*. Islamic Research Foundation International, Inc. Louisville, Kentucky, www.irfi.org.

Tabari, Ahmad ibn 'Abd Allah. *Dhakha'ir al-'Uqba*. Qum: Maktabat al-Amin. 2001.

Tabarsi, Shaykh Abu Ali al-Fadl. *Tafsir Majma' al-Bayan*. Tehran: Intesharat-e-Farahani, Vol. 27, 1981.

Tahmasebi, Muhammad Husayn. 2013. *Imam Ali: Sunshine of Civilized Islam*. CreateSpace Independent Publishing Platform.

The Encyclopedia of Islam. Vol. 7. Leiden: E. J. Brill (1965–1986): 3.

The Holy Bible: New International Version. London: Hodder & Stoughton, 2011.

The Islamic World to 1600. Online book developed by the Department of History, Applied History Research Group, University of Calgary.

Turfe, Tallal Alie. *Patience in Islam: Sabr.* Elmhurst, New York: Tahrike Tarsile Qur'an, Inc., 1996.

Turfe, Tallal Alie. *Unity in Islam: Reflections and Insights.* Elmhurst, New York: Tahrike Tarsile Qur'an, Inc., 2004.

Turfe, Tallal Alie. *Energy in Islam: A Scientific Approach to Preserving Our Health and the Environment.* Elmhurst, New York: Tahrike Tarsile Qur'an, Inc., 2010.

Turfe, Tallal Alie. *Children of Abraham: United We Prevail, Divided We Fail.* Bloomington, Indiana: iUniverse, 2013.

Watt, William Montgomery. *Islamic Political Thought: The Basic Concepts.* Edinburgh: University Press, 1968.

Wikipedia Encyclopedia.

Ya'ghoubi, Mohammad Taher and Asghar Montazerolghaem. *The Shi'a of Baghdad at the Time of the 'Abbasid Caliphs and the Seljuq Sultanate (447–575 AH).* University of Isfahan, Iran: Journal of Shi'a Islamic Studies, Vol. VI, No. 1. (Winter 2013): 53–74.

Yaqub, Abu Yusuf. *Kitab al-Kharaj (Taxation in Islam).* Luzac, 1st ed., 1969.

Yildirim, Yetkin. *Peace and Conflict Resolution Concepts in the Madina Charter.* Athens, Georgia: Interfaith Cultural Organization, 2005.

Zaman, Muhammad Qasim. *Religion and Politics Under the Early Abbasids: The Emergence of the Proto-Sunni Elite.* Leiden, The Netherlands: E. J. Brill, 1997.

Zaynali, Gulam Husayn. *The Twelve Imams in the Sunni Sources: Fiqh ul-Hadith.* Translator: Ahmad Rezwani; Editor: Mahdi Baqi. Qum, Iran: Dar ul-Hadith Scientific Cultural Institute, 2010.

Name Index

A

Aaron (prophet). *See* Prophet Aaron

Abbas, 104, 105

Abd Allah ibn Abbas, 16

Abd Allah ibn Umar, 16

Abd al-Ra'uf Muhammad al-Munawi, 45

Abd al-Salih, 187

Abdul Mutallib, 41

Abdullah, 41

Abdul-Rahman ibn 'Awf, 106, 107

Abi Talib, 41

Abraham (prophet). *See* Prophet Abraham

Abu al-Muayyid Khatib al-Khawarizmi, 46

Abu Amr Usman Ibn Saeed Amri, 214

Abu Bakr, xix, 16, 46, 63, 82, 103, 104–105, 106, 109, 115, 116, 119, 120, 121, 129, 131, 201–202, 231

Abu Dawud, 3, 12, 14, 25, 69, 70, 88, 116, 194, 195, 217, 218, 272, 275, 285, 286, 288, 308, 309

Abu Hanifah, 95, 143, 158, 205

Abu Hurayra, 16, 18

Abu Jafar Mohammad Ibn Usman Ibn Saeed, 214

Abu Lahab, 128, 129

Abu Musa Jabir Ibn Hayyan al Azdi (Geber), 186–187

Abu Nu'aym al-Isfahani, 113

Abu Said al-Khudri, 16

Abu Sufyan, 138

Abul Hasan Ali Ibn Mohammad Seymouri, 214

Abul Qasim Husain Ibn Ruh Nawbakhti, 214

Adam (prophet). *See* Prophet Adam

Ahl al-Sunnah wal Jama'a, 123

Ahmad ibn Hanbal, viii, 3, 9, 13, 17, 19, 22, 25, 40, 44, 45, 47, 48, 51, 52, 53, 58, 63, 64, 72, 75, 82, 88, 110, 113, 130, 195, 285, 286, 287, 288, 307, 311, 312, 316

Aisha, 16, 72, 73, 131, 204

Al Mu'jam al Kabir (al Tabarani), 17

al-Alama al-Hilli, xvi

Al-Baghdadi, 113

Al-Bayhaqi (al Baihaqi), 17, 113

martyrdom of, 107

as member of Ahl al-Kisa and Ahl al-Bayt, 72, 199

as most knowledgeable authority on Islam after Prophet Mohammad, 110

name of as linked to idea of justice, 65–66

oppression and persecution of, 131–133

patience of, 155–156

people as holding erroneous views against, 15

periods in life of, 213–215

Prophet Mohammad as entrusting guardianship of Islam to, 95

as reclaiming right to become caliph, 107

resentment toward followers of, 20

as sinless and infallible, 71

as successor to Prophet Mohammad, 48–52, 62–63, 79–80

as taking place of prophet, 128

and unity of Imamat, 201–203

Imam Hassan al-Askari ibn Ali (Imam Hassan)

energy of, 192–193

as Imam after his brother's martyrdom, xxi

Imam Ali al-Rida compared to, 189–190

as member of Ahl al-Kisa and Ahl al-Bayt, 72, 199

Muawiyah breaking truce with, xxii

Muawiyah scheming to take caliphate away from, 107–108

objective of peace of, 188

as one of Imam Ali's four children, 41

oppression and persecution of, 149–151

patience of, 161

poisoning of, 142

as rightly guided caliph, 120

as second Imam, 55

as sinless and infallible, 71

Imam Hassan ibn Ali, 55, 133–134, 142, 156, 159, 171–172, 248, 266–267

Imam Hussein ibn Ali (Imam Hussein)

agony and affliction of, 69

in chronology of Twelve Infallible Imams, 55

energy of, 172–175, 177

as hero of Islam, 181

Imam Ali al-Rida compared to, 190

key achievements of, 249–250

Lady Zainab standing over remains of, 175

martyrdom of, xxii–xxiii, xxv, 94, 137, 231

massacre of, 140

as member of Ahl al-Kisa and Ahl al-Bayt, 72, 199

mental and spiritual anguish of, xxii

objective of revolution of, 188

as one of Imam Ali's four children, 41

Malik ibn Anas, 9, 16, 95, 143, 158, 205

Marjanah, 137

Marwan ibn Hakim, 115

Mary (mother of Jesus), 27

Masabih al Sunnah (al Baghawi), 17

Mohammad (prophet). *See* Prophet Mohammad

Mohammad ibn Ya'qub al-Kulayni, 23, 24–25

Moslem ibn Aqil, 200

Muawiyah, xxi, xxii, 14, 16, 17, 18, 107, 131, 133, 134, 138, 156, 171

Musannaf al Sanani, 17

Musnad al Bazzar, 17

Musnad al Mawsili, 17

Musnad al Najjar, 17

Musnad al Tayalisi, 17

Mustadrak al Hakim al-Nishaburi, 17

Mutawakkil, 20, 148, 149, 150, 160, 191, 192

Muwatta Imam Malik, 17

P

Pharaoh Ramses II (*Fir'awn*), 34, 120, 320

Plato, 127

Prophet Aaron, 230

Prophet Abraham, 8, 9, 27, 33, 35, 37, 38, 60, 80–81, 172, 174

Prophet Adam, 38, 50

Prophet David, xix, 33

Prophet Jesus, 9, 27, 35, 92, 151, 161, 174, 193, 194, 200, 221, 223, 236

Prophet Mohammad
appointment by of companions to various positions, 82–83
attributes of, 37
characteristics of, 41
as descendant of Prophet Abraham, 35
as embodiment/personification of *sabr*, 155
as final prophet, 35–36
funeral of, 103–105
as Imam, 36
key achievements of, 243–244
loyalty of Imam Ali to, 42, 168
as manifestation, demonstration, and fulfillment of light of divine energy, 163–165
naming of Imam Ali by, 41
as one of five Great Messengers, 27
oppression and persecution of, 128–129
relationship of with Imam Ali ibn Abi Talib, 39–40
as self-actualized in concept of Imamat, 37
Sunni perspective on errors of, 70–71
Umar ibn Khattab as denying request for pen and paper, 229
and unity of Imamat, 197–199

Prophet Moses, 8, 9, 27, 34, 35, 165, 230

Prophet Noah, 8, 27, 174, 223

Prophet Solomon, 92

Q

Qadi Ayad ibn Musa, 113
Queen Elizabeth I, 120
Queen Victoria, 120

S

Sahih Abu Awana, 17
Sahih Bukhari, 2, 3, 12, 13, 14,
    15, 16, 21, 23, 24, 25, 45, 47, 64,
    69, 71, 72, 82, 86, 87, 88, 109,
    110, 114, 115, 116, 118, 119,
    120, 130, 132, 166, 217, 230,
    271, 278, 285, 286, 287, 288,
    308, 309, 311, 316
Sahih Ibn Hibban (al Busti), 17
Sahih ibn Khuzaymah, 17
Sahih Muslim, 3, 12, 13, 14, 15,
    21, 25, 44, 45, 47, 48, 60, 64, 69,
    72, 73, 82, 85, 88, 113, 114, 115,
    116, 118, 119, 120, 217, 230,
    285, 286, 287, 308, 309, 313,
    316
Sa'id, 149
Salih bin Wasif, 151
Sarah (wife of Abraham), 27
Sayed Musa al-Sadr, 183
Sheikh Mahmood Shaltoot, 204
Soumaneh, 147
Stalin, Joseph, 34
Sunan al Daraqutni, 17

T

Talha, 106, 131
Tannoudjii, Claude Cohen, 183

U

Ubaydullah ibn Ziyad (Ubaydul-
    lah), 136, 137, 200
Umar ibn Abdul Aziz, 119, 120,
    123, 231
Umar ibn Khattab, 16, 46, 63, 64,
    82, 103, 104, 105, 106, 109, 110,
    115, 116, 119, 120, 121, 123,
    202, 229, 230, 231
Umul Fadhl, 147
Usama ibn Zayd, 82, 119
Uthman, 16, 63, 103, 105, 106,
    107, 115, 116, 119, 120, 124,
    131, 202, 231
Umm Kulthum, 41

W

Walid ibn Abdul Malik, 140, 141

Y

Yazid (Yazid ibn Muawiyah), xxi,
    xxii, xxiii, 34, 94, 108, 134, 135,
    137, 138, 139, 140, 156, 157,
    173, 175, 176, 177, 178, 179,
    180, 181, 200

Z

Zain al-Mutjahideen, 187
Zayd ibn Ali, 141
Zubair (Zubayr), 106, 131

Subject Index

magnetic energy, 177

mental energy, 177

one of characteristics by which Imams were molded, 152

positive energy. *See* positive energy

potential energy, 177, 178, 179

spiritual energy. *See* spiritual energy

vibration energy, 177

expectation, 225

explicit designation, 83, 84, 85

F

fadak, 129, 130, 229

fajr prayer time, 70

Farewell Sermon, 51, 52, 63, 66, 82, 83, 84, 85, 98, 106, 229, 230, 289–308

Fatimid caliphs, 309

Fayd al Qadir fi Sharh al-Jami' al-Saghir, 45

fiqh (Islamic jurisprudence), 320

First Law of Thermodynamics, 174

forgiveness, 99

four elements, theory of, according to Imam as-Sadiq, 185–186

Four Rightly Guided Caliphs, 120

free will, xviii, 163

furqan (criterion), 320

furu' al-din (practical principles of beliefs) (secondary principles of practices), 199, 320

G

Ghadir Khumm, 49, 50, 51, 66, 82, 98, 106, 107, 203, 289

Ghayat al-Maram, 52, 63, 83

ghayba (absence) (occultation), 213, 223, 320

ghaybat-ul-kubra (major occultation), 213, 320

ghaybat-us-sughra (minor occultation), 213, 320

ghusl (honorary bathing), 103, 104

gift of guidance, 6, 8

glossary, 319–324

Gospel of Jesus, 29, 31, 32–33, 34, 46

Great Messengers, 27

The Great Muslim Scientist and Philosopher Imam Jafar ibn Mohammed As-Sadiq, 183

guardianship, 94–102

H

habib Allah (Allah's beloved friend), 37, 320

hadi (guidance) (guide), 30, 31, 81, 321

Hadith al-Thaqalayn, 25

Hadith Qudsi (Sacred Hadith), 321

hadiths (traditions)

on Ahl al-Bayt Six Books of major Sunni sources, 285–288

classification of, 11–12

fabricated hadiths, 17–19

glossary, 321

overview, 11

Shi'a hadiths, 22–23

Imam(s). *See also specific Imams in* NAME INDEX
of Ahl al-Bayt, 309
as book, 29–34
concept of, 26–38
as destination, 28–29
evil Imams, 34
glossary, 321
legitimacy of, 60
main function of, 37
major role of, xviii
oppression, persecution, and martyrdom of, 122
as person, 34–38
responsibilities of, 81–82
role of, 196
Shi'as use of term, xix
use of term, xvi, 59
various forms and significance of, 27–28
Imamun-Mubeen (Manifesting Guide), 46
iman (faith), 321
implicit designation, 83, 84
imprisonment, 140, 149, 150, 158, 161, 181, 192
inertia energy, 178
infallibility, 70–78, 89
infallible Imams
concept of, 58
Twelve Infallible Imams of Ahl al-Bayt. *See* Twelve Infallible Imams of Ahl al-Bayt
Injil (Gospel), 31, 34, 46, 321
inner guidance, 75, 76, 77
inner knowledge, 75, 77
iqamah (call to prayer), 321

Islam
as submission to the will of Allah, 321
threats to, xxiv
Islamic events, timeline of, 239–242
Islamic morality, 226
'ismah (infallibility), 70, 89, 112, 321
isnad (chain of transmission), 12, 18, 321
Isra' and Mi'raj (Night Journey of the Ascent), 92, 163, 164, 165, 321
'itrah (Ahl al-Bayt), 91, 321

J

Ja'far school of thought, 204
jahil murakkab (closed-minded ignorance), 208–209, 321
Jews/Judaism, 129, 197, 204, 221
jihad (struggle), xxii, 135, 138, 175, 179, 321
jinn (unseen beings), 92, 321
jurisprudence, 101
justice, 65–67, 101, 225–226

K

Ka'bah (sacred house in Mecca), 41, 49, 321
Kalim Allah (he to whom Allah has talked), 37, 321
Kanz al-Ummal fi Sunan al-Aqwal Wa'l Af'al, 45
Karam Allahu Wajhah (may Allah bless his face), 110, 111, 321

Karbala, Iraq, xxii–xxiii, 98, 135, 136, 137, 138, 139, 140, 156, 157, 158, 175, 176, 179, 181, 189, 191, 200, 231

kawthar (fountain), 27, 322

khalifah (khalifa) (steward, trustee), xix-xx, 26, 38, 50, 189, 201, 322

khalifat Allah (Allah's deputy), 124, 125

khalifat rasul Allah (Allah's messenger's successor), 124

khalifati (caliph), 47, 84

khalil (ideal character/role model) (good friend), 37, 80, 322

Khawarij, 133

kindness, 99

kinetic energy, 177, 178, 179

kitab (book), 322

Kitab Al-Manaqib, 46

knowledge, necessity of, 67–68

Kufa, Iraq, xxii, 134, 136, 137, 138, 141, 176, 179, 200

Kutub al-Sittah (The Six Books), 12, 16, 17, 18

L

La Ilahi Illalah (There is no Allah but Allah), 322

leadership, xx, 64–65

light, theory of, according to Imam as-Sadiq, 183–184

light of the stars, according to Imam as-Sadiq, 184–185

lutf (Allah's grace), 61, 68, 70, 76, 322

M

madhhab (school of thought), 208, 322

magnetic energy, 177

mahdi (guide), 322

majalis (meetings), 189, 322

Majlis-Ash-Shura (Consultative Council), 108, 322

major occultation, 38, 55, 69, 96, 151, 161, 195, 198, 200, 213, 215, 220, 221, 222, 223, 224, 236

Man la Yahduruhu al-Faqih, 22

Manzilah, 107

marja'a (fully qualified jurist) (Islamic jurist), 96, 322

marja'a al-taqleed, 96

martyrdom, xxi–xxii, xxiii, xxiv, xxv, 107, 122, 123, 128, 131, 132, 135, 136, 137, 140, 147, 149, 156, 160, 169, 170, 174, 175, 181, 189, 190, 231, 234

masjid (mosque), 158, 322

Masjid al Haram, 110

ma'sum (sinless), 70, 73, 89, 322

matn (text), 12, 322

matter and anti-matter, according to Imam as-Sadiq, 184

mawdoo' (fabricated), 12, 322

mawla (successor) (master), 51, 322

Mecca, xxii, 42, 43, 104, 128, 139, 155, 197

Medina, 42, 43, 82, 86, 103, 104, 107, 128, 129, 139, 140, 141, 156, 159, 160, 168, 169, 197

mental energy, 177

messengers

compared to Imams, 27
main function of, 37
responsibilities of, 81–82
Messiah, 221
mihna (inquisition), 19, 20
minor occultation, 23, 161, 213,
214, 220, 222, 223
mi'raj (ascension of Prophet Mohammad), 322
muazzin (one who summons people to prayer), 139, 322
mujtahid (authority in Islamic
law), 96
mu'min (believer), 322
munafiqin (hypocrites), 133
munajaat (whispered prayers), 139
musannaf (collection of hadiths),
13, 322
Muslims, agreement among,
206–207
musnad (chain of transmitters of
hadiths) (traditions), 13, 322
*Mustadrak al-Wasa'il wa Mustan-
bat al-Masa'il*, 23
mustaqim (straight), 7
Mu'tazilite doctrine, 19
mutjahid (authority in Islamic law),
322

N

nabi (prophet), 27, 322
nabuwwat (prophecy), 38
nafs (self), 179, 322
*Nahj al-Balagha (Nahjul Balagha)
(Peak of Eloquence)*, 23, 154, 203,
322
Najran tribe, 133

nass (designation for appointment), 84, 189, 322
necessity
of justice, 65–67
of knowledge, 67–68
of leadership, 64–65
of obedience, 68–69
of succession, 62–64
Night Journey of the Ascent (Isra'
and Mi'raj), 92, 163, 164, 165,
321
ni'mah (blessing), 6, 7, 322
nur (light), 6, 39, 40, 322

O

obedience, 68–69, 89, 92, 100,
115–119
occultation. *See also* major occultation; minor occultation
of Imam Mohammad al-Mahdi,
217–220
opposing views relative to,
222–224
oppression, 122, 123, 128–152
Ottomans, 122
outer guidance, 76

P

PBUH (Peace be upon him), 322
peace, objective of, 188
pen and paper issue, 229–230
perfect perfection, 73
perfect purification, 73
perpetual motion, theory of, according to Imam as-Sadiq, 185
persecution, 122, 123, 128–152
personality, 225, 226, 227

poisonings, 55, 108, 134, 140, 141, 142, 145, 147, 149, 150, 156, 160

Polarization around the Character of 'Ali Ibn Abi Talib (Mutahhari), 169

positive energy, 168, 169, 171, 172, 174, 176, 178, 180, 187, 189, 192

potential energy, 177, 178, 179

power, authority compared to, 92–93

pragmatic infallibility, 74–78

prayer, xxiii, xxiv

preparation, 224, 225, 227

The Prince (Machiavelli), 127

prophets, number of, 27

Psalms of David, 29, 33, 34

psychological health, 7–8

purification, 235

purity, as criteria for *ulu 'l-amr*, 89

Q

Qayyamat (Day of Judgment), 38, 56, 322

qiblah (direction of prayer), 322

Qur'an
  according to Mu'tazilite doctrine, 19
  according to Sunnis, 19
  and Ahl al-Bayt as complementing each other, 235
  Imam Ali as being first to compile and codify, 49
  as one end of rope of Allah, xviii, 27
  as one of Allah's books, 29, 30–31, 34

as one of two weighty things (*thaqalayn*), 91

only Prophet Mohammad and infallible Imams as having light and inspiration to interpret all verses of, 78

Quraysh tribe, 41, 42, 87, 88, 103, 108, 128, 129

R

RA (Rathie Allahu Anhu) (may Allah be pleased with him), 322

rafidis (rejectionists), 123

rahma (mercy), 31, 34, 36, 323

rahmatun-lelalamin (universe), 4

raj'a (return), 213, 323

rakats (parts) (units of prayer), 5, 323

rasul (messenger), 27, 323

Rathi Allahu Anhu (may Allah be pleased with him), 110, 111

reason, use of, 60

The Republic (Plato), 127

Research Committee at Strasbourg, France, 182–183

revolution, objective of, 189, 190

ritual purity, 235

rotation of the earth on its axis, according to Imam as-Sadiq, 186

S

sabr (patience), xxiii, 99, 136, 150, 152, 153–161, 208, 225, 323

Sacred House (Ka'bah), 42

Safi Allah (Allah's sincere friend), 37, 323

Safinah, 107

sahaba (companions), 323

Sahib al-Zaman (Master of the Age), 213, 323

sahih (authentic), 12, 24, 323

salawat (blessings), 1–4, 323

Saqifah, 103, 105

Sassanid dynasty, 202

Satanic Verses (Rushdie), 204

SAWS (SAW & SAAS) (Sallallahu Alahi Wa Sallam) (may Allah honor him and grant him peace), 323

schools of thought, 42, 142, 143, 203, 204, 205, 206, 207, 208, 229

Scrolls of Abraham, 29, 33, 34

self-actualization, 59, 73

self-criticism, 227, 228

self-efficacy, 178

self-forgiveness, 227

self-realization, 10

self-sacrifice, 227

shari'ah (divine law), 59, 76, 323

shaykh (spiritual master, cleric), 323

Shi'a (followers of Ahl al-Bayt), 8, 323

Shi'a hadiths, 22–23

shura (council) (consultation), 26, 323

Shura Council, 106

Sirat-al-Mustaqim (Straight Path), xxiii, 6, 29, 199, 323. *See also* Straight Path

sociopathic personality, 126

spiritual energy, 162, 163, 165, 172, 187, 188, 191, 192

spiritual happiness, 7

spirituality, 227

stars, light of the, according to Imam as-Sadiq, 184–185

Straight Path, xxiii, xxiv, xxvi, 1, 4, 5, 6, 7, 8, 10, 28, 29, 51, 53, 59, 60, 62, 66, 70, 74, 79, 89, 94, 100, 103, 135, 140, 147, 151, 157, 165, 187, 188, 190, 198, 199, 201, 222, 224, 225, 226, 228, 235, 237, 250, 253, 300

successor to Prophet Mohammad, Shi'as criterion for, xix

sunnah (path or way of Prophet Mohammad) (sayings and doings of the prophet and his companions), 21, 25, 323

Sunni
as denomination of Islam, 323
origin of word, 25

Sunni hadiths, 12–17

Sunni-Shi'a relations, during Abbasid Dynasty, 19–22

supplications, xxiv, 8, 139, 140, 158, 179, 180, 181, 186, 187, 192

sura (chapter), 5, 323

SWT (Subhanahu Wa Ta'ala) (Glorious is He, and He is exalted), 323

Syria tribe, 133

T

Tabligh, 86

Tabouk, Battle of, 82

tafsir (explanation), 59, 323

203, 205, 206, 207, 214, 215,
223, 224, 230, 231, 233, 234,
323

ummat-e-wasat (group of middling
stand), 67

'umra (lesser pilgrimage), 323

unification, price for not unifying,
231

unity
achievement of, 207–212
as Allah's gift, 236
of Imamat, 196–212
importance of reviving passion
for principle of, 236
message of, 234
personalities of Imams molded
in part by, 152
roadblocks to, 233
of ummah as preached by
Twelve Infallible Imams, 231

Usama, 107

usul al-din (theoretical and fundamental principles of beliefs)
(faith), 64, 199, 323

V

vibration energy, 177
volition, xviii, 163

W

wali (guardian) (nearest of kin),
104, 324

*Wasa'il al-Shia'ah ila Tahsil Masa'il
al-Shari'ah*, 22

wasi (spiritual heir) (successor), 7,
49

wassiyyi (successor), 47, 84, 324

wila'-e Imamat (spiritual guidance),
96, 97, 324

wila'-e muhabbat (love and devotion), 96, 97, 324

wila'-e tasarruf (universal nature),
96, 97, 324

wila'e zi'amat (sociopolitical guidance), 96, 324

wilayat (guardianship), 96–100,
324

wilayat-ul-faqih (guardianship-based political system), 96,
324

Y

yoreedo (intends), 3, 324

Z

Zabur (Pslams of David), 33, 324
zakat (tax, alms), 324

TRUE DIRECTIONS

An affiliate of Tarcher Books

OUR MISSION

Tarcher's mission has always been to publish books
that contain great ideas. Why? Because:

GREAT LIVES BEGIN WITH GREAT IDEAS

At Tarcher, we recognize that many talented authors, speakers,
educators, and thought-leaders share this mission and deserve to be
published – many more than Tarcher can reasonably publish ourselves.
True Directions is ideal for authors and books that increase awareness,
raise consciousness, and inspire others to live their ideals and passions.

Like Tarcher, True Directions books are designed to do three things:
inspire, inform, and motivate.

Thus, True Directions is an ideal way for these important voices to
bring their messages of hope, healing, and help to the world.

Every book published by True Directions– whether it is non-fiction, memoir,
novel, poetry or children's book – continues Tarcher's mission to publish works
that bring positive change in the world. We invite you to join our mission.

For more information, see the True Directions website:
www.iUniverse.com/TrueDirections/SignUp

Be a part of Tarcher's community to bring positive change in this world!
See exclusive author videos, discover new and exciting books, learn about
upcoming events, connect with author blogs and websites, and more!
www.tarcherbooks.com

TRUE DIRECTIONS
AN AFFILIATE OF TARCHER BOOKS